TRADITIONS AND TALES OF THE NAVY

Dr. Martin Davis

Pictorial Histories Publishing Co., Inc.
Missoula, Montana

LIBRARY OF CONGRESS
CONTROL NUMBER
00 135706

ISBN 1-57510-081-9

First Printing: November 2000
Second Printing: November 2001

PRINTED IN CANADA

Cover Graphics and Design: Mike Egeler, Egeler Designs
Typography and Layout: Leslie Maricelli

PICTORIAL HISTORIES PUBLISHING CO., INC.
713 South Third St. West, Missoula Montana 59801

~ INTRODUCTION ~

The seeds for this book were planted when I was very young. At that time, my brother Bill was a member of the pre-war Navy, and he bought a subscription to *Our Navy* magazine for me. This gave me my first exposure to the Navy, and I greatly enjoyed reading monthly features such as *Fleet News, Foreign Naval News, Salty Rhymes, Salt Shakers,* and *Letters to the Editor.* However, I was fascinated by the work of Cedric W. Windas and his *Traditions of the Navy* drawings and text. It was these tidbits of naval lore and language that helped direct me toward a lifelong interest in the English language, word evolution and naval history.

Using Cedric Windas' drawings as an illustrative base for this book, I researched and collected almost 600 nautical words and phrases that have become part of our common language. Included in this number are short stories that provide an opportunity to expand and explain.

The scope of *Traditions and Tales of the Navy* purposely entails much more than nautical etymology. Included in the structure of this book are sections that focus on the naval and maritime atmosphere that caused, and continues to cause, the formation of tradition and the expansion of our vocabulary. This is the reason for inclusion of John Charles Roach's *"Anatomy of U.S. Frigate Constitution,"* as well as *"Images of the Navy"* and other segments.

It is important to note that a fair portion of text and illustrations in this book deals with the era prior to 1948, with emphasis on the '20s, '30s and '40s. This time period encompassed the post-World War I period, the depression, World War II and the immediate post-war. In most cases, these were the years prior to the wave of equal opportunity movements of women, African-Americans, the handicapped and disabled, and before the sexual revolution. This was a time before we were fully aware of the real dangers of smoking, alcoholism and drug addiction. We had come out of the decade-long depression economy due to World War II, and the full force of America's technological revolution had not yet begun. As a result of the great changes that have taken place in 60 years, some of the illustrations and humor may appear to be dated, provincial, naïve and even "corny." This is to our advantage because it gives us the opportunity to view changes in history and culture from the perspective of today.

It is hoped that readers of this book find it informative, enjoyable and stimulating.

NAVAL TRADITION

"The worth of sentiment lies in the sacrifices men will make for its sake. All ideals are built on the ground of solid achievement, which in a given profession creates in the course of time a certain tradition, in other words, a standard of conduct."
—— *Joseph Conrad*

ACKNOWLEDGMENTS

A central theme of *Traditions and Tales of the Navy: Volume I* is that many persons over the years throughout the world have contributed to the development of our English language. Being more specific, this book focuses on nautical words and phrases that have crept into our normal everyday American English. Many people, over many centuries, sailed the sea or were affected by the sea, and it is they who have produced a legacy of speech that has brightened and enriched the English language.

If one performs research and strives for accuracy, it is necessary to turn to many sources. A review of the bibliography indicates that a relatively large amount of references were turned to for that purpose. My sincere thanks and gratitude to the authors and research facilities that I referred to. On a more personal level, I express my deep appreciation to the following individuals who served as important sources of knowledge and assistance.

Cedric W. Windas is the author of *Traditions of the Navy*, which was published in 1942. His artwork first appeared as a monthly feature in *Our Navy* magazine in 1936, and when his book was printed, it contained his *Our Navy* drawings that were published between 1936 and 1942. Included in this book is that artwork plus selections from his drawings covering the 1943 through 1948 period.

Cedric Windas was born in Richmond, Australia in 1888. He went to sea as an apprentice on the steel-hulled, full-rigged ship *Segura*. He eventually became second mate of the inter-island trading schooner *Amy Moir*. Windas entered the field of commercial art and advertising in Melbourne, and then in Honolulu, where he became feature writer and cartoonist for the *Honolulu Morning Advertiser*. He later served in the same capacity with the *Los Angeles Evening Express*. Operating on a freelance basis, Mr. Windas contributed articles and artwork to some 35 national magazine, including *Argosy*, *Adventure* and *Power Boating*.

Commander Arnold S. Lott, USN (Ret.) recognized the historical significance of Cedric Windas' *Traditions of the Navy*, and he wanted to keep this book alive. In 1978, Arnold Lott published a revised copy in which he modified Windas' original art format. Unfortunately, this version had limited circulation. This book contains a portion of Mr. Lott's material, and I am pleased to bring it forward to a new generation.

While serving in the Navy, Commander Lott wrote *A Long Line of Ships*, *Most Dangerous Sea* and *Brave Ship, Brave Men*. He was co-author of *America's Maritime Heritage* and *Man in Flight*. Arnold Lott retired from the Navy in 1961, lived in Annapolis and worked as an editor with the U.S. Naval Institute until he passed away in November 1992.

Captain John Charles Roach, USNR is a recognized Navy Combat Artist who has many notable paintings on exhibit in the Pentagon, the Naval History Center and its museum in the Washington Navy Yard. Captain Roach's drawings were the centerpiece of the April 1976 United States Bicentennial Celebration, in which the Navy paid national tribute to the historic *Constitution*. The Navy published his exhibit drawings in the book, *An Essay in Sketches of Old Ironside*. Some of these drawings are included in this book's section, "Anatomy of *U.S. Frigate Constitution*."

As a veteran naval officer with 30 years of service in both active and drilling reservist status, John Roach has held a wide number of prestigious naval posts throughout the world. He was issued a Presidential Recall to serve on the staff of the Commander Implementation Force in Bosnia and, following that, on the staff of Commander-in-Chief of U.S. Naval Forces in Europe. In March 1999 Captain Roach was reactivated to assume the post of Director of the Secretary of the Navy's Drug Demand Reduction Task Force. In his civilian career, John Roach is the Public Affairs Officer for the Office of Naval Intelligence, with sub-assignments to the Defense Intelligence Agency.

Commander John W. Alexander, USN (Ret.), is the author of *A Living Tradition: The United States Navy Memorial*, which was published by the Navy Memorial Foundation in 1987. Through his efforts, and that of the Memorial's President and CEO, Rear Admiral Henry C. M\^cKinney, USN (Ret.), it was possible for me to use important material that was created for *A Living Tradition*. John Alexander has been a very helpful resource in connection with historic research. As far as Admiral M\^cKinney is concerned, he has provided strong support to this project, and he has made the research facilities of the U.S. Navy Memorial available to me.

Commander John Alexander's 22-year Navy career demonstrates the U.S. Navy's broadened role in public relations and communications. While on active duty, he redesigned *All Hands Magazine* and produced a video documentary, *United States Navy Around the Clock & Across the Globe*. In addition to *A Living Tradition*, he has published two other books: *Liberty*

Centennial—The Fourth of July Weekend and *From the Sea: The Navy-Marine Corps Team Into the 21st Century.* Upon retirement, John Alexander was appointed as the Director of Communications and Public Affairs of the Navy-Marine Corps Relief Society.

Alex Gard is a World War II sailor who became a well-known artist after the war. It is my understanding that he graduated from the Russian Naval Academy prior to joining our fleet. His distinctive signature can identify his humorous sketches of boot camp, life aboard a "tin can" and a "DE." Mr. Gard received his basic training at Norfolk (VA) Naval Training Station in 1942. He then served as a quartermaster aboard the destroyer *USS Chauncey* (DD-667) and the destroyer escort *USS Dobler* (DE-48).

Other persons have contributed in their own way toward the publication of this book. They include: Rear Admiral Sheldon H. Kinney, USN (Ret.), who wrote the Foreword for this book; Captain Channing Zucker, USN (Ret.), Executive Director of the Historic Naval Ships Association, assisted greatly by reviewing the text and making important suggestions. Others include: Joe Gerson, the driving force behind the creation of the Maritime Industry Museum at New York State Maritime College at Fort Schuyler, NY; Myrna Lewis, Assistant Superintendent of Schools at Cold Springs Harbor (NY) School District; John Cosgrove, past President of the National Press Club; Sam Saylor, President of the Destroyer Escort Historical Foundation/*USS Slater*; Dr. Edward J. Price Jr., Naval Historian and Linguist; Gordon McKean, a World War II veteran of service aboard *USS Lansing* (DE-388), whose cartoons in this book demonstrate the "bucking bronco" aspects of a DE in the North Atlantic and Stan Cohen, Publisher, Pictorial Histories Publishing Company. Special thanks go to Leslie Maricelli, also of Pictorial Histories, who assisted me in structure and layout. Strong credit must also go to my wife, Shain Davis, not only for helping in research, but also for having to put up with my constantly exclaiming, "I just found a new fact!!!"

Thar She Blows!

❦ FOREWORD ❦

When I reflect on the Navy of the '30s, nothing brings back more poignantly my days as a seaman and signalman than recollections of *Our Navy* magazine. Leaving high school to enlist in 1935, my first ship was the light cruiser *Omaha*. I still have the flat hat ribbons from her and my next ship, the battleship *New York*.

There were no official publications such as today's *All Hands* and *Surface Warfare* magazines. *Our Navy*, however, more than filled the bill. Each ship had a member of the crew who received a small stipend from the publisher to act as agent for information and sales. At a time when an apprentice seaman received $21 a month, a seaman second class $36 and a seaman first $54, this provided him a little extra. The monthly delivery of *Our Navy* magazines to our ship was as welcome as the receipt of The *Saturday Evening Post* was to our parents back home.

The magazine augmented my enthusiasm and enjoyment of being a "man-o'-warsman," as I liked to be thought of. (Certainly not as a "gob," though "sailor" or "bluejacket," and later, "white hat" was fine.) In each issue there was a full-page photo of a ship of the fleet, news of the Navy, Letters to the Editor, original poetry, Naval Traditions articles and, of course, the incomparable illustrations of Cedric Windas.

This was a small but highly professional Navy. The high degree of competence, officer and enlisted, provided a foundation for the tremendous expansion of World War II which produced promotions, commands and responsibilities unheard of in the peacetime Navy. The success of that Navy was vitally fueled by the remarkable augmentation of young Americans who transitioned from civilian life to naval life. They quickly acquired new skills and exercised them with courage in combat to win victory at sea. This was matched by an amazing American industrial capacity that rapidly produced an unprecedented number of ships, aircraft and weapons.

The young American Navy of the Revolution inherited the traditions of the Royal Navy, and lived to build upon them. As recruits, we were told that the three stripes on the dress jumper stood for Admiral Lord Nelson's victories at Trafalgar, The Nile and Copenhagen; and that the thirteen buttons of the blue trouser's front flap closure stood for the thirteen colonies. We learned the bugle calls that signaled battle stations, the movies, payday, meals, reveille, tattoo, taps, church, and fire. Since there was no ship announcing system, the bosuns' mate made the rounds of the main deck hatches—piping and passing the word.

In the *New York*, 1937, we represented the United States at the Coronation Fleet Review of the Queen's father, King George VI. Moored alongside the battleship *Queen Elizabeth* in Portsmouth harbor prior to the review, I had the signal bridge watch on a Sunday morning and was observing her activities with great interest. The bosun's mates were summoning worshippers with the words, "Now fall in the church parties on the fantail. Church of England to starboard, Romans to port, and the fancy religions amidships." This Congregationalist knew just where he stood!

The *New York* was a veteran of World War I in which she had been flagship of the Sixth Battle Squadron, the United States battleships that cooperated with the British Grand Fleet. The Admiral, Hugh Rodman, long on the retired list, was returned to the active list and embarked in his former flagship to represent the United States at the coronation.

The *New York* returned to American waters and proceeded to Annapolis Roads to embark midshipmen for the annual training cruise. Here, I experienced the benefit of a Navy tradition, the opportunity for an enlisted man to enter the Naval Academy. The regulations provided that each year 100 bluejackets could be appointed midshipmen if they had served a minimum of one year in a ship in full commission, were under twenty years of age, and had passed the entrance examination. A signal from the station ship *Reina Mercedes* ordered my transfer to the Academy. A year later, I again embarked in *New York* for the training cruise in Europe. But, this time, I was aboard as a midshipman.

In the '30s a sailor's life was far from luxurious. We slept in hammocks swung from overhead billet hooks in the passageways and gun compartments, just inches below the wooden mess tables stowed above us. We stowed our clothes and ditty bag in a canvas sea bag lashed to a jackstay. It was an art to fold and roll uniforms and then fasten them with clothes stops. Uniforms had to emerge from the folding fit for Captain's Inspection or pass the Officer of the Deck's inspection of a liberty party. This skill, and that of sleeping in a hammock six feet off the deck, was learned during recruit training at San Diego, Newport, or Norfolk. A "belly band" left you hanging from the middle if you overturned. It was up to a fellow sailor on watch to turn you back over.

As for sea bag stowage, the traditional three inverse creases in the dress jumper derive from it being turned inside out before folding and rolling. Inverse creases were also produced on the sides of the bell-bottomed blue trousers, as they too were rolled. The "bell-bottom" facilitated turning the trousers up before, barefoot, you washed down, holystoned, and squeegeed the teak decks of battleships and heavy cruisers.

The morning routine commenced with the 0530 reveille. Coffee was issued in the living compartments, followed by "turn to" for one hour before breakfast. *Omaha* had but a single scuttlebutt with multiple spigots, and single washroom. You were allowed but one bucket of fresh water per day (but all the salt water you could use). This fresh water was for brushing your teeth, washing your body and clothes. The water was heated by inserting it under a pipe that bubbled steam from the boilers through it.

But to the minority enlistment sailor (enlistment under the age of 18 and discharge before the 21st birthday to permit an "adult" decision about reenlistment!), the life was an adventure. And to the enlisted man, it was simply accepted as the way sailors lived. The executive officer of *Reina Mercedes* discharged me on a June evening of 1937, and with an air of fatherly advice suggested that I should not leave the ship until I was sworn in as a midshipman the next morning. Since I was a civilian for the night with neither Navy protection nor benefits, in true naval tradition, I replied, "Aye, aye, sir! I have heard the order. I understand the or-der. I will carry out the order."

I found, and continue to find, tradition in the Navy inspiring. The routine use of expressions founded many years ago in sailing ships and carried on, was fascinating. The captain, in concluding each case at disciplinary mast orders the man on report, "Lay forward," from the days when mast was held aft, and the crew lived in the forecastle. When a junior overtook a senior on foot he passed only with the request, "By your leave, Sir." The usual response was, "Granted." The Officer of the Deck's noon report to the captain included the words, "The chronometers have been wound and compared." This was vital to navigation before time ticks by radio. Though I had trouble one time keeping a straight face when the bridge messenger reported to me, "The officer of the deck reports twelve o'clock, Sir. The chronometers have been ground and repaired."

And so it is that in my friend Martin Davis' book, *Traditions and Tales of the Navy*, I find refreshing reminders of tradition, and to my delight, tales previously unknown to me. So, reader, carry on, with one of the finest wishes a seafarer can convey.

"Fair Winds and Following Seas."

Sheldon H. Kinney
Rear Admiral, USN (Ret.)

About Admiral Sheldon H. Kinney.....

In April 1943, 23-year-old Lt. Sheldon H. Kinney became the youngest commanding officer of a major combatant vessel, *USS Edsall* (DE-129). During the first patrol of his next command, *USS Bronstein* (DE-189), his ship sank three German U-boats and sent a fourth to the scrap yard. The Chief of Naval Operations described this as "the most concentrated and successful action against U-boats by a ship in World War II."

During his 47 years in the Navy, Admiral Kinney had 11 commands at sea that placed him in combat in World War II, Korea and Vietnam. He led ships, a squadron and a flotilla, including command of 125 ships and 60,000 sailors of the Cruiser-Destroyer Force, U.S. Pacific Fleet. His 25 awards include the Navy Cross, Distinguished Service Medal and decorations from Poland, the Soviet Union, South Korea and South Vietnam. Sheldon Kinney served as Commandant of Midshipmen at Annapolis and Director of Navy Education and Training. While on active duty, he found time to earn three college degrees: BS, MA and JD.

Admiral Kinney's post-Navy career continued in the direction of education and training others. He served as President of New York State Maritime College at Fort Schuyler, Bronx, NY, President of the World Maritime University of the United Nations (Sweden), and Special Adviser to the Secretary-General of the International Maritime Organization (London).

In 1991, Sheldon and I traveled to Uruguay under the auspices of the Destroyer Escort Sailors Association (DESA) to determine the feasibility of bringing back to the United States his ship, ex-*USS Bronstein* (DE-189) or ex-*USS Baron* (DE-166). We found it impractical to acquire either vessel. However, the lessons learned on that trip enabled DESA to be successful in its 1993 acquisition and return of *USS Slater* (DE-766). This warship is now undergoing full restoration in Albany, New York.

In many ways, Admiral Sheldon H. Kinney symbolizes what this book is about. He has seen it all. He has been witness to the depression, the pre-war Navy, the development of the World's greatest navy, participation in three wars. He has seen victories and tragedies. (Admiral Kinney's brother rests with his comrades in the hull of *USS Arizona*.) Sheldon Kinney is representative of our highly able career members of the United States Navy, Coast Guard and Marine Corps. I feel fortunate in having had his help and guidance in matters far beyond the scope of this publication.

Martin Davis

Contents

A SCRAMBLE FOR SALT-JUNK.

A scramble for chow on a Whaler, 1846.

Salty Words, Phrases and Sea Stories

A-1 at Lloyds
When one is questioned as to his health and state, if he replies that he is feeling "A-1," he is borrowing an old marine insurance term. Lloyds, the largest marine insurance company in the world, rated first class ships by registering them as A-1. Thus, the reply of A-1 means one is feeling absolutely at his best or that the condition of something is excellent. (See Posted at Lloyds.)

Above Board
In nautical language, an honest person is one who is "above board." The phrase originated in the days when pirates hid most of their crews behind the bulwarks in order to lure some unsuspecting victim into thinking they were an honest merchant vessel. It followed that anyone who displayed all his crew openly on deck was obviously an honest seaman. Therefore, the captain of a legitimate vessel would command his men to stand tall behind the bulwarks in order to show the other vessel that he is "above board."

Acey-Ducey
This is a seagoing version of backgammon, a game for two persons in which pieces are moved around a board having two tables or parts, and then removed according to throws of the dice. The game had its beginning between 1635 and 1645.

Admiral
Admiral is the senior officer rank in the U.S. Navy, but the title comes from the name given the senior ranking officer in the Moorish army of many years ago. A Moorish chief was an "emir," and the chief of all chiefs was an "emiral." Our English word is derived directly from the Moorish.

Admiral Penn
The Royal Navy's Admiral Sir William Penn, who conquered the island of Jamaica, actually had nothing to do with American history, yet one of the states is named for him. The wealthy admiral loaned money to the Duke of York and left a fortune to his own son, William. When son William acquired from the Duke the land that is now Pennsylvania, he named it after his admiral father.

Admiral's Eighth
This expression relates to the old practice of paying prize money to admirals in the Royal Navy for all ships captured by the fleet under their command. The admiral got one-eighth of the value of all captured ships, as allowed by the prize courts, whether he was present at the time or not.

Air Conditioned Ships
The first completely air-conditioned ships in the Navy were the heavy cruisers *Newport News* and *Salem,* built in 1947.

Airdale
Carrier deck crews have given their naval aviators the good-natured nicknames of "airdale"" and "flyboy." In turn, the flyers refer to the deck crews as "deck apes."

American Clipper Racing
In 1851, three fast clipper ships raced from East Coast ports to San Francisco. The *Sea Witch* left New York on August 1, followed by the *Typhoon* a day later. The *Raven* sailed from Boston on August 5. The *Typhoon* reached San Francisco on November 18 after a run of 108 days. The *Raven* arrived the next day, after sailing only 106 days. The *Sea Witch* made port the day after that, for a run of 111 days. Naturally, they had to sail around the tip of South America.

Amidships
Frequently, and mistakenly, this term is used to designate the center of a ship at the waist. Actually, this word refers to a line running the length of a ship from bow to stern. Thus, the masts are stepped "amidships."

Anchor
The name for the weight used for mooring a ship comes from the Latin "anchora." Stone anchors were used

• WORKING FOR A DEAD HORSE •

This expression, meaning that one is working at some job for which he has already been paid, dates back to early days, when it was customary to advance a sailor his first month's pay. After the ship had been thirty days at sea, the crew would construct a horse out of a barrel and odd ends of canvas. It would be hoist overside and set on fire, and as it drifted astern, the men would sing the old chantey "Poor Old Horse." This indicated that they would once again be working for wages, and not alone for "Salt Horse" (food).

• PENNSYLVANIA •

Contrary to the general belief, the state of Pennsylvania was not named for its founder, William Penn, but for his brother Admiral Penn, as a mark of the King's favor.

• FIRST NAVAL COLLEGE •

The first naval college of which there is any record was established at Sagres Portugal, in 1415 A.D. Here King Henry (known as Henry the Navigator) called together famous seamen from every nation to instruct his young countrymen.

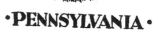

• NELSON'S EYE-SIGHT •

The famous statue of England's brilliant sea-lord which stands in Trafalgar Square London, is, oddly enough, not true to history. It depicts the admiral as being blind in his right eye, when as a matter of record, it was his left eye that was sightless.

by the Chinese as long ago as 2000 BC. Anchors range in weight from little ones that a man can lift, to the anchors of 30 tons and more aboard our modern aircraft carriers.

Anchor Watch
Originally, an anchor watch was stood only when the ship was tied up in dock and with her anchors stowed on deck. Then watch was posted, "Lest," says a serious chronicler of early days, "some miscreants from ye other ships about, steal ye anchors while they (the crew) sleep."

Anchor's Aweigh
It is customary to note in the ship's log when an anchor is dropped and when it's raised again. Usually, the dropping and hauling of anchors is a routine undertaking, but this is not always the case. The following episode is an illustration of this point: The British warship, *HMS Centurion* anchored off Juan Fernandez Island one day in 1742, during the round-the-world cruise made by Commodore Anson between September 1740 and June 1744. The *Centurion* noted in the log that when the anchor was being hauled in, the cable broke and the anchor went to the bottom. In 1882, 140 years later, *USS Lackawanna* stopped at Juan Fernandez, anchored, weighed anchor, and brought up the one the *Centurion* had lost long before. The *Centurion's* anchor was brought to Mare Island Navy Yard at Vallejo, California for display.

Army at Sea
Until 1546, seamen were hired to only work a ship. An army officer was responsible for the supervision of battle at sea.

Arrive
To reach one's destination, is to arrive. It was once a purely nautical expression, and it comes from the Latin "arripare," to come to land.

At Loggerheads
This term, descriptive of an angry relationship between two parties, dates back to the days when tools called "loggerheads" were used for spreading hot pitch along deck seams. The tool consisted of a wooden pole with an iron head similar to a flattened adz.

Men doing this work for long hours were apt to grow nerve-raw and quarrelsome, and their loggerheads made effective and ugly weapons. A fight with these tools was a deadly battle. Mutual dislike or hatred between two people is aptly described as, "they are at loggerheads."

Avast
To stop or hold fast. It comes from a combination of two words: the Dutch "houd vast," for hold fast, and from the Portuguese "abasta," enough.

AWOL
Absenting oneself from a Navy ship or base without permission, and it is an acronym for "Absent Without Leave." The phrase evolved from 17th century France, where it was accepted that a French person could properly leave a party without bidding farewell to the host or hostess. Unauthorized absence became "French Leave" for the Allied forces in Europe during World War I, and AWOL (sometimes described as "Over the Wall") during World War II.

Aye, Aye Sir!
This reply by a junior to the order of a senior means that he understands the order and will carry it out. The expression has a very interesting evolution. It is a corruption of the words "yes, yes," which in Cockney accents became "yea, yea," and then "yi, yi." The last stage of the evolution was "aye, aye."

Backing and Filling
"Backing and filling" describes the motions of a sailing vessel holding her position without actually heaving-to. She would back her yards to spill the wind and stop forward motion; then, when tide and breeze tended to move her too far away, she would square her yards and run up to her original position. The modern application of this phrase refers to actions of an indecisive person.

Balaclava Helmets
In the old British Navy, it was a common stunt to cut the foot off a woolen sock and wear the leg of it pulled over one's head in cold weather. It was called a "Balaclava helmet" because British soldiers started the practice during the Crimean War. The Battle of Balaclava was fought during that war, on 25 October 1854.

Balloon Carrier
Long before airplanes were invented, the U.S. Navy had an aerial spotter. During the Civil War, the armed transport *Fanny* launched a manned balloon to make observations of Confederate positions at Fortress Monroe, Virginia. The balloon reached an altitude of 2,000 feet.

WINDAS 1935

The 'HORSE' LATITUDES

Roughly, the area between North latitudes 30°-40°. The term was coined in the days when ships carrying horses from Europe to America were often becalmed in the region of the Indies. To conserve drinking water for the horses, some of the animals would be thrown overboard in an effort to save the others.

FIRST TELESCOPE

The first telescope was invented by a Dutch spectacle maker. Experimenting in 1608 with one lens placed over another he accidentally discovered the optical principle for bringing distant objects nearer to vision.

TARPAULIN MUSTER

Old Navy slang for helping a shipmate in distress. A tarpaulin was rigged and the crew would file past, contributing whatever they could spare to help their financially embarrassed comrade.

PATAGONIA

This South American country received its name when Portugese sailors noted with amazement the huge feet of the natives. They promptly nicknamed them "PATA GONES" (big feet).

Bamboozle

In today's Navy, when you intentionally deceive someone, usually as a joke, you are said to have "bamboozled" him. The word was used in the days of sail, but the intent was not hilarity. Bamboozle meant to deceive a passing vessel as to your ship's origin or nationality by flying an ensign other than your own,—a common practice of pirates.

Banian Days

The British Navy, as a measure of economy, ruled that sailors would have two meatless days per week. Sneering sailors referred to such days as "Banian Days," naming them for the Hindu Banians, a tribe whose religion permitted only a vegetarian diet.

Batten Your Hatch

Once a hatch was battened down, it was tightly closed. "Stop talking!" "Shut up!" and "Button your lip!" join "Batten your hatch!" in drawing upon the closing of a hatch for common origin. In order to add a measure of refinement among members of his crew, legend has it that a World War II destroyer skipper issued an experimental order for "Please" to be used at the beginning of the previous statements. The experiment failed.

The Battle of Santiago

This combat between American and Spanish forces was fought off the coast of Cuba on July 3,1898. As the Spanish fleet left the harbor, American forces took up the chase and in four hours the entire Spanish fleet was sunk or run ashore. Spanish losses were 350 killed and 150 wounded. One American sailor was killed. When sailors on the *Texas* cheered as a Spanish ship burned, Captain John Philip called out, "Don't cheer, boys. Those poor fellows are dying!"

Beachcomber

A term for a ne'er-do-well or loafer along the waterfront that originated in the islands in the South Pacific. It described the outcasts who had lost all ambition, and preferred to comb the beaches for findings.

Bean Jockey

A member of the crew who is assigned to mess duty is a "bean jockey."

Bean Rag

The flag that is flown aboard ship during meal hours is called the "bean rag." The men who help to serve the meals are referred to as bean jockeys.

Before the Mast

Literally, this was the position of the crew whose living quarters on board was on the forecastle (foc'sle or foc'sul), the section of the ship forward of the foremast. As a result, the phrase, "he sailed before the mast," is understandably more applicable to seamen rather than officers

Being Over a Barrel

During the middle 19th century, Navy captains sometimes preferred to punish the young ships' boys and midshipmen for infractions in a unique way. Instead of traditional flogging, the young men were ordered to expose their bare buttocks, bend over a cannon and to receive a whipping in which a "cat-o-nine tails" was used. Aboard ship, this punishment was known as "kissing the gunner's daughter." From this saying derived the phrase, "being over a barrel."

Belay

To cease hauling on a line or stop what you are doing. The word was originally "delay" before being corrupted to its present form.

Bell Bottom Trousers

These wide-legged pants were cut with a flare in the legs for several reasons: They were easier to roll up  for a man swabbing decks, but primarily the flare permitted sailors to remove trousers quickly without removing their shoes first. This was a safety feature in case their ship sank or if they were knocked overboard. In such instances, sailors were taught to tie a knot in each pant leg and force air into the trousers through the top, thus making a natural air pocket life preserver.

Bells

When time was kept aboard ship by means of a half-hour glass, it was the job of the ship's boy to turn the glass as the sands of

· BLUE MONDAY ·

The term "Blue Monday" came into being as early as the 18th century. It originated because of an old custom aboard ships, whereby a man's misdeeds were logged daily, and the culprit flogged weekly, on the following Monday.

· DINGHY ·

This name for a ship's smallest boat, is a contribution to our nautical vocabulary from India. Dinghy means "small", and from this same word we get also our slang term "Dinky".

· SHIP'S MASTER ·

The official title for the sailing-master of a ship was created centuries ago, during the Punic Wars, when he was known as "Magestis Navis."

· HAWSER ·

The word "Hawser" is derived from the old English "Halter," meaning a rope for the neck.

time ran out. With each turn, he gave the bell on the quarterdeck a lusty swing to show that he was on the job. Eventually, quartermasters found it convenient to show the passage of their watches by having the bell rung at the end of the first half hour, twice at the end of the second and so on. Eight bells indicated the end of a four-hour watch and the beginning of a new one.

Berserk
Meaning "violently and destructively frenzied," this word comes down from the Vikings. It was common for them to tear off their shirts and fight half-naked. Hence the term "berserk," with "ber" meaning bare, and "serk" the Norse word for shirt.

Best Girl's on the Towrope
An old Navy term descriptive of fair weather and easy going on the homeward passage. If the ship was making good progress, the seamen would say, "Ah! The best girl is on the towrope."

Big Ocean Waves
Large waves can be whipped up by the wind and their height in feet will usually be half of the wind speed in miles per hour. In illustration, an 80-mile per hour hurricane will produce waves 40 feet high, but sometimes they are bigger. The *SS Queen Mary* was off Greenland, and her bridge, which was 90 feet above the sea, was flooded by a huge wave. One of the biggest waves recorded was seen from the *USS Ramp* in the Pacific on February 7,1933; it was 112 feet high. In 1944, Admiral William B. Halsey's Pacific Fleet Task Force encountered high waves in a major storm and three destroyers were overturned and sunk.

Bilge
This word now means nonsense or filth, and it came from the sea term that described the dirty water that collected in the bottom of a ship. "Bilge" was first spelled "bulge," which referred to the fact that water accumulated in the bulge or curve at the bottom of a straight-line ship.

Binnacle List
This is a ship's sick list. A "binnacle" was the stand on which the ship's compass was mounted in the eighteenth century and probably before. A list was given to the officer or mate of the watch and it contained the names of men unable to report for duty for health reasons. This list was kept at the binnacle and, although the procedures for listing men on sick call have changed, the binnacle list is in use today.

Bird Farm
This is one more nickname for an aircraft carrier. The air control officer's station on the island of the carrier is called the birdcage, and the platform where off-watch sailors watch landing operations is known as the vulture's roost.

Biscuits
These were cooked a second time to keep them from spoiling too quickly during a sea journey. Their name originated from the Latin "bis," meaning twice and "coctus," which means cooked. Joined together, the words became "cooked twice."

Bitter End
As any able-bodied seaman can tell you, a turn of a line around a "bitt," those wooden or iron posts sticking through a ship's deck, is called a "bitter." Thus, the last line secured to the bitts is known as the "bitter end." Nautical usage has somewhat expanded the original definition in that today the end of any line, secured to bitts or not, is  called a bitter end. The landlubbing phrases, "stick to the bitter end" and "faithful to the bitter end," are derivations of the nautical term. These phrases refer to anyone who insists on adhering to a course of action without regard to consequences.

Black Gang
During coal-burning days, the engineers were usually black with coal dust. In addition to being members of the "black gang," they were also called "bilge rats" or "snipes." These descriptions are with us to the present day.

Blasphemy
A definition for this word is to speak impiously or irreverently of God or sacred things, and it is also interpreted to include the use of obscene or profane language. In Queen Elizabeth's reign, a person convicted of blasphemy received a punishment of having his tongue burned with a hot iron.

WINDAS

CROSSING THE LINE

This traditional ritual, now introducing the greenhorn to King Neptune in fun and merriment, was originally a very serious procedure amongst the Vikings, and was practised with all kinds of severe tests to see if the novice could really stand the hardships of the ocean.

PRESENT ARMS

The 'present arms' salute was originally a pacific and friendly gesture, meaning literally 'Presented for you to take if you wish'.

THE OLD "RED DUSTER"

The British flag was first named the 'Union Jack' in the reign of Queen Anne. Even at that date its design was practically what we now know as the Red Ensign or British Merchant Navy flag.

NO PROHIBITIONIST

Water was used to christen the U.S.S. Constitution on the first two attempts to launch her. She wouldn't budge. Then someone produced a bottle of Madeira, smashed it against her bow, and she slid gracefully into the stream.

Blazer

Officers in the British Navy were outfitted with regulation uniforms in the 18ᵗʰ century while the crewmen had to wait another century for theirs. However, certain captains took to outfitting the crews of their personal boat (gig) in special uniforms to reflect the ship's identity and individuality. The captain of one British warship, in the mid-1800s, had his gig crew dress in white trousers with a dark blue jacket on which were sewn large brass buttons. This type of dress became popular aboard other ships and with people on shore. The casual jacket that we call a "blazer" comes from the name of the ship that initiated sartorial creativity, *HMS Blazer.*

Bloody

When used by the British, this expression can mean almost anything, good or bad, depending on the tone of voice, but it usually serves as a substitute for damned or extraordinary. Once, it was a pious oath: "By our Lady!" Poor pronunciation and hurried exclamations shortened it to "By oor Leddy," then to "B'oor Luddy," and finally to "Bloody."

Blue Nose

Nova Scotia fishermen worked in cold weather and, as a result, they were referred to as "Blue Noses." This was also the name of the most famous fishing schooners on the Grand Banks. In the Navy, someone who has crossed the Arctic Circle is qualified to become a "blue-nosed polar bear."

Blue Monday

This expression came into use as early as the 18th century, when it was a custom aboard ship to log a man's daily misdeeds. On the following Monday, all culprits were flogged for their bad behavior.

Blue Moon

The expression, "once in a blue moon," means very rarely. Under certain atmospheric conditions, the full moon has a blue tinge to it, and it is seen relatively few times a year. (For readers interested in the technical aspects of a blue moon, see *Sky and Telescope Magazine*, March 1999 in which scientists have challenged existing theory.)

Blueprints by the Mile

The first ship built in America, back in 1607, was a little 30-foot craft called *Virginia of Sagadahock*. Shipbuilding was simple at that time. Men cut some logs, trimmed the timbers to shape, put them together and it then was complete. In order to build the Navy's nuclear-powered aircraft carrier *USS Enterprise*, some 350 years later, it was necessary to draw over 16,000 different plans and to produce 2,400 miles of blueprints enough to sink the little *Virginia*.

Bluff

This is the blunt bow of old sailing ships and emanated to a meaning of "stout" or "hearty."

Blunderbuss

This clumsy firearm with a trumpet-shaped muzzle got its name from the Dutch "donder-bus" (thunder-gun). The buss is a corruption of Bess, from the English weapon of the same time, called "Brown Bess." Specifically, this firearm was a short musket of wide bore and expanded muzzle that could scatter shot at close range. It was invented between 1645 and 1655. In modern language, "blunderbuss" is used to describe an insensitive, blundering person.

Boatswain, Cockswain and Skiffswain

As required by 17ᵗʰ century law, British-ships-of war carried three smaller boats: the "boat," the "cockboat" and the "skiff." The boat, or "gig," was usually used by the captain to go ashore and it was the largest of the three. The cockboat was a very small rowboat used as a ship's tender. The skiff was a lightweight all-purpose vessel. "Swain" means keeper. Thus, the keeper of the boat, cock and skiff were called boatswain, cockswain and skiffswain, respectively.

As described, a coxswain (or cockswain) was at first the swain (boy servant) in charge of the captain's boat. The term has been in use in England dating back to at least 1463. With the passing of time, the coxswain became the helmsman of any boat, regardless of size. Until 1949, a Navy boatswain's mate 3ʳᵈ class was called a cockswain. Boatswain is pronounced "bosun."

Boatswain's Pipe

No self-respecting bosun's Mate would dare admit he

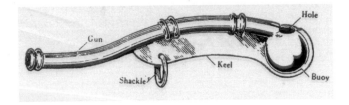

· DUTCH COURAGE ·

Slang-term for bolstered heroism. It was coined to describe a custom of the old Netherland's Navy, when it was common practise to serve schnapps or gin to the gun-crews of fighting ships prior to engaging in battle.

· EIGHT BELLS ·

This measure of time originated in the days when a half-hour glass was used to tell off the four-hour watches. Each time the sand ran out, the ship's boy, whose job it was to reverse the glass, struck a bell to show he was attending to his business. Thus, eight times he turned the glass, and eight times struck the bell.

· IN MUFTI ·

Meaning dressed in "Civvies". The word is a corruption of the West Indies "MUF-TEE", which means civilian.

· BULLY~BOYS ·

Nickname for sailors in Colonial days. However, it did not refer to any bullying or bad-tempered characteristics, but to the "Bully-Beef", standard ship grub of the time.

couldn't blow his pipe in a manner above reproach. This pipe, which is the emblem of the bosun and his mates, has an ancient and interesting history.

On the ancient row-galleys, the bosun used his pipe to "call the stroke." Later, because its shrill tune could be heard above most of the activity on board, it was used to signal various happenings such as knock off and the boarding of officials. This signaling device was important to the successful operation of a ship, and it became a badge of office and honor in British and American Navy sailing ships.

Bokoo

Often an old salt will boast that he had "bokoo" this or has done something "bokoo" times during his seafaring years. The picturesque sound of the word bokoo may cause one to wonder how it came to mean many or a lot.

Actually, bokoo is a legitimate French word, "beaucoup," meaning "very many." Americanization changed the spelling and pronunciation but the meaning remains unchanged. Like many foreign terms that have crept into our nautical lingo, bokoo is the inevitable product of generations of American seamen meeting people of other nations and adopting bokoo phrases from their languages for everyday shipboard use.

Bomb Alley

"Bomb Alley" is what the World War II British Navy termed the Strait of Sicily. This was because of the constant air attacks on British shipping at that location. (See Torpedo Junction.)

Boondocks

A remote out-of-the-way place is called a "boondock." The term reportedly comes from the relatively isolated Philippine village of "Bondoc," across the bay from Manila. Heavy boots are called boondockers.

Boot Camp

During the Spanish-American War, Navy and Marine recruits wore canvas leggings called boots. The recruits were trained in boot camp and the trainees, and others with little service or sea time, were called "boots." In modern civilian parlance, a boot is someone who has little experience or knowledge in a particular industry or setting.

Bootlegger

A bootlegger is one who conducts an illegal trade in liquor. This was first used during the reign of King George III to describe smugglers who hid valuables in their huge sea-boots when dodging His Majesty's maritime inspectors.

Botany Bay

This port is five miles south of Sydney, Australia. Captain Cook, the famed navigator, named it "Botany Bay" because of the great number of strange new plants he found there.

Bottle Message

In old sea tales, shipwrecked sailors scribbled a message, stuffed it in a bottle and tossed it into the sea, hoping someone would find it and learn what happened to them. For many years the U.S. Navy furnished "bottle papers" to mariners who dropped them overboard with notations as to when and where they were launched. The finders of these papers were encouraged to return them to the Navy for study of ocean currents.

One of the longest trips made by a message bottle began when it was dropped overboard from the *SS Linfield Victory* off Japan in March 1948. It finally turned up on the beach at Reedsport, Oregon twenty-seven years later.

Bottled Up

For many years sailors carved miniature ships which were placed in bottles. The phrase, "bottled up" or "jammed up," derived from this practice. Today, saying "traffic is bottled up or jammed up on the freeway" evolved from this hobby.

Bowsprits

"Bowsprits" are an integral part of a ship to which the figurehead is secured. The descriptive word comes from the Old Saxon "sprit," meaning, "to sprout."

Brick Battleship

The *USS Illinois*, a ship that never went to sea or even served in the Navy, was visited by an immense number of people. She was an exact replica of an *Oregon* class battleship and was built on a platform resting on pilings in Lake Michigan for the 1893 Chicago World's Fair. The ship was built of bricks covered with cement, but many of the more than 3 million people who went aboard her were certain they had been aboard an actual battleship.

Brigantine

A brigantine is a two-masted and square-rigged type of ship. It derived its name from "brigandine," a name for pirates and outlaws in the Levant, the eastern part of the Mediterranean. The term "brig," which is the

• IN THE DOG~HOUSE •

If you think this is modern slang, please note that it was coined in or around 1800. When slaves were bringing big prices on the American auction-blocks, it was the brutal custom to pack them into every available niche aboard the slave-ships. Even the officer's cabins were filled with them, while the officers had to sleep on the poop-deck in semi-cylindrical boxes, six or seven feet long, and about thirty inches high. These boxes were nicknamed "Dog-houses," and because they were so horribly uncomfortable to sleep in, the term "In the Dog-house" grew to describe being in a tough spot.

FLYING~FISH SAILOR •

Old Navy slang to differentiate between a seaman on duty in Asiatic waters, and one in a Mediterranean squadron. The latter was known as a "Sou'Spainer."

• PAINT WASHERS •

Term of contempt, used by the hairy-chested sea-dogs of wind-driven warships, to describe the young "upstarts" who served aboard the new-fangled steam-driven battle wagons..... and dared to call themselves sailors.

• BLOODY •

A meaningless expletive much in use among British Sailors. Originally a pious oath "By Our Lady," rough seamens' talk corrupted it to "By oor Leddy" "Boor Luddy," and finally, "Bloody."

compartment aboard ship in which prisoners are confined, evolved after Admiral Horatio Nelson used a brigantine to confine prisoners taken during a naval engagement.

Brightwork
"Brightwork" referred to polished metal objects. Wood that was scraped, rubbed and polished was called bright woodwork.

British Clipper Racing
One of the greatest sea races of all time ended in London, in September 6, 1866 when the clippers *Taeping, Ariel* and *Serica* arrived after a 14,060-mile run from Foochow, China. All three ships sailed from Foochow on May 30 and were extremely close to each other for the entire distance. *Taeping* docked in London at 9:45 PM, the *Ariel* docked 30 minutes later and the *Serica* came in an hour and 15 minutes after the *Ariel.*

Broad in the Beam
It is obvious that this jocular anatomical description is of nautical origin and it needs no explanation.

Brown Bagger
This is someone who carries lunch to work. It originally applied to married men on shore duty who brought lunch from home in a brown bag. Today, anyone who takes lunch to the office "brown bags" it.

Buccaneers
Buccaneers were the pirates who raided Spanish ships and colonies along the American coast in the second half of the seventeenth century. These sea rovers came to piracy from England, France and Netherlands. Buccaneer comes from the French "boucanier," which derives from the Caribe word "boucan" (dried meat.) The pirates learned how to prepare dried meat through the smoking process, and they carried on an illegal trade in it. It is somewhat amusing to know that the buccaneers acquired a name that includes a heritage of being expert beef smokers rather than one of a swashbuckling nature.

Bucket of Grog
In the old days, the Swedes knew how to make their holidays happy. It was the custom, aboard Swedish vessels, to place a bucket of grog at the wheel for whoever wanted a drink during the period between December 24 and January 1.

Bully Boys
"Bully Boys," a term prominent in Navy shanties and poems, means in the strictest sense, "beef-eating sailors." Sailors of the Colonial Navy had a daily menu of an amazingly elastic substance called "bully beef," which was actually beef jerky. The item appeared so frequently on the mess deck that it naturally lent its name to the sailors who had to eat it. As an indication of the beef's texture and chewability, it was also called "salt junk," alluding to the rope yarn that was used for caulking the ship's seams.

Bumboat
In spite of their name, "bumboats" are not boats piloted by bums or hoboes. They are small boats used

by natives and commercial salesmen to sell their wares to sailors on ships anchored in a harbor. The name is a hand-me-down from "boom boats," as the craft were once permitted to tie up to the boat boom of a ship. An early Low German spelling was "bumboat," and in that form it was taken by American sailors.

Buoy
This is any kind of float used to mark a channel or carry a navigational aid. The word evolved from the old English "boye," meaning "float."

Burnt Offerings and Admiralty Ham
Sailors of the old Royal Navy gave the nickname of "burnt offerings" to roasted beef and mutton, and they referred to canned fish as "admiralty ham."

Buttons on Sleeves
The sleeves of midshipmen in the British Navy had to have buttons sewed on them at the orders of Admiral Nelson. In those days, midshipmen had no pockets in their uniforms in which to carry a handkerchief; and

· DEAD MARINES ·

This slang-term for empty bottles was coined when, at a banquet aboard ship in his honor, the Duke of Clarence ordered the removal of the "empties," saying "Take away those dead marines." A major of marines asked haughtily "Why nickname empty bottles after my honorable corps?" "Because," replied the ready witted Duke, anxious to give no offence, "they are fine fellows who have nobly done their duty, and, if filled once more, would be willing to do so again."

· JOSS ·

Chinese name for a god. It is really a corruption of the Portugese "Dios" and was learned from Magellan's sailors when they visited the Orient.

· FIRST NAVY UNIFORMS ·

Until the year 1747 the dress of sailormen was very nondescript. At that time King George II ordered uniforms to be worn by all navy men, as a means of boosting their appearance and morale.

· ONCE *in a* BLUE MOON ·

Believe it or not, this phrase is not just a whimsical saying used when expressing any unusual happening, but actually refers to a condition of the moon, which on certain rare occasions assumes a bluish color. It was last reported by the British Navy in 1883.

the buttons were so placed to discourage them from the practice of wiping their noses on their sleeves.

By the Great Horn Spoon
This sea-going oath is supposed to refer to the constellation known as the Big Dipper, which early mariners knew as "The Great Horn Spoon." This name, in turn, referred to the days when feeding utensils were primitive and few. During this time, the wives and families of lowly people had small spoons carved from horn. The head of the house had a large horn spoon, which served the double purpose of helping the family from the common bowl and by which he fed himself.

Camel
"Camels" are used in port as floating fenders that are made up of beams or logs. Used singly or in clusters, they are placed between a ship and her pier when moored to the shore. When used as a floating dock, camels can be used to help lift a vessel over shallow water when entering or leaving port. It is believed that this device was first used in Amsterdam as early as the 14th century.

Camel Cargo
In 1856, the United States sent *USS Supply* to Smyrna, formerly Izmir, to bring back a load of 50 camels, which it believed could replace Army mules in the southwest. The camels were unloaded in Powder Horn, Texas in May 1856. Soldiers preferred mules and they did not care for camels, and apparently, the camels did not care for Texas. Sold out of the Army, a few of the camels went to a circus and the rest were turned loose in Arizona. A few survived until about 1905.

Canoe
It is believed that this small, light, double-ended boat originated with the Indians of North America. However, it is understood that the name of "canoe" came from the West Indies Haitian word, "canne," which means boat.

Canteens
Canteens aboard naval vessels are not as new as some people might think, because the Romans had them too. A street called "Via Quintana" in Rome was the place where Julius Caesar's legionnaires went to shop when they went to town, and it is from that street that canteen received its name.

Cape Cod Turkey
In the old sailing ship days, "Cape Cod turkey" was the nickname for salted codfish.

Cape of Good Hope
The Cape of Good Hope is located at the extreme southern tip of the African continent. It was first rounded by Phoenician sailors who took their ships from the Red Sea clockwise around the continent to the Strait of Gibraltar and back to Egypt about 600 B.C. In 488, the Portuguese explorer Bartholomeu Dias, rounded the Cape in an eastward direction for the first time. Because of the fierce storms, he named it the Cape of Torments. Later, King John of Portugal changed the name to Good Hope. Until the Suez Canal was opened, all ships had to round the Cape. Today, the super tankers are so large that they cannot go through the Suez Canal, and they must travel around the Cape.

Cape Horn Fever
This is an old-time description for malingering when in far southern and stormy latitudes. Sailors developed "sudden and mysterious maladies" that they originated in order to keep them in their bunks instead of working on deck. A mate with a rope-end in his hand usually cured the "fever" in a hurry.

Captain
Captain evolved directly from the Latin "caput," for head. Captains were the highest-ranking officers in the Navy until 1862, at which time the rank of Admiral was instituted.

Captain of the Head
In Navy parlance, he is the enlisted man whose undesired assignment is to keep the head tidy and complete with necessary supplies. Thankfully, this is a temporary duty assignment, not a permanent one.

Captain's Mast
The term "mast" refers to the ceremony that takes place when the captain awards non-judicial punishment for regulation infractions or official recognition for jobs well done. In the days of sail, ceremonies were held under the mainmast on a regular basis and usually on a Sunday morning just before divine services. Consequently, the ceremony came to be known as mast in recognition of the locality of the presentation.

Careen
"Careen" came from the French "carin," which translated into "turn over." In sailing ship days, it was not unusual to run a ship onto the beach and careen her, first to one side and then to the other, to clean her bottom.

· BERSERK ·

This word, denoting ungovernable rage, was coined from a custom of the Vikings, who, to prove their courage in desperate fights, would tear off their shirts of mail, and fight half-naked. Hence the term "Ber-serk" or "Bare-sark", meaning literally "Bare of Shirt", as sark is the Norse word for shirt.

· DERRICKS ·

Ship's loading booms received their name from an enterprising hangman of Queen Elizabeth's reign. Mr. Derrick was a true artist, and invented a swinging beam for his gallows, with topping lift 'n' everything.

· PORTHOLES ·

Port holes were originally gunports. In early days no provision whatever was made for admitting air or light into the crew's quarters, which remained foul and gloomy until recent times.

· CAREEN ·

This method of cleaning or repairing ship's hulls, was named for the French word "carin", meaning "to turn over."

Careful With Them Cannons!

The old sloop of war *Constellation*, now a permanent exhibit in Baltimore, carries cannons that never could fire. The original iron guns cost too much to maintain, so they have been replaced with exact copies made of plastic. Since the vessel was reduced in weight by 80 tons with the departure of the original weapons, she rode too high in the water. This was corrected by using lead ingots as ballast.

Cargo

This is a word that came from the Latin "carga," meaning a load. It applies to anything carried by ships, barges, and aircraft.

Carry On

In the days of sail, the officer of the deck kept a weather eye constantly on the slightest change in wind so sail could be reefed or added as necessary to ensure the fastest headway. Whenever a good breeze came along, the order to "carry on" would be given. It meant to hoist every bit of canvas the yards could carry. Pity the poor sailor whose weather eye failed him and the ship was caught partially reefed when a good breeze arrived.

Through the centuries the term's connotation has changed somewhat. Today, the Bluejacket's Manual defines carry on as an order to resume work, but not the grueling work of two centuries ago.

Cash for Columbus: An Angel

Nothing could be more romantic than the story of Queen Isabella of Spain pawning her jewels in order to finance the voyage of Columbus to the New World, but it didn't happen. The Queen didn't provide any money. Columbus borrowed the money from Luis de Sant-Angel, keeper of the treasury of Spain.

Catamaran

The "catamaran" was developed in Ceylon where it was called a "tamil kattumaran." It is from this that the name generated. Initially, the boat was not much more than a sailing raft of logs lashed together. The double canoes seen in the Pacific islands by early explorers more nearly resemble the modern catamaran.

Catheads

"Catheads" were short heavy booms extending from the rail to port and starboard, near the bows. Secured slightly aft and above the hawseholes, they were used for the hauling of anchors. They were found on most ships until the beginning of the 20th century, when they became obsolete. They were so named because in very early times they were decorated with carvings representing cat's heads. In those days, cats were highly favored as ship pets.

Cat-O'Nine Tails

The British Navy authorized this instrument of punishment in the late 1700s and it was used as recently as 1881. A 1788 description says, "it consists of a handle or stem, made of rope 3-1/2 inches in circumference and about 16 inches in length, at one end of which are fastened nine branches or tails, composed of log line, with three or more knots upon each branch." Although the number of lashes was limited in accordance with the infraction, a number of sadistic or angry captains far exceeded the amount. In a number of instances, the use of Cat-O'-Nine Tails caused death by shock or infection.

Caulk Off

Pronounced "cork off," this refers to sleeping. It comes from the time that men sleeping on deck in sailing ships had their backs marked by the pitch used to fill seams after they were caulked or packed with oakum.

Chains

Originally, chains were used to brace the platform on which the leadsman stood when "heaving the lead." Gradually, the term chains was used to designate the platform itself. Today, any place where a man stands when heaving the lead, platform or otherwise, is called the "chains."

Chaplain

"Chaplains," the military men of the cloth are rightly named according to French legend. It seems that Saint Martin of Tours shared his cloak by splitting it in half with a beggar (Christ) on a wintry day at the gates of Amiens, France. On this basis, the cloak was preserved, and it became the sacred banner of French kings. The officer tasked with the care of the cloak and carrying it into battle was called the "chaplain" or "cloak bearer." Chaplain comes from the French word "chapele," meaning a short cloak. Later, priests or chaplains, rather than field officers were charged with the care of the sacred cloak.

Chaplains served aboard warships of many nations and in the British and American navies they collected four pence per month from each member of the crew. In return, they rewarded every seaman who learned a psalm by giving him six pence. Besides holding divine services, chaplains were charged with instruction of midshipmen and the moral guidance of officers and men alike. It wasn't until the 18th century that chaplains were permitted to dine in the wardroom. Previously,

· BOOTLEGGER ·

This is a modern term with an old origin. Bootleggers got their name from smugglers in King George the Third's reign. The nickname derived from the smuggler's custom of hiding packages of valuables in their huge sea-boots when dodging His Majesty's coastguardsmen.

· HOG - YOKE ·

Old Navy slang for that indispensable instrument of navigation ....the sextant.

· SCOTTISH ENGINEERS ·

So strong is the tradition that Scotchmen are born marine engineers, that many folk maintain you can yell "Are you there, Mac?" into the engine-room of any ship afloat (regardless of nationality) and receive an affirmative answer.

· ONE CASUALTY ·

Amazing as it seems the American fleet in the Battle of Santiago lost but one sailor, while the Spanish Admiral Cerveras lost every vessel under his command and 500 men.

they messed in their own cabins, although they were frequently invited to dine with the captain.

Charley Noble
The enlisted man's name for the galley smokestack is "Charley Noble." The funnel is named after a stern old merchant captain who discovered that the galley's smokestack was made of copper and therefore should receive a daily polishing. In today's Navy, it is the custom to send green recruits to find Charley Noble, a hunt that causes endless amusement for the ship's veterans.

Charts
It is believed that the first charts to be used by European seamen were made by the Italians in 1351. They were called "portolani" or "portolans," and they were usually printed on sheepskins. The U.S. Navy began printing charts in 1883. Now, more than thirty million are produced every year.

Cheese It
No matter how one slices it, cheese is cheese. That is, until it's fired out of a cannon. Cheese actually was used in a naval battle in 1841, when ships of the Uruguay and Argentine navies met in battle. Several of the Uruguayan ships were low on cannon balls, so the sailors loaded their guns with hard round cheeses. History records that the Uruguayan fleet won the fight.

Cheese-Paring
This much-used term has lost much of its original meaning. Today, it describes the acts of a niggardly, miserly person. Originally, "cheese-paring" meant petty theft. Some shipmasters that carried cargoes of cheese from Holland to London would steal the mold ridge from the balls of cheese, and press them into extra balls for their own profits. Since they used knives in the whittling-down process, they became known as "cheese-parers."

Cheesebox on a Raft
That was the derisive term applied to the *USS Monitor*, the Civil War ironclad. Using its revolving turret, this ship fought the Confederate ironclad *CSS Virginia* in the famous Battle of Hampton Roads on March 9, 1862. The *Monitor-Virginia* battle doomed all wooden ships; after that, the navies of the world built steam-powered, iron-hulled ships. The *Monitor* sank off Cape Hatteras in a storm the night of December 31, 1862, and for over a hundred years her exact location was a mystery. Finally, in 1973, she was discovered through the endeavors of midshipmen at the U.S. Naval Acad-

emy. The area of the ocean bottom where the *Monitor* lies has been declared the first Marine Sanctuary in the United States.

Chief Housemaid
The old British Navy gave the first lieutenant this nickname because this officer was responsible for the cleanliness of the ship between decks.

Chinese Gangway
This type of gangway is one that leads forward instead of aft, which is opposite to the traditional manner. A boat that makes a "Chinese gangway" goes alongside a ship with its bow facing the stern of the ship, instead of the customary bow-to-bow approach.

Chipping with a Rubber Hammer
An old-time superstition regarding eternal punishment for wicked seamen pictured them forever hopelessly chipping with a hammer made of rubber.

Chit
One tradition carried on in the Navy is the use of the "chit." It is a carryover from the days when Hindu traders used slips of paper called "chitthi" for money, so they wouldn't have to carry heavy bags of gold and silver. British sailors shortened the word to chit and applied it to their mess vouchers. Its most outstanding use in the modern Navy is for drawing pay and a form used for requesting leave and liberty. But the term is currently applied to almost any piece of paper from a pass to an official letter requesting some privilege.

Chop
When used in radio communications "chop" means to transfer control from one command to another. It is also to indicate approval on paper. This word is from the Hindu "chap," meaning "stamp."

Chow
The Far East represented a challenge for English-speakers because they found it difficult to pronounce native words, so they adopted singsong versions of them. Such was the case with an ancient name of a recipe for mixed pickles. Unable to accurately repeat the Chinese name for this concoction, they called it "chow-chow." No one could tell what it was composed of, so this name was given to any dish in which the contents could not be distinguished. On long voyages between the Orient and London, the cooks ran low on food and had to serve any kind of stew that they could make. Seamen complained about having to eat so much indescribable food or chow-chow. They cut

· YANKEE ·

The nickname of YANKEE was first applied to Americans by merchants of Holland. Because of the argumentative traits of certain American captains trading with the Netherlands, Dutchmen jeeringly called them "Yankers" (wranglers), and the name stuck..

· DAVITS ·

These devices for hoisting boats were named for their inventor, a Welshman named David, and given the Welsh pronunciation of that word viz. Davit.

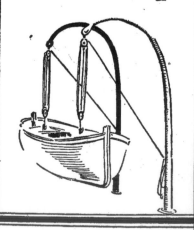

· LISTLESS ·

This good dictionary word, meaning dull or lifeless, was coined in the days of sail, when, under a good breeze, ships would list sharply to port or starboard. When there was no wind, they would ride without any list (listlessly) sluggishly, devoid of pep.

·LATITUDE and LONGITUDE·

Latitude and Longitude were first arrived at by astronomical observation, by Arabian ship-masters way back in the 15th. century.

the name in half to "chow" and eventually, chow reached its present meaning of any food-mixed or pure. The use of chow as a word is almost as varied as the ingredients in the original menus: chow down; chow up; chow hall and chow time.

Christening Ceremony

When a ship is launched, she is officially named by a sponsor who breaks a bottle of champagne over the bow of the ship as she says, "I christen thee . . ." A bottle of water was used when the *Constitution* (Old Ironsides) was launched, but the ship refused to budge. The launch succeeded when a bottle of Madeira wine was brought forth. The first woman sponsor of a naval vessel was a Miss Watson of Philadelphia, who christened the *USS Germantown* on October 22, 1846.

The only woman non-American citizen to christen a Navy ship was Lady Dixon, wife of Australian Minister Sir Owen Dixon. In 1943, she christened *USS Canberra*. This ship was named for *HMAS Canberra*, which was lost in the Battle of Savo Island.

Christmas Tree

A modern vessel's lighted control panel of red and green lights is known as a "Christmas tree."

Chronometers

"Chronometers" are the precision instruments that navigators and quartermasters treat with tender care. They are absolutely necessary in navigation. More specifically, they are time pieces or timing devices for use in determining longitude at sea or for any purpose where very exact measurement of time is required. Until they were invented, navigators had no way of timing their celestial observations. John Harrison, an English carpenter, made the first successful chronometer. Harrison's invention was made mostly of wood, and it weighed 66 pounds. The instrument proved itself aboard *HMS Centurion* in 1735. (See latitude and longitude for additional detail.)

Clawing Off

"Clawing off" is an old sea-going term for anyone stuttering, stammering or trying to side step an embarrassing question or argument. It is related to the back-breaking task of "kedging" (clawing) sailing ships past calms to catch a breeze. The task itself consisted of conveying a kedge anchor a cable's-length ahead of a becalmed vessel; dropping it over and rowing back to the ship. Then, with the cable bent onto a windlass, men heaved the ship forward to the kedge and repeated the operation until they encountered the desired breeze.

Clean Bill of Health

This widely used term had its origins in the document issued to a ship showing that the port it sailed from suffered from no epidemic or infection at the time of departure.

Clipper Ships

These sharp-bowed, fast sailing ships were an American development. The first clipper, *Rainbow*, was built in 1845; the last one was put to sea about 1860. In that time more than 400 of the tall ships were constructed. The *Sea Witch* could spread more than an acre of canvas.

Close Quarters

This term, now used to express hard fighting, was originally "closed quarters." The phrase referred specifically to special deckhouses where the crew could take refuge if boarders tried to take the ship. The doors were barred and loopholed, so a deadly fire could be poured into the enemy.

Coast Guard

The United States Coast Guard was formed in 1915 by a combination of the Revenue Cutter Service and the Lifesaving Service. The motto of the Coast Guard is "Semper Paratus," meaning "always ready." The history of the Coast Guard goes back to 1790 when the Revenue Service was created by Secretary of the Treasury, Alexander Hamilton. The first vessels were ten cutters, ranging from 30 to 50 tons in size. During wartime, the Coast Guard operates as a branch of the Navy.

Coffin Ships

This refers to old and non-seaworthy craft that were over-insured by their owners and sent to sea with the idea of deliberately sinking them for the maritime insurance proceeds.

Coins for Charon

The custom of placing coins in the step beneath a mast when a ship is being constructed had its origin with the ancient Romans. It was their custom to place coins in the mouth of a dead person in the belief this would enable him to pay "Charon" to ferry him across the river Styx. This custom continued to some extent; a Spanish wreck that was found off England had a coin dated 1618 under its mast.

Collision Mats

The huge mats used to place over a hole in the hull of a ship to prevent flooding. Sailors also use "collision

· SEA SHANTIES ·

Sea chanteys (or shanties) received their name from an old custom of the negroes in the West Indies. When these men moved from one job to another, they would drag their shanties (huts) with them, what time one of their number would sit astride the hut and sing melodies to put a swing into the work of hauling. English sailors watching the manoevers forever afterwards associated the hut with the tunes, and gave the nickname of "sea-shanties" to all sea songs.

·LIBERTINE ·

Today a word implying, a a person of easy morals, its origin meant nothing of loose living, but was the name for sailors on Roman ships of war.

·CHAIN CABLES·

"Old Ironsides" was one of the last American ships to use hemp cables for her anchors. In 1812 chain cables were introduced, and quickly demonstrated their superiority over rope.

·KEEP A SHOT *in the* LOCKER·

Old navy slang which was the early equivalent of the modern "put a little bit away for a rainy day." It got its meaning from an admiralty order advising captains to "Keep always good reserve supplies in the shot-locker."

mats" as a name for pancakes.

Columbia
The *Columbia,* a three-master out of Boston, was the first American ship to sail around the world. She made the trip in 35 months, from 1787 to 1790. The Columbia River in Oregon is named for this vessel.

Commander
When it was first used as a designation of rank in the Navy in 1838, it was for the purpose of replacing "master commandant." The rank comes from "commandeur" that was introduced in the British Navy by William III (1553-1584).

Commissioning a Navy Ship
The commissioning ceremony celebrates a ship's entry into active service of the United States Navy. When a "commission pennant" breaks for the first time, a ship officially becomes a Navy vessel and takes her place alongside the remainder of the fleet.

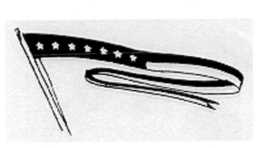

The commission ceremony itself continues a 325 year old tradition observed by navies throughout the world, and by the U.S. Navy since the frigate *Alfred,* the first ship of the Continental Navy, was placed in service in December 1775. It is one of the most significant events in the life of a ship.

Though no written procedure was laid down for early U.S. ships, the commission ceremony would have been familiar to sailors accustomed to Royal Navy tradition. In most cases, The commanding officer came aboard, called the crew to quarters and read his orders appointing him to command. He then ordered the ensign and commission pennant be closed up and directed that the first entries be made in the deck log.

The commission pennant is the outward symbol of an active Navy ship. The American commission pennant is a narrow red and white streamer with a blue hoist with seven stars. Narrow pennants of this type have been used on naval vessels for thousands of years and are seen in ancient Egyptian artwork and medieval manuscripts. The pennants were originally used to help mariners tell the differences between a man-o'- war and a merchant vessel at a distance. As professional national navies emerged, they adopted the colors of the national flag. The practice became

standard and continues today as the distinctive mark of a commissioned ship.

Commodore
William III first introduced this title into the British Navy. It was one rank above captain. This designation was first used by the U.S. Navy in 1862, abolished in 1899, revived during World War II and abolished postwar. The equivalent rank in today's Navy and Coast Guard is rear admiral, lower half. As a matter or courtesy, the title applies to any officer commanding a squadron or flotilla of destroyers or smaller ships. This is also a popular name for the head of civilian yacht and boat clubs.

Compass
The magnetic compass was first used by the Chinese as early as 2600 BC. An oddity of their compass was that the south end of the needle is marked, not the north end. Compasses were next used by the Arabs in the 8th century and finally reached northern Europe in the 13th century. Several hundred years ago, many compasses used in the Mediterranean had their east point marked since that indicated the direction to Mecca. Early compasses were marked four points-north, south, east and west, and eventually 32. The United States Navy adopted the 360-degree compass at the beginning of the 20th century, while the British Navy did not follow suit until during World War II.

Continental Navy
The "Continental Navy" was the forerunner of the United States Navy. It was established on October 13, 1775. The first four ships in the Navy were all named for foreigners. They were: (1) *Alfred* (for King Alfred the Great who founded the British Navy between 878-900 AD); (2) *Columbus* (for Christopher Columbus who discovered the New World in 1492); (3) *Cabot* (for John Cabot, who was really an Italian named Giovanni Caboto, the first English explorer of America); and (4) *Andrew Doria* (for Andrea Doria, a Genoese admiral who lived at the same time as Columbus).

Coxswain
During the 15th century, a ship captain had for his use a small rowboat called a "cockboat," a "swain" was in charge and he was called a "cockswain." Whether oars, sail or motor in future years, he served as "helmsman." The change in spelling from cockswain to "coxswain" occurred during the 17th century. During World War II, a Navy or Coast Guard coxswain held the rate of

· BOTTLED UP ·

Today a term in naval par-lance, indicating that an enemy fleet is so completely hemmed in that it cannot manoeuver, the phrase itself was coined to illus-trate the quaint custom of old sailormen, who would carve little models of ships on which they had served, and put them in bottles.

WINDAS

· CARRY ON ·

While the order "Carry On" now means only to proceed with any duty, it was originally a specific order not to shorten sail, but to carry on all canvas the ship would stand unless stress of bad weather dictated otherwise.

· BUCCANEER ·

Alas for the dreams of boyhood! The original buccaneers were not romantic pirates, but only a bunch of hard-working swabs who made "Boucan" (smoked beef) for a living. Hence Boucan or Buccan-eer.

· MIND YOUR P'S and Q'S ·

Nowadays a term meaning "Be on your best behavior." In old days, sailors serving aboard government ships could always get credit at the waterfront taverns until pay-day. As they would only pay for those drinks which were marked up on the score-board, the tavern-keeper had to be careful that no Pints or Quarts had been omitted from the customer's list.

third class petty officer. His promotions would lead him to boatswain mate second class and upward to chief boatswain's mate. The modern Navy now has the rating of boatswain's mate third class.

Crew
Originally applying to the men in a ship's company, the meaning has been extended to groups of people working together. In illustration, there is a flight crew, stage crew, train crew, wrecking crew and many more. The word comes from the French "creue," meaning "augmentation or reinforcements."

Crossing the Line
When a ship crosses the Equator, all those aboard who are doing so for the first time are known as "Pollywogs." They are initiated into the "Ancient Order of the Deep" by "Shellbacks," those who have crossed before. This ceremony had its origin long ago, and such initiations were held when ships sailed south across the 30th parallel of latitude, or when they passed through the Straits of Gibraltar. It is believed that the ceremony started with the Vikings, who passed it on to the Anglo-Saxons and Normans.

In the U.S. Navy, men who cross the line are given an elaborate certificate attesting to their shellback status, as well as a small card for their wallet. Probably the biggest mass initiation of pollywogs in the Navy took place in 1935, when the entire Pacific Fleet steamed south from Panama just far enough to cross the line. A crossing-the-line party can be very elaborate, with sailors costumed as King Neptune, Davey Jones, Queen Amphritite, the Royal Baby, Royal Bears, Royal Cops, Royal Barber, Royal Chaplain, Royal Navigator and any number of other characters. When a ship crosses the line, rank has no privilege a senior officer who is a pollywog is initiated along with all the lesser ranks and rates.

Crow's Nest
The crow (the bird) was an essential part of the early sailors navigational equipment. These land-lubbing fowl were carried on board to help the navigator determine where the closest land lay when

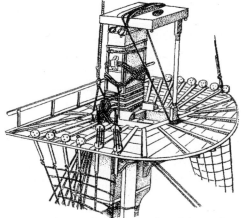

the weather prevented sighting the shore visually. In cases of poor visibility, a crow was released and the navigator plotted a course that corresponded with the bird's flight because it invariably headed toward land. The crow's nest was situated high in the main mast where the look-out stood his watch. Often, he shared this lofty perch with a crow or two since the crow's cages were kept there: hence the "crow's nest."

Cruiser
This fast, well-armed warship takes its name from the Dutch "kruise," which means "to cross."

Cuban Souvenir
During the Spanish-American War of 1898, American troops staged a landing at a small Cuban town no one had ever heard of. The local residents treated some of the officers to a cool, refreshing drink. When they came home, they brought back the recipe and named the drink after the town where they found it. This is how we got the "daiquiri."

Cumshaw
"Cumshaw" is Navy jargon for, "a little extra on the side," or "something for nothing." It comes from the Chinese "kam sia" used by beggars to express grateful thanks.

Cute
The 14th century saw increasing interest in geometry as a result of the expanding activities of sailors, explorers and scholars. The word "acute" was derived from an ancient Latin word for needle, and any sharp-pointed angle was referred to by that name. The word was shortened to "cute," describing "intellectual sharpness" and became synonymous with an appreciation for clever inventions or gadgets. Over the years, the word was given a twist and is used to describe something or someone that is attractive or pretty.

Cut of His Jib
This is another phrase pertaining to a person's general appearance. It is derived from the days when it was possible to distinguish French ships by their two small jib sails while British ships had one large single jib.

Dago
This word, which has been a disparaging nickname for Italians or Portuguese, is at least 400 years old. The name of their patron saint was "St. Diego," which was pronounced incorrectly and shortened to "Dago" by rival seamen.

· KNOTS ·

To ascertain the speed of his vessel, a British commander had knots tied at regular intervals in a coil of rope. The rope was then bent onto a log, and the log hove overboard. With an hour-glass, he timed each knot as it disappeared over the taffrail ... thus originating the custom of telling off a ship's speed by knots instead of miles.

· HALLIARDS ·

Originally an order "Haul Yards", these two words were corrupted into one which now designates any lines used for hoisting sails, flags etc.

· JACK TAR ·

International nickname for government sailors, because of the custom among old navy men of giving their work-clothes a light coating of tar to water-proof them.

· THE CUT of HIS JIB ·

An everyday phrase referring to a man's general appearance. The term derives from the days when it was possible to distinguish French vessels at a distance because of their two small jibs, and a British ship by her huge single jib.

Dandyfunk

"Dandyfunk" was a messy concoction of broken ship biscuit smeared with molasses, but it was one of the few desserts ever served aboard the old wood ships. Understandably, it is composed of the words dandy and funk.

Davey Jones' Locker

Since the mid-1700s seamen have used the saying, "going to Davey Jones' Locker" to point to death, very possibly by drowning. It is believed that the saying came forth from the Bible story in which Jonah is described as having stowed away in a whale for three days. In connection with this rationale, it is thought "Davey" evolved from St. David, the patron saint of Welsh sailors and that "Locker" refers to the storage chest of a seaman.

Davits

These small crane-like fittings are used for hoisting boats, anchors, etc. aboard ship. They were invented by, and named for a Welshman with the name of David. In Welsh, it is pronounced "davit."

Dead Horse

British seamen, apt to be ashore and unemployed for considerable periods between voyages, generally preferred to live in boarding houses near the piers while waiting for sailing ships to take on crews. During these periods of unrestricted liberty, many ran out of money so the innkeepers carried them on credit until hired for another voyage.

When a seaman was booked on a ship, he was customarily advanced a month's wages, if needed, to pay off his boarding house debt. Then, while paying back the ship's master, he worked for nothing but "salt horse" the first several weeks aboard.

Salt horse was the staple diet of early sailors and it wasn't exactly tasty cuisine. Consisting of low quality beef that had been heavily salted, the salt horse was tough to chew and even harder to digest.

When the debt had been repaid, the salt horse was said to be dead and it was a time for great celebration among the crew. Usually, an effigy of a horse was constructed from odds and ends, set afire and then cast afloat to the cheers and hilarity of the ex-debtors. Today, just as in the days of sail, "dead horse" refers to a debt to the government for advance pay.

Dead Marine

The Duke of Clarence originated a term for an empty bottle. At a banquet aboard ship in his honor, he ordered the removal of empty bottles by saying, "Take away those dead marines." A Marine major objected to calling the bottles dead marines, and the Duke responded, "They are fine fellows who have nobly done their duty and, if filled once more, would be willing to do so again."

Dead Reckoning

A method of navigation by which the position of a ship is fixed by plotting the distance steamed and course steered from the last well-established position. It was originally called "deduced reckoning," then shortened to "ded reckoning," but somewhere along the line, someone thought the "a" had been left out of "ded" so he put it in. That's how it's been ever since.

Deck Ape

This is another example of nautical lingo for a sailor working on the topside of a ship. Such a seaman is also known as a "swab jockey."

Deep Six

"Deep six" is the nautical way of saying, "throw it away," or "get rid of it." The expression comes from the leadsman taking soundings and shouting, "By the deep six!" when the water is six fathoms, or 36 feet deep. In modern times, deep six retains its original nautical meaning.

Derricks

Whether they are cargo booms rigged to a kingpost aboard ship, or towering above an oil well, "derricks" take their name from a 17th century hangman who plied his trade at Tyburn, England during the reign of Queen Elizabeth. Mr. Derrick invented a swinging boom for his gallows with topping lift and boom step bracket, just as they are fitted today.

• SIRENS •

Ships' foghorns got their name from the women of Greek mythology known as SIRENS. Beautiful but cruel, they used their marvellous voices to lure sailors to destruction. Ulysses outwitted them by having himself bound to the mast, while his seamen, their ears plugged so that they could not hear the enticing voices of the women, rowed him safely past the danger zone.

• CUTTING A DIDO •

This term to describe some smart-aleck cutting monkey-shines, was coined because the commander of H.M.S. DIDO used to delight showing off the superior sailing qualities of his brig by sailing in circles around the slow moving old ships-of-the-Line.

• FOUNDER of NAVAL POWER •

The first known to recognise the importance of maritime power was King Minos of Crete. He established the first navy in 3,000 B.C.

• BOOBY •

Here is a perfectly legitimate dictionary word used to describe a foolish person. It gets its meaning from the crazy antics of the booby bird.

Devil to Pay

Today, the expression "devil to pay" is used primarily as a means of conveying an unpleasant and impending happening. Originally, this expression denoted a specific task aboard ship: caulking the ship's longest seam. The "devil" was the longest seam on the wooden ship, and caulking was done with pitch, which was known as "pay." The task of "paying the devil" was a grueling one, and this expression was used to describe any unpleasant task.

Different ships . . . Different Long Splices

Is an old Navy colloquialism meaning there is more than one side to an argument and more than one way of doing a shipshape job.

Dinghy

The name of the smallest boat on a ship comes from India. In Hindu, "dinga" means boat and "dingi" is the diminutive of dinga.

Dipping of the National Ensign

This is a relic of an old-time custom by which a merchant vessel was required not only to heave to when approaching a warship on the high seas, but also to clew up all her canvas. This was to indicate her honesty and willingness to be searched. Delays resulted and in later years the rule of dipping the flag was authorized as a time-saving substitute. Merchant ships dip first, naval vessels answer. Ships of the United States Navy return dip for dip.

Ditty Bag

"Ditty bag" (or box) was originally called the "ditto bag" because it contained at least two of everything: two needles, two spools of thread, two buttons, etc. With the passing of years, the "ditto" was dropped in favor of "ditty," and remains so today. Before World War I, the Navy issued ditty boxes made of wood and styled them after footlockers. These carried the personal gear and some clothes of the sailor. Today, the ditty bag is still issued to recruits and contains a sewing kit, toiletry articles and personal items such as writing paper and pens.

Doctor Discharge

In the last days of sail, when experienced sailors were at a premium, ordinary seamen would pay the ship's cook to alter their discharges into the higher rating of able-bodied seaman (ABS). Since the cook was traditionally called "Doc" aboard ship, the faked tickets became known as "Doctor Discharges."

Dog House

"In the dog house," indicates that one is in disfavor or disgrace, and it originated in the early 1800s during the slave trade. Slave ships filled every nook and cranny with their unfortunate cargo, and sometimes the slaves were crowded into the officer's cabins. Disliked or unpopular officers were usually chosen to give up their quarters and to sleep on deck in small box-like structures, which were referred to as "dog houses." They were most uncomfortable, so the term "in the dog house" came to describe being "in an unfavorable position in the view of someone."

Dog Watch

"Dog watch" is the name given to the 1600-1800 and the 1800-2000 watches aboard ship. The 1600-2000 four-hour watch was originally split to prevent men from always having the need to stand the same watches daily. As a result, sailors dodge the same daily routine; hence they are dodging the watch or standing the dodge watch. In its corrupted form, "dodge" becomes "dog" and the procedure is referred to as "dogging the watch" or standing the dog watch.

Donkey Engine

The small auxiliary engine used on deck in merchant ships was so called because it replaced the donkey, which once powered hoisting gear along the waterfront.

Donkey's Breakfast.

In old sailing ships, sailors slept on the deck or on bare bunk boards, and later in hammocks. Any kind of a mattress was a great luxury. Because the first sea-going mattresses were usually filled with hay or straw, "donkey's breakfast" became a synonym for such beds.

Don't Give Up the Ship

Legend has it that Captain James Lawrence shouted these immortal words while mortally wounded on board the U.S. frigate *Chesapeake* during its battle with *HMS Shannon* off Boston in the War of 1812. His actual words were, "Tell the men to fire faster and not give up the ship; fight her till she sinks!" The *Chesapeake*'s rigging was cut away in an exchange of broadsides and she lost maneuverability. Despite the valiant crew's struggle to carry out their captain's last order, they were overwhelmed. *Chesapeake* was repaired, taken into the Royal Navy and broken up at Plymouth, England, in 1820.

• RAISING THE WIND •

This popular slang term for raising funds for some specific purpose dates back to early days, when a shipmaster would go to a witch or fortune-teller and pay big money for the old harridan's assurance that good winds would surely drive his vessel for the entire voyage and bring her safely back home.

• FIRST U.S. NAVAL COMMISSION •

The first U.S. Naval commission was that given to Captain Samuel Nicols of the U.S. Marines by the Continental Congress Nov. 28th. 1775.

• LIFE-BUOY •

The life-buoy got its name by the simple expedient of dropping the last three letters from the word "buoyant."

• SHROUDS •

The side and backstays of a mast were called "shrouds" because in early times the quality of these standing ropes was so poor, that the vast number which had to be used for strength shrouded (hid) the mast from view.

Don't Sink Our President!

On November 14, 1943, the destroyer, *USS William D. Porter*, nicknamed "Willie Dee," accidentally sent a live torpedo at the 52,000 ton battleship, *USS Iowa*. As bad as this may appear, it was even worse since *Iowa* was carrying President Franklin D. Roosevelt, Secretary of State Cordell Hull and the country's top military leaders to the Casablanca Conference. Roosevelt and his entourage were on their way to meet with Joseph Stalin of the Soviet Union and Winston Churchill of Great Britain. Had *William D. Porter*'s successfully launched torpedo struck its *USS Iowa* target, who knows what the impact on history might have been?

When east of Bermuda, the *Iowa*'s commanding officer wanted the President to see how the big ship could fight off an air attack, so a number of weather balloons were released in order to serve as antiaircraft targets. When the firing by *Iowa* began, the captain of "Willie Dee" sent his crew into battle stations so that they could shoot down the balloons missed by the *Iowa* that had drifted into his ship's proximity.

Meanwhile, at "Willie Dee's" torpedo mounts, the torpedo crew prepared to fire unarmed practice shots at the big battleship. Unfortunately, one of the torpedo men forgot to take the primer out of torpedo tube three, causing that torpedo to remain alive.

At the bridge, a new torpedo officer ordered the releasing of torpedoes at the *Iowa* and he commanded: "Fire One!" "Fire Two!" "Fire Three!" When Torpedo Three was launched, its distinct and unique hissing sound told everyone that a **LIVE ARMED TORPEDO** was on its 6,000 yard journey toward *USS Iowa*.

The next five minutes aboard the *Porter* were pandemonium. Despite strictly enforced radio silence, the radio operator on the destroyer yelled to the *Iowa* radiomen that a live torpedo was launched toward their ship! This information was immediately conveyed to the *Iowa* bridge and the helmsman turned his course, causing a large wake. Reportedly, within moments of the warning, a huge explosion occurred behind *Iowa*. The torpedo apparently had been detonated by the wash kicked up by the battleship's increased speed and turn.

A major investigation of the incident took place after the ship docked in Bermuda. In addition to officer reassignments, the enlisted man that acknowledged failure to deactivate torpedo tube three was sentenced to 14 years at hard labor. However, President Roosevelt intervened and the sailor's punishment was eliminated.

USS William D. Porter went on to distinguished accomplishment in the Battle of Okinawa and downed a Japanese Val Bomber on June 10, 1945. The plane exploded in the water under the ship's hull, seriously damaging the vessel's plates. The "Willie Dee" then slipped stern first into 2,400 feet of water without loss of life.

This story of the live torpedo was kept under naval wraps until the 1958 reunion of the *William D. Porter* crew, and the veterans could recall the incident with amusement in place of the heart-stopping anxiety of fifteen years before.

Down the Hatch

This is another of the many drinking euphemisms of men at sea. It came from the time when cargoes started to be lowered into hatches on freighters. Seamen began using this phrase at the turn of the 20th century.

Drinking a Toast

The word for drinking to one's health or in honor of someone was coined in early days along the waterfront. It was customary, during this honor, to place a small piece of toast in the hot toddy and mulled wine popular with seamen of the time.

Duffel

This is a name given to a sailor's personal effects. It refers to his principal clothing as well as to the sea bag in which he carried and stowed it. The term comes from the Flemish town of Duffel, which is near Antwerp, and it relates to a rough woolen cloth made there.

Dungarees

Webster's Dictionary defines "dungaree" as "a coarse kind of fabric worn by the poorer class of people and also used for tents and sails." We find it hard to picture our favorite pair of dungarees flying from the mast of a sailing ship, but in those days sailors often made both their working clothes and hammocks out of discarded sail cloth.

The cloth used then wasn't well-woven, nor was it dyed blue, but it served the purpose. Dungarees worn by sailors of the Confederate Navy were cut directly from old sails and remained tan in color just as they had been when filled with wind. Naturally, they would not dye them blue.

After battles, it was the practice in both the American and British navies for captains to report more sail lost in battle than actually was the case so the crew would have sail cloth to mend their hammocks and make new clothes. Since the cloth was called "dungaree," clothes made from the fabric borrowed the name.

WINDAS

· ADMIRAL ·

It seems a far cry from a Moorish chief to a senior ranking officer in the Navy. Yet, a Moorish chief is an Emir, and chief of all the chiefs is the EMIR-AL, from which we get our English word "Admiral!"

· FLEUR de LIS ·

The fleur de lis, which points the North on all compass-cards, was put there originally by the 14th. century Neapolitan pilot who designed the card; it was a tribute to his king, who was of the house of Bourbon.

N

SON of a GUN ·

This term dates back to when men of certain ratings, including gunners and gunners' mates, were allowed to take their wives along to sea with them. If a boy was born on the voyage, he was half-humorously, half-contemptuously referred to as "a son of a gun."

· IN THE BRIG ·

Because Admiral Nelson once assigned a small brig to carry captives taken in one of his naval engagements, and because his seamen ever afterwards associated that vessel with prisoners, the name 'brig' became sailor's universal slang for JAIL.

Dunnage

This is a term for a seaman's personal gear, including his clothes. The term derives from the lumber known as "dunnage," used in shoring up and dressing the cargo stowed in the ship's hold.

Dutch Courage

The false courage or bravado inspired by drunkenness is known as "Dutch courage." During the 17th century war between Holland and England, it was the practice of the Old Dutch Navy to serve a significant amount of liquor to the gun crews of ships before going into battle.

The Eagle Screams

Another way of saying that it's payday, with reference to the eagle on a coin.

Early Royal Marines

Companies of British Army troops served aboard British warships in the 1790s under the command of a Marine captain, assisted by an army lieutenant. In the wartime year of 1815, marines had supplanted the army troops to such an extent that they averaged about 20 per cent of a ship's complement. The marines served as infantry in shore operations, provided disciplinary measures to the sailors and were a defense against mutiny. During combat, marines were the boarding party, acted as snipers, manned the guns with the sailors and guarded the captain. The marines were a separate shipboard community that wore uniforms, while the sailors had none. The seamen treated the marines with scorn otherwise reserved for idlers.

East Indian

The big ships of the British East India Company (the Honorable John Company) came into prominence early in the 19th century, although smaller ships of the same line had been trading with India years before that time. They were huge, compared to the earlier vessels, and were really a compromise between a man-o'-war and a merchant vessel.

They carried both passengers and cargoes, were heavily armed and carried crews trained to fight. These features made them almost invincible to the pirates who infested the sealanes.

These vessels were such a source of pride to the British public that young men of good education and social standing preferred service under the British East India Company house flag to a commission in the Navy.

Eight Bells

Most landlubbers know that eight bells means eight o'clock. Not many persons realize that it can also mean four o'clock and twelve o'clock. In days when time was marked by a 30-minute glass, the boy whose job it was to turn the glass struck the bell once the first time, twice the second time, and so on for every half-hour through a four-hour watch, after which the routine started all over again. It was customary in the old Navy to measure time by glasses, meaning half-hours. A 90-minute battle might be recorded in the log as, "We then fired our guns for three glasses."

Ensign

"Ensign," the name given to the Navy's most junior officers dates to medieval times. Lords honored their squires by allowing them to carry the ensign (banner) into battle. Later, these squires became known by the name of the banner itself. In the U.S. Army, the lowest ranking officer was originally called ensign because he, like a squire of old, would one day lead troops into battle and was training to that end. It is still the lowest commissioned rank in the British Army today. When the United States Navy was established, the Americans carried on the tradition and adopted the rank of ensign as the title for its junior commissioned officers.

Exonerate

Ships of ancient times could not carry much cargo because they had small holds. These boats could operate better when empty and the crew was glad to unload after a voyage. "Exonarare" in Latin means "to take off a burden." This word passed from Old French into English about the time of Henry VIII and by then it meant to relieve of any burden. This old sea term was borrowed by lawyers and used to describe the clearing of a client from accusation of blame.

Eyes of the Ship

Ships in the early days generally had carved heads of mythological monsters or patrons in the bow. The fore part of the ship was called the "head." The term, "eyes of the ship" followed from the eyes of the figures placed there.

• BRINGING THE WAR CLOSE HOME •

To the JACOB JONES belongs the distinction of being the first U.S. destroyer ever to be sunk by enemy action in <u>home</u> <u>waters</u>.

BLUFF OLD SEA-DOG DIES

In view of the battle now raging in the Crimea, it is of more than passing interest to note that there died recently in Brisbane Australia, an ancient mariner named Charles Longden who served in the Crimea War of 1854. He was 105 years of age.

• FIRST U.S. OCEAN MAIL •

In 1847 Congress ordered built a fleet of steamers under the great Commodore Perry to carry the first U.S. Government Ocean Mail Service

• BLUFF •

And speaking of the word "bluff" (meaning stout or hearty) the word was coined from the general appearance of stoutness or strength of old ships' bows.

Far Distant Shores

Navy men on shore duty might get a duty far from salt water, but in February 1971 Captain Alan B. Shepard Jr. set a record for that time. He went to work 250,000 miles from the sea on the moon. A member of the Apollo 14 mission, he was the first Navy man to walk on the moon.

Fathom

"Fathom" was derived from the Anglo-Saxon word "faetm," meaning literally "the embracing arms." In

those days, most measurements were based on average size of parts of the body such as the hand or foot, or came from average lengths between two points of the body. A fathom came to be regarded as the average distance from fingertip to fingertip of the outstretched arms of a man, about six feet.

Even today in our nuclear Navy, sailors can be seen "guesstimating" the length of a line by using the Anglo-Saxon fingertip methods: crude but still reliable. And every woman measuring cloth today knows that from the tip of her nose to the tips of her fingers on one outstretched arm equals a yard.

Feather Merchant

Navy nickname for a person holding a yeoman rating. It is also applicable to an enlisted man who has been retired and recalled to active duty.

Feeling Blue

Having the blues means to feel melancholy or sad. It was the custom among deepwater sailors, when a ship lost a captain or officer during a voyage, to fly blue flags and paint a blue band along the ship's hull when entering port.

Fid

A "fid" is a multi-use device aboard vessels whose nautical source of origin is uncertain. Made of wood or metal, it is shaped like a baseball bat and pointed at one end. It was used to open strands of rope for splic- ing, stretch- ing eyes for rigging and to support anything such as the 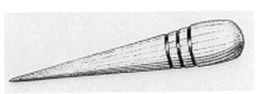 topmast of a ship. Fids are designed in various forms and are in use aboard modern ships. In naval language, it can be equated with "raw deal" or "double-crossed," as illustrated by "he was given the 'fid' (shaft)," or, "I got even with him by giving him the 'fid.'" "Fidding," which also evolved from this device, means to "put into place and secure."

Fife Rail

The "fife rail" is located at the base of the mainmast of a sailing vessel. It has holes into which belaying pins can be inserted. The fife rail was named for the little fife-and-drum boys who perched there, out of the way, while men drilled to the shrill note of the fife and drum tattoo. Fife and drum have long since disappeared, but the fife rail still retains its old name.

Fighting Ferryboat

During the Civil War, the Union Navy was hard pressed for ships, and took over almost anything that floated and had an engine. One such craft was an unfinished ferryboat. She was sheathed with iron and named *Essex*. Surprisingly, she met, fought and sank the Con- federate ironclad *Arkansas*.

Figurehead

This is the carved wood figure or bust of a person, very often quite awe-inspiring, placed beneath the bowsprit at the extreme bow of the ship directly above the water. The figure had no function, and so it is to- day, with someone who is appointed to a position that carries no duties or responsibility, but yet that person may receive prestige and income.

Find an Angel

This theatrical wish has a nautical origin. It pertains to finding someone with sentiment and wealth that will provide the funds necessary to produce a sure- hit show. The phrase is said to have originated when Luis de Sant-Angel helped finance the voyage in which Columbus discovered America.

° FORECASTLE °

This name (fo'c'stle to you) for the crew's quarters, is a relic of the days when huge wooden castles actually were, built on the fore and after ends of ships, from which fighting men could throw spears, arrows, stones etc., onto the decks of an enemy.

°EXECUTION DOCK°

A familiar phrase today for any place of legal lethal dispatch. However, there was actually a place by that name, situated near Blackwall (England) next to the East India Docks on the Thames.

° QUARANTINE °

This term for medical detention derives its name from the French "Quarant," meaning forty. The first known case of isolating a ship for reasons of plague, was at Marseilles, and the vessel was held for FORTY days.... hence the name..

° LIMEY °

Because it was practically impossible to carry fresh fruits and vegetables on protrated voyages years ago, British Parliament decreed that each sailor must drink a pint of limejuice daily as a preventative against scurvy. Thus came the nickname for British ships, and Britishers in general.

Firecrackers

Invented by the Chinese, "firecrackers" were first used in America in 1787 when the merchant ship *Grand Turk* returned from Canton with a cargo of silk, tea, and the noisy fireworks.

Fire Chiefs

The pre-War Asiatic Fleet included five gunboats that patrolled China's Yangtse River. Chinese workmen were hired to work aboard these vessels for pennies a day to perform duties that would normally be done by the crew. As a result, the ship's company had the luxury of having servants handle much of the vessels cooking, tailoring, ship maintenance and operation. These conditions are well portrayed in the book and film, *The Sand Pebbles*. The expression of "fire chiefs" originated aboard these vessels because of publicized instances where angry and unhappy Chinese workers used a fire-ax to seek vengeance on a ship's company.

Firing a Bale of Hay

A gunnery error in which a powder charge is fired without a projectile in the gun.

First Atlantic Crossing by a Steamship

The record for the first crossing of the Atlantic by a steamship is attributed to the *SS Savannah*, which completed the trip in 1819. The voyage took 29 days, and she used her engines for only three of those days. Although this vessel was technically a steamship, the crossing was not made totally by steam because sails did most of the work. In 1831, the Canadian steamship, *Royal William*, made the Atlantic trip in 19 days with the complete use of its engines.

First Family Allowance

In the 13th century, Irish shipmasters were compelled by law to provide for the needs of the families of every man in their crews. This included "his sisters and his cousins and his aunts."

First Fort in America

The first structure built by Europeans in the Western Hemisphere was a fort erected in December 1492 on the island of Haiti. It was made out of timbers from the wreck of Columbus' *Santa Maria*, which ran aground at that location.

First Iron Ship

An iron vessel about 70 feet long was built in England in 1787 and an iron sailing ship named *Vulcan* was launched in 1818. The first iron steamship, the *Aron Manby* was built in London and began operating in 1822. The first ocean-going iron ship was the *SS Great Britain*, completed in 1845. The first American ship built of iron was the *USS Michigan*, a side-wheeler launched at Erie, Pennsylvania, in December 1843. The following year, the *SS Forbes*, a screw-steamer with an iron hull, was launched. The Navy's first steel-hulled ships, the early cruisers *USS Atlanta, USS Boston,* and *USS Chicago*, were authorized in 1883.

First Lady of the Seas

The *SS United States* made her first Atlantic crossing in 1952 in the record time of three days, ten hours and 2 minutes, cutting the 14-year record of the *Queen Mary* by 10 hours. She averaged 40.98 miles an hour. In 17 years of service, the *United States* made 726 Atlantic crossings, and carried a million passengers.

First Lighthouse

One of the Seven Wonders of the ancient world was the Pharos, a beacon light that was erected by Ptolemy at the harbor of Alexandria, Egypt about 274 B.C. The light has been estimated to be from 375 to 475 feet high. An earthquake destroyed it during 1375.

The first successful lighthouse in relatively recent times was the Eddystone Light near Plymouth, England. John Smeaton built the structure during 1756-1759, and lighting was produced through the use of candles. The Eddystone Light was replaced by a new structure after 120 years.

The first lighthouse in America was built in 1716 on Little Brewster Island at Boston Harbor. Eventually, hundreds of lighthouses were built at locations along the coasts of the United States and its possessions. Early lighthouses used a variety of fuels that included lard, fish oil and kerosene.

First Man Around the World

Fernao de Magelhaes, better known as Ferdinand Magellan, is credited with being the first man to sail around the world. He led an expedition sent out by Spain in 1519, but only one ship, under the command of Sebastian del Cano, returned to Spain in 1522. Magellan didn't complete the trip; natives in the Philippines killed him. However, a native named Molucca Henry had been taken to Spain from the Philippines earlier by another explorer, and he sailed with Magellan as interpreter. When Henry's vessel stopped at Leyte, he had returned home. Henry was, in fact, the first man to sail around the world, having gone to Europe across the Indian Ocean and returning to the islands by crossing the Atlantic and Pacific.

The FIRST SUBMARINE

In the present war in the East, Dutchmen are really living up to the best traditions of their race. Particularly is this true of their submarine successes. And rightly so, for it was Cornelius Van Drebel, a famous Dutch scientist, who invented the submersible in 1622.

The worthy Hollander interested King James of England in his ingenious product, and actually sailed it both on the surface and underneath the Thames River.

The craft was built of wood and was propelled by six oars.

The 'HUNGRY HUNDRED'

In the gay '90's, this was the nickname bestowed on the first group of Royal Navy Reserve officers to be assigned to duty with the fleet; the significance of the term referred to the insignificance of their pay.

DAGGER-RAMMER-REES

This is the awesome pronunciation given the name of Diego Ramirez Island by unscholarly seamen in the early days; and "Dagger-Rammer-Rees" it remains to this day in sea-going circles.

The SAGRES

The beautiful Portugese naval training ship which recently visited the U.S. was named for the first Naval Academy ever to be established. This institution was founded at Sagres Portugal, by Henry the Navigator in 1415.

First Sea-Going President

Franklin D. Roosevelt was the first U.S. president to sail his own vessel to a foreign port. He took his schooner *Amberjack* to Campobello, Canada, on a vacation cruise.

First Ship Through the Panama Canal

The crane ship *Alex Lavalley* sailed though the Panama Canal on January 7, 1914. The first Navy ship to transit the canal from Pacific to Atlantic was the collier *USS Jupiter* on October 12, 1914. The first transit from Atlantic to Pacific by Navy vessels was made on July 16, 1915 by the battleships *USS Ohio*, *USS Missouri* and *USS Wisconsin*. The first cargo ship through the canal was the *SS Azores*, just after the start of World War I. The Panama Canal was officially opened on July12, 1920.

First Steamboat

Robert Fulton is generally credited with inventing the steamboat. His boat, the *Clermont*, traveled on New York's Hudson River in 1807. But Fulton was not the first to develop such a boat. John Fitch built a steamboat that operated out of Philadelphia from 1788 to 1790, during which time it covered more than 2000 miles.

Flag at Half Mast

At times of mourning in old sailing days, the yards were "cockbilled" and this rigging was slacked off to indicate that the grief was so great that it was impossible to keep things shipshape. Today, the half-masting of the colors is in reality a survival of the days when a slovenly appearance characterized mourning on board ship.

Fleet

A "fleet" is a group of ships operating together for tactical and other purposes, and it is the largest organization of vessels under the command of a single officer. Fleet is an adaptation from the Anglo-Saxon "floet."

Fleur-De-Lis

The symbol that marks the north point on the compass takes it names from the French word meaning "lily flower." The symbol resembles a lily. It was used on the coat of arms for France in the 14th century. However, the claim that the "fleur de lis" was adopted for the compass to honor Henry IV of France has no merit. Early compasses had the letter T for "tramontana" (Italian for north), marking the north point. Some embellishment of the T turned it into a design that resembled the royal French symbol.

The Floating Bawdyhouse

The Confederate stronghold of Nashville, Tennessee, had fallen to Union forces during February 1862. Many prostitutes inhabited Smoky Row, the City's red-light district, and a large number of Union soldiers were being infected with venereal disease. By July 1863 Nashville's military commander, Brigadier-General Robert S. Granger, had become exasperated by the impact on his troops. Daily complaints by his regimental surgeons convinced him that the only way to get rid of this situation was to clear Nashville of its prostitutes. On this basis, Granger ordered the Provost Marshall, Lieutenant Colonel George Spalding, to seize all the city's prostitutes and transport them by river to Louisville, Kentucky. Spalding's choice for the job was Captain John Newcomb and his paddle wheeler, *Idahoe*.

Spalding then started to round up the women, most of whom resisted fiercely. In some cases, they had to be driven at bayonet point. Reportedly, some ladies of blameless reputation were mistakenly forced to the vessel, but ultimately released. Eventually, more than 150 prostitutes were placed aboard the *Idahoe*.

Unfortunately, no one told Colonel Spalding that arrangements had never been made to accept the unusual cargo in Louisville. In addition, Captain Newcomb had to depart without provisions for his passengers, without medical resources and with no guards to maintain order. As a result, he provided funding from his own pocket with the understanding that he would be fully reimbursed.

The *Idahoe* paddled up the Cumberland River and reached Louisville in five days, but military authorities would not accept Newcomb's cargo. Instead, he was told to take the women to Cincinnati and he was given a supply of guards. News of the vessel's coming passed up the river like wildfire and Newcomb was met in Cincinnati by grim-faced Union troops assigned to "protect the harbor at Cincinnati from the 'sinners' aboard the *Idahoe*." The *Idahoe*'s plight was beginning to resemble that of the *Flying Dutchman*. Was the paddle wheeler doomed to sail forever without reaching a haven?

Newton managed to inform Secretary of War Stanton in Washington by telegraph of the situation, and Stanton immediately decided that General Granger exceeded his authority and used poor judgment. Stanton ordered Newcomb to take the women back to Nashville and, as a result, *Idahoe* returned to that city after its 13-day ordeal.

General Granger responded with an innovative solution that was years before its time. He legalized prostitution in Nashville, established a venereal disease

The • MIDNIGHT LEADSMAN •

Just in case you didn't know it, every time you steer your vessel safely past a rockbound coast during a fog, you are indebted to the "Midnight Leadsman." This gent was frozen to death while heaving the log some hundred and twenty years ago, but his obliging ghost stands by to give guidance through foggy weather near land. However, it appears that he always quits at midnight, after which time you must do the best you can.

• PUFFING BILLY •

Term of derision for the first steam-propelled battle-ships, by old seamen of the square-rigged era.

• SHIP'S GALLEY •

This name for a vessel's cookhouse is supposed to be an abbreviation of the word "gallery", because originally, fires were lit and food cooked on a platform or gallery of bricks built in the ship's waist

• WARTS •

This term for British naval cadets was bestowed on them for the purpose of making the youngsters realize they are positively of NO importance whatever.

education program for his troops and demanded that prostitutes comply with a schedule of medical inspections.

Captain Newcomb did not find his future as fortunate. It was difficult for him to obtain reimbursement for his personal expenditures or for the damage inflicted on his vessel by the passengers. Further, as he and *Idahoe* traveled the rivers of the south after the war, viewers on the banks would point and yell, "Here comes the floating whorehouse!"

Flying Dutchman

The *Flying Dutchman* is supposed to have set sail in 1600 and disappeared without a trace. Legend has it that Captain Van Der Decken, trying to take his ship around the Cape of Good Hope, cursed the stormy ocean and, in punishment for his blasphemy, was sentenced to sail his ship at that location forever. The tale of the *Flying Dutchman* failing to round the Cape of Good Hope against strong winds, then trying Cape Horn and failing there too, has been the most famous of maritime ghost stories for more than 300 years. The legend of the cursed ship sailing back and forth on its endless voyage, with its ancient white-haired crew crying for help while hauling at her sail, inspired Samuel Taylor Coleridge to write his classic, *The Rhyme of the Ancient Mariner*. In 1843, the German composer Richard Wagner completed an opera titled, *Der Fliegende Hollander* (*The Flying Dutchman*), based on the legend. A superstition that remains with us to the present is that any mariner who sees the "ghost ship" will die within a day.

Flying-Fish Sailors

This is an old Navy description of those who were assigned to Asiatic waters. Those who served in the Mediterranean were known a "Sou' Spainers." In four-piper days, Asiatic sailors referred to those who were based in U.S. waters as "popsicle sailors."

Follow a Red Herring

Red herring was abundant off the coast of northern Europe. This fish was favored by seamen during long voyages because it could be preserved through salting, sun drying or smoke curing. When smoked, it took on a reddish color, and the trainers of hunting hounds found it a unique and effective way to train hunting dogs. They would drag a pungent fish through the countryside during a training session for young hounds. If a dog was diverted from the trail of the fox by following the herring, the dog chose a false clue and was in need of additional training. In this case, the animal was said to have "followed a red herring." The phrase now stands for "misleading information" or a device to "throw one off the track."

Follow the Leader, Regardless

He was the "Old Man," a 30-year-old commanding officer of a destroyer escort on South Pacific patrol duty during the spring of 1945, and he was experienced beyond his years. Not only was he a highly skilled warship skipper, but he was a natural leader who was respected by everyone aboard the vessel. His sense of humor was legendary, and his personal charisma and cheerfulness caused officers and men to respond positively and enthusiastically to him. This Captain's personality was such that he disdained from using the loud speaker from a remote location because, when possible, he preferred to speak directly to the crew from the bridge facing aft.

As a result of the good-natured spirit that existed among them, the men took to imitating some of the Captain's actions. One example occurred when the C.O. grew a Groucho Marx-type mustache. As a result, it wasn't long before most people aboard the ship were sprouting similar bristles on their upper lips. On another occasion, the skipper appeared on deck in British-type short trousers. Almost immediately, out came the scissors and, as a result, practically everyone sported knee-level dungarees.

One particularly hot day, the Captain stood at the bridge facing the men who gathered on the gun deck to hear his personal report. After he finished, he exclaimed, "Damn, it's hot!" In the same motion, he yanked off his cap and revealed a bald and gleaming scalp to the surprised and laughing sailors. Naturally, out came the scissors, razors and shaving cream, and there was not a full head of hair anywhere.

The next day it was announced that the Captain would make a special report to the crew. He faced his assembled, bald sailors and announced, "I've got great news! We are going home to the States immediately!" With that statement, he pulled off his fake novelty store bald scalp and displayed, with a broad and mischievous grin, his uncut, bushy brown hair.

Forecastle

Seamen pronounce this word as "focsul" or "foc'sle." It is the forward main deck of a ship. In sailing ships, it included the crew's quarters. In antiquity, ships had large raised platforms resembling wooden castles, built at bow and stern, from which spears, arrows and fire-bombs were thrown at an enemy.

Fouled Anchor

The "fouled (rope or chain entwined) anchor" so

⚓ TRADITIONS OF THE NAVY by CEDRIC·W·WINDAS

WINDAS 1840

◦ GUN WALES ◦

Gun'nles to you; one of three wales, or strengthening pieces, secured around the entire length of a wooden ship's hull. Originally there were only two, the bilge wale and the main wale. Then openings were cut through the bulwarks for cannon, and the gun wale was added to strengthen the bulwarks.

◦ CHAPLAIN ◦

The chaplain received his name from an ancient legend in which it appears Saint Martin gave his cape one wintry night to a freezing beggar. This cape was preserved by the King of France, and kept in a chapelle. The keeper of the chapelle was called a chaplain...hence the title.

Keep Your ◦ WEATHER-EYE ◦ Lifting

This modern admonition to take care of yourself, was originally an order to the helmsman to keep his eyes constantly on the weather leeches to see that they didn't shiver, and the sails spill the wind.

◦ BO'S'UN'S PIPE ◦

The bo's'un's pipe was introduced by one Andrew Barton, a thrifty and ingenious pirate of Scotch extraction. With it he could give signals above the roar of storm and strife, thus saving the cost of maintaining a special bugler for that purpose.

prevalent in our Navy's designs and insignia is a symbol more than 500 years old. It has its origins in the British traditions adopted by our naval service. The fouled anchor was used as the official seal of Lord High Admiral Charles Lord Howard of Effingham during the late 1500s. A variation of the seal had been in use by the Lord High Admiral of Scotland about a century earlier. The anchor, both with and without the entwined rope, is a traditional heraldic device used in ancient British coats of arms. As a heraldic device, it is a stylized representation used mostly for decorative effect.

Foxtail
A "foxtail" is a counter brush that resembles the tail of a fox. It is used in various shops of a ship.

Fresh Water King
The ship's evaporators produce the fresh water. The sailor in charge of this equipment holds this euphemistic title.

From Down South to Down Under
The *SS Edina*, which gained fame as a blockade-runner and dodged many Union ships during the Civil War, had a long life after the war ended. She was sold to a group of Australians who put her on a run between Port Melbourne and Geelong. *(Illustrator of this book, Cedric Windas, made many trips on her as a young man.)*

Frosty Flight Deck
Inventors have come up with many unusual ideas for ships, but one of the most interesting was a World War II plan to construct an aircraft carrier out of ice. The ship was to be 2,000 feet long, 300 feet wide and 200 feet deep. She was to operate in the cold North Atlantic, but would carry refrigeration equipment to keep her from melting in case she had to go south. The ice ship was estimated to cost $70 million but was never built.

Full Monty
An immensely popular British motion picture, *The Full Monty*, played before world-wide audiences in 1998, but relatively few viewers had knowledge as to the meaning and derivation of the film's title. This humorous film dealt with the plight of four unemployed British men. Although untrained in dance, the men comically performed for an audience composed entirely of women and, in their conclusion stripped totally naked before the raucous spectators.

The title of the film evolved from World War II, when it was mandated by British Field Marshal Bernard L. Montgomery that his cooks be prepared to serve him a full and total breakfast whenever he wanted it, regardless of time of day or location. It is with this background the term, "Full Monty," has come to mean "complete, total or all the way." General Montgomery's desire to be perpetuated in memory is legendary. As a result of this motion picture, his role in history is further solidified.

Futtock Shrouds
These are the short shrouds extending below (and securing) the lower edges of the tops to the masts. "Futtock" is a combination and corruption of the English words, "foot" and "hook."

Gadget
A gadget is any mechanical contrivance or device, or anything whose proper name can't be brought to mind instantly. It was originally a proper nautical name for a hook. It emerged from the French "gachette," the "catch of a lock."

Galley
A galley is the kitchen aboard anything from a 30-foot boat to an aircraft carrier. It is probably a corruption of "gallery," the stone or brick platform amidships on Roman ships in which mariners cooked their meals.

Galley West
The expression, "knocked him galley west," is a reminder that when a Viking chief died, his body was placed aboard his galley or long boat and, after setting it on fire, started "sailing toward the west." The old English term for this was "gollywest."

Galley Yarn
In the Navy or merchant marine, this is a doubtful piece of information from the cooks. It has the same ring of

_ and a COIN for CHARON ·

In the good old days, when a seaman 'slipped his cable' and was buried at sea, his messmates placed a coin in his mouth "to pay Charon the Boatman to ferry the corpse across the River Styx."

· SEA-GOING 'COPS' ·

The British Admiralty was first organized as a Marine Police Dept. Maybe our Anglo-Saxon cousins have therefore 'got something' when they claim to have been "policing the high seas for centuries."

· CHITS ·

This name for notes or vouchers is a contribution to our nautical vocabulary by the Hindu sailormen in the service of the Honorable East India Company.

· The O·A·O ·

Ask any Annapolis grad and he'll tell you; that's the right and proper term for one's best girl......the One and Only.

uncertainty that is implied in the more familiar phrase, "that's scuttlebutt."

Gangboard to Gangway
On ancient galleys the "gangboard," deriving from "gang" (old English for way or passage), was the narrow boardwalk the rowers used to walk from forward to stern. The meaning of gangboard then related to the board with railings that passengers use on entering or leaving a ship, with the word eventually becoming "gangway."

Gangway
Narrow platform by which one boards or leaves a ship became known as the "gangway." It received its name from the plank or platform that extended from bow to stern on slave-galleys, where the whip-master beat time to a count and used a lash on the oarsmen.

Geedunk
To most sailors, the word "geedunk" means ice cream, candy, potato chips and other assorted snacks or even the place where they can be purchased. However, no one knows for certain where the term originated. There are several plausible theories:

In the 1920s, a comic strip character named Harold Teen and his friends spent a great amount of time at Pop's candy store. The store's name was the Sugar Bowl, but Harold and his pals always called it "The Geedunk" for reasons never explained.

The Chinese word meaning "a place of idleness" sounds something like "geedung." In addition, "geedunk" is the sound made by a vending machine when it dispenses a soft drink in a cup.

Finally, the word may be derived from the German work "tunk," which means "to dip or sop either in gravy or coffee." Dunking was a common practice in days when bread, not always obtained fresh, needed a bit of "tunking" to soften it. The "ge" is a German unaccented prefix denoting repetition. In time, it may have changed from "getunk" to "geedunk."

Get the Point?
When a British officer is court-martialed, the verdict of the court is made plain to him by placing his sword on a table. If the hilt is toward him, he has been found not guilty; if the point is toward him, he has been found guilty. In this manner, he "gets the point" without a word being said.

Golden Dragon
A sailor who has crossed the International Date Line has entered the "Realm of the Golden Dragon," and is eligible for a Golden Dragon Certificate so attesting.

Grab the Money and Run
During the Civil War, Asbury Harpending secured a commission in the Confederate Navy for a very specific purpose. It was his plan to fit out a fast schooner in California with the hope that he could capture two ships, USS Constitution and the USS Oregon. Each of the vessels was supposed to carry more than a million dollars in gold. His schooner, Chapman, was ready to proceed with the plan, but word had leaked out about the plot. As a result, USS Cyane and two boatloads of marines captured Harpending, his schooner and his Confederate adventurers before the goal could be accomplished.

Great Lakes Navigation
Sailing in the Great Lakes began in 1679 when the French explorer LaSalle built a small ship named Griffon and sailed it in Lake Michigan. The first naval vessel on the lakes, and the first iron ship built for the Navy, was the side-wheeler Michigan that was launched on December 5, 1843. The first vessel from overseas to operate on the lakes was the steamer Madeira Pet, which reached Chicago from London (via the Welland Ship Canal) in 1874, after a voyage of 80 days.

The Great White Fleet and Segregation
In 1907 the United States desired to dramatically demonstrate it's position as a great naval power. Painted a dramatic white, 16 battleships and four destroyers were sent on a world cruise. This group of warships was known as the "White Fleet" or "Great White Fleet."

History shows that black sailors were removed from the vessels because their dark complexions "clashed"

·ARCHIMEDES' WAR MACHINE·

Strangely enough, though he was neither sailor nor soldier, Archimedes invented the earliest machines of war which proved so devastating to the Roman fleet at Syracuse. They were huge grapnels which lifted a vessel's bows from the water, smashing and then dropping her under stern first.

·DISCHARGING RIFLES *at* SUNSET·

The custom of Royal Marine sentries in discharging their rifles at sunset is a relic of ancient times, when small arms were fired to prevent possible misfiring later on, owing to dampened priming. Each new sentry, of course, used fresh charges and priming.

·BOX *the* COMPASS·

This term for reciting the points of the compass is claimed by some to have originated from the Spanish word "Boxar", meaning 'to sail around.'

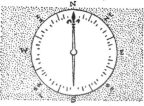

·WEST COAST MOUNTAINS·

Three famous Pacific coast mountains were named for British Admirals: Hood, Ranier and Helena.

with the desired overall whiteness of the ships. From that point until 1942, African-Americans totaled less than one per cent of naval personnel, and they were primarily relegated to the role of officers' stewards. The civil rights movement, led by Eleanor Roosevelt and national black leaders, caused Navy rates, ranks and assignments to be partially opened to the expanded wartime group of sailors. President Harry S. Truman's 1948 Desegregation Order was a landmark action that mandated racial integration in the armed forces. As a direct result of this Order, a number of landmark equal opportunity laws were enacted that applied to the civilian population. By 2000, African-Americans made up approximately 20% of the services, with all assignment restrictions removed.

Green Oil and Whistle Steam

Old salts liked to send a new man to the bosun's locker to get some green oil for the starboard running light, or perhaps red oil for the port running light. If a man couldn't find either, he might be sent back for a bucketful of whistle steam.

Greenwich Time

Although Greenwich, England was established in 1675 as the international Prime Meridian or time center for mariners, it was not until World War I that French navigators used any other than Paris time for their measurements. The world is now divided into 24 time zones, and all navigation and communication is based on Greenwich Mean Time (GMT). (See Latitude and Longitude.)

Grog

The mixture of alcoholic liquor and water was first issued in the British Navy. The sailors drank straight rum until 1741, when Admiral Edward Vernon suggested that the government could save money by diluting it fifty-fifty, with water. As the Admiral always wore a cloak of "groggam," a half mixture of silk and wool, his men nicknamed him "Old Grog." Jeering sailors at once nicknamed the new drink "grog," together with the related "groggy" and "grogginess." The rum issue to sailors stopped in 1970, but the words to describe its effects remain a part of the English language.

Gundecking

In the modern Navy, falsifying reports, records, and the like is often referred to as "gundecking." The origin of the term is obscure, but at the risk of gundecking, here are two plausible explanations for its modern times usage.

The deck below the upper deck of a British sailing ship-of-war was called the gundeck although it carried no guns. This false deck may have been constructed to deceive enemies as to the amount of armament carried; thus the gundeck was a falsification.

A more plausible explanation may stem from shortcuts taken by early midshipmen when doing their navigation lessons. Each mid was supposed to take sun lines at noon and star sights at night and then go below to the gundeck, work out their calculations and show them to the navigator.

Certain of these young men, however, had a special formula for getting the correct answers. They would rise at noon, or last position, on the quarterdeck traverse board and determine the approximate current position by dead reckoning plotting. Armed with this information, they proceeded to the gundeck to "gundeck" their navigation homework by simply working backward from their dead reckoning position.

Gun Salute

Theoretically, all salutes are the act of the one who first salutes, rendering himself or his ship powerless for the time during which the honors are rendered. For example, in the days of Columbus, after firing a salute, an appreciable time of approximately half an hour was required before the guns could be fired again. Then, the ship first rendering the honors feared no attack and the gesture was one of friendship and confidence. Firing blank cartridges is a comparatively modern invention, occasioned, it is said, by the fact that a complimentary cannon ball once proved fatal to an honored personage. It should be noted that the "present arms salute" of today was originally a gesture to present the arms for taking.

United States Navy Regulations proscribe that only those ships and stations designated by the Secretary of the Navy may fire gun salutes. A national salute of 21 guns is fired on Washington's Birthday, Memorial Day, and Independence Day, to Honor the President of the United States and to Honor Heads of Foreign States.

Additionally, ships and stations may, with approval of the Office of the Secretary of the Navy, provide gun salutes for naval officers on significant occasions, using the following protocol: Admiral, 17 guns; Vice Admiral, 15 guns; Rear Admiral (upper half), 13 guns; Rear Admiral (lower half), 11 guns. All gun salutes are fired at five-second intervals and the salutes will always total an odd number.

· STARBOARD SIDE ·

Because the Vikings shipped their star (steering) oar on the right hand side of their vessels, and called the side of a ship its "board", the right hand side of vessels has ever since been designated as the "star-board" side.

· PILOT ·

From two Dutch words "Peil" (to mark with pegs) and "Loth" (lead). Strangely enough the name was conferred on persons who could navigate a vessel into port without the use of the "Peil-loth" (lead line).

· DEAD RECKONING ·

This navigation term was originally spelled "ded" (the abbreviation for deducted) reckoning. An unscholarly British shipmaster thought the "a" had been ommitted, so inserted it. Ever since then, even the officially printed forms spell it "dead" reckoning.

· LOG BOOK ·

As early ship's records were inscribed on shingles (cut from logs) and hinged so that they opened like a book, the name "Log-book" was logical and lasted to this day.

One school of thought traces the salute back to a Roman custom at the time of the Borgias. Assassinations by dagger were apparently not uncommon at that time, so it became the custom for men to approach each other with raised hands, palms to the front, thus offering assurance that there was no dagger concealed.

Another school of thought places the origin of the salute in the days of chivalry, when knights in mail, upon meeting others, would raise their visors with their hands, enabling others to see the face. Eventually this gesture came to signify membership in the same order, or at least, in a friendly order. It is also believed that, because of the strict gradations in rank, the junior was required to make the same move.

Others place the origin of the salute in the days of chivalry and tournaments. After the Queen of Love and Beauty was crowned, the knights passed in review before her throne. Each knight, as he drew near, raised his mailed fist to shield his eyes—a subtle way of letting the Queen know that her beauty blinded him.

However, in the American Navy, it seems reasonable that the "hand salute" came to us directly from the British Navy. There is general agreement that the salute, as now rendered, is really the first part of the movement of uncovering a hat. From the earliest days of military units, the junior uncovered when meeting or addressing a senior. Gradually, the act of taking off one's cap was simplified to merely touching the cap and this finally evolved into the present hand salute.

Hardtack
During the 1800s, "tack" was understood to be food of any sort. "Hardtack" was a food of more than ordinary hardness and durability to have on hand in rough weather. It was the modern equivalent of dog biscuit.

Hash Mark
This stripe is worn on the sleeve of a Navy enlisted man to denote four years of service. The inference is that he ate a lot of hash during his tour.

Hawsehole
This is a hole in the bow of a vessel for the anchor cable. Many times there are two such holes and they bear a resemblance to a pair of eyes. Originally, eyes were carved or painted on the bows of ancient ships for the purpose of allowing the vessel to "see" if there were evil spirits ahead, and to veer away from her course until they had been left astern.

Hawser
A "hawser" is any heavy line, five inches or more in circumference, used in towing or mooring a ship and also to hoist. It evolved from the Latin "altaire," meaning "rise," by way of old English "haelfter."

Head
This is the toilet of a ship and its name dates back to ancient vessels, when it was located forward, or "ahead," of the main body of the ship. In fact, the original location of the "head" was on a beam that projected from the stem, or foremost part of a ship. It became somewhat less precarious in later days when a small deck was constructed on heavier timber that also protruded forward and above the water. In time, shipbuilders installed wide grates in the deck that stretched both port and starboard directions, forward of the forecastle and directly above the water. In this manner, waste was disposed of directly into the sea, and seamen were expected to use the lee (down-weather side) in order to keep the area and hull clean. Head is now a word of colloquial use.

Helped By a Poem
USS Constitution, better known as "Old Ironsides," was built in 1797. In her battle with *HMS Guerriere* on 19 August 1812, British shells bounced off her stout plank sides and, according to Moses Smith, sponger of No. 1 gun, someone said, "Her sides are made of iron! See where the shots fell out!" The nickname of "Old Ironsides" soon became familiar. In 1830 the ship was ordered scrapped. When Oliver Wendell Holmes learned of this, he wrote the famous poem that begins, "Aye, tear her tattered ensign down! Long has it waved on high . . ." The poem was printed in nearly every newspaper in the country and it contributed greatly to the saving of the vessel.

Hijack
The popular greeting of "Hi, Jack!" was given to seamen by prostitutes along California's infamous Barbary Coast, where there was a constant scarcity of crewmen due to the gold rush. After being drugged or knocked unconscious, the sailor would find himself sold and shanghaied. "Hijack" is a contraction of "Hi, Jack," and its current meaning is to steal.

Holy Joe
The friendly nickname for a member of the Navy Chaplain Corps is "Holy Joe."

Holystone
A block of soft sandstone used for scrubbing wooden decks aboard ship. It was called "holystone" because a man using the block usually worked on his knees

SWIFT JUSTICE

By old British Naval Law, any seaman who was found guilty of having murdered a messmate aboard ship was forthwith tied to the corpse and flung overboard.

FIRST NAVAL COMMISSION

The first commission granted to a U.S. Naval officer was to Captain Hopley Yeaton, March 21st, 1791. He was master of a revenue cutter, then the sole maritime defense of our young republic.

IT'S AN ILL WIND.....

The old saying "It's an ill wind that blows nobody any good," was originally exclusively nautical, and meant that no matter which way the wind blew, some ship must surely profit from its direction.

CRUISERS

The word cruiser is derived from the Mediterranean word CRUSAL meaning "fast."

and, as a result, resembled his being in prayer. The use of holystones was reduced because they wore down expensive teak decks.

Homeward Bound Pennant
This pennant is a flag flown by a ship returning to the United States after she has been overseas for nine months or more. It flies from the time she starts home until sunset of her first day in a U.S. port. Next to the hoist, the flag carries a star for the first nine months overseas, and additional stars for every six months. It is one foot long for each man on board, but never longer than the length of the ship. Frequently, balloons are used to keep a long pennant from dragging in the water. After the pennant is taken down, it is cut up and a piece of the flag is given to every person on board the ship.

Homeward Bound Stitches
In the old days, sailors were particularly neat with their sewing. Careless sewing was referred to as "homeward bound stitching," the idea being it was only a temporary makeshift until port was reached. When reaching port, the mother, wife or girlfriend could be counted on to finish the job properly.

Hooker
British descriptive word for certain small, single-masted vessels trading between British ports and the Hook of Holland. The word now means any small or clumsy seagoing craft. The same term evolved independently in America during the Civil War when hordes of prostitutes followed the Army troops of Union General Hooker. As a result, "hooker" is also a nickname for prostitutes.

Horn Pipe
A frisky sailor's dance that was named for the two instruments usually found aboard deep-sea ships, a horn and a pipe.

Horse Latitudes
The words of Samuel Taylor Coleridge, "Idle as a painted ship upon a painted ocean," well-describe a sailing ship's situation when it entered the "horse latitudes." Lo-

cated near the West Indies between 30 and 40 degrees north latitude, these waters were noted for unfavorable winds that becalmed cattle ships heading from Europe to America. Often, ships carrying horses would have to cast several overboard to conserve drinking water for the rest as the ship rode out the unfavorable winds. Because so many horses and cattle were tossed to the sea, the area became known as the "horse latitudes."

Hospital Ships
The first hospital ship to be built from the keel up for the Navy, was the *Solace.* This vessel was commissioned in 1920 and decommissioned in 1946. During World War II, the Navy had 12 full-time hospital ships in service. The first hospital ship used by the Navy was the *Red Rover*, a steamboat converted for such use during the Civil War. The job was fairly simple then. It consisted of not much more than painting the words "hospital ship" on the side of the ship.

House Flag
The flags of the various shipping companies are known as "house flags" because the device borne on such flags is the insignia of the company or house, which operates the ships. Their origin dates back to medieval days, when crusaders, off to the Holy Wars, carried on their ships a banner showing the crest or coat-of-arms of the house or company to which they belonged. Many modern-day merchant marine officers wear an enameled replica of the company's flag in the badge on their caps.

How Deep is the Ocean
It all depends on where one drops the sounding lead. Along the continental shelf, which may be from 30 to 800 miles wide, the sea slopes from the beach line down to 100 fathoms. Beyond the shelf, it drops down two or three miles. The average depth of all oceans is about 13,000 feet. To date, the deepest known part of the ocean is Challenger Deep, in the western Pacific, where the depth is 35,760 feet. Two men have ventured there; Jacques Piccard and Don Walsh made the trip in the *Trieste* in 1960.

Hugh Williams
The name "Hugh Williams" is used to refer to the sole survivor of a sea tragedy. This is the result of the odd coincidence that for greater than 200 years, more than 40 sole survivors of shipwrecks and ship sinkings were named Hugh Williams.

· DIPPING THE FLAG ·

Dipping the flag is a survival of a very old custom when merchant ships were required to clew up all their canvas and wait until the adjacent man-o'-war either sent a boat off to inspect their papers or signalled them to proceed. The flag salute was later adopted as a time saver.

· BO'SUN'S PIPE ·

The present form of the bo'sun's pipe is actually a facsimile of that taken from the body of the infamous pirate Andrew Barton by Admiral Lord Howard.

· PALE ALE ·

Old Navy slang for a drink from the scuttle butt.

· FOR BLASPHEMY ·

Despite Hollywood and popular opinion, cuss words have always been frowned upon aboard ship. In Queen Elizabeth's reign, blasphemy was punished by burning the offender's tongue with a hot iron.

Hull Down

"Hull down" is the description of a ship when it is just far enough beyond the horizon so that only masts and superstructure are visible.

Hunky Dory

A slang term meaning everything is OK. One theory is it was coined from a notorious street named "Honkidori" in Yokohama. Since a sailor could find women, liquor and anything he wanted in that street, its name became synonymous for anything that is enjoyable or satisfactory. Another theory is that it evolved from the Dutch *honk* for home to *hunk* to *hunky*. The full hunky dory appears to have come into use as the result of a post-Civil War blackface minstrel show in which a song was introduced that contained the phrase, "a red hot hunky dory contraband."

Idlers

Members of the ship's company who stand no regular watch are known as "idlers." This does not include members of the medical staff, the stewards, messmen and others who work on a different schedule.

I Have Not Yet Begun to Fight

John Paul Jones made many contributions to the Navy. However, none stands out more conspicuously than his display of daring and enterprise. At the time of the American Revo-

lution, in the classic action between Jones' ship, *Bonhomme Richard*, and the British frigate *Serapis*, Jones faced an enemy of vastly superior strength. During the early stages of the battle, a steady flow of cannon fire poured forth at close range, and Jones' inferior and aged craft was rapidly reduced to a deplorable state. Finally, in a sinking condition, *Bonhomme Richard* got alongside and lashed with the other vessel for the purpose of hand-to-hand combat. When a gunner in panic cried for quarter and rushed to haul down the American flag, Jones hurled his pistol at the fellow, fracturing his skull and knocking him down a hatch. Captain Pearson of *Serapis*, having heard the cry, called to Jones asking whether he had struck his colors. Though barely able to keep her afloat, Jones thundered back his famous answer, "I have not yet begun to fight!" This proved to be no idle boast as history has proved, and John Paul Jones' action established an early and major tradition of the Navy.

In Mufti

These are civilian clothes, also known as "civvies," when worn by a person who normally wears a uniform. "Mufti" comes from West Indian "muf-tee," meaning "a civilian."

In Through the Hawsepipe

Sometimes we hear an old chief petty officer claim he "came into the Navy through the hawsepipe," and it makes one wonder if he is referring to some early enlistment program. Actually, it was an enlistment program of sorts; it means "a person is salty and savvies the way of the sea because he began  his nautical career on the lowest rung of the deck force ladder." A "hawsepipe" or "hawsehole" is a hole in the bow of a ship that the anchor chain runs through.

Irish Hurricane

An "Irish Hurricane" is the lighthearted description of a dead calm.

Irish Pennant

Any piece of line or rope not properly secured and hanging in an untidy manner is referred to as an "Irish pennant." This is also applicable to a loose rope end.

Iron Ships

If properly shaped, iron can float as well as wood. However, in the early days of metal ships, there was considerable doubt about it. British seamen protested in Parliament against sending iron ships to sea on the grounds that, "Everyone knows that metal cannot float!" Actually, a ship constructed of iron weighs only half as much as a similar one that is constructed of wood, and a steel-hulled ship is 15 percent lighter than

• SAILORETTE •

Just in case you should think it a modern innovation to grant commissions and ratings in the navy to the weaker (?) sex, remember that Mary Ann Talbot received a pension of twenty pounds per annum for wounds received in action many years before Nelson's time. Also note that Ann Johnson died at the Battle of Copenhagen while serving as a member of a British gun crew.

• SHACKLE •

This word is derived from the old Anglo-Saxon "sceacul" meaning a link of chain.

• OAK LEAVES •

Oak leaves are used in insignia as a tribute to the memory of the staunch ships of oak in the good old days of sail.

• MEGAPHONE •

.....and if you think this is a modern instrument, be advised that Alexander the Great used one 335 years B.C.

one of iron.

Island On the Starboard Side
The island on all U.S. aircraft carriers is on the starboard side. Propeller-driven airplanes have a tendency to pull to the left due to torque effect when power is suddenly applied, as when a plane making a carrier landing takes a wave-off. The Navy's first carrier, *USS Langley*, had no island, but when the *USS Lexington* and *USS Saratoga* were designed, it was only natural to put the islands on the right hand side, out of the way. Jet aircraft on our modern carriers, of course, are not bothered by the torque effect but traffic patterns continue on the left with the island on the right.

It's an Ill Wind
The old saying, "It's an ill wind that blows nobody any good," was an exclusively nautical expression. It meant that no matter which way the wind blew, some ship would profit from its direction.

Jack of the Dust
This is a euphemism for the enlisted sailor in charge of the provision storeroom.

Jack Tar
"Tar," a slang term for sailor, has been in use since at least 1676. The term of "Jack Tar" was in use by the 1780s. Early sailors wore coveralls and broad-brimmed hats made of a tar-impregnated fabric called tarpaulin cloth. The hats and the sailors who wore them were called "tarpaulins," later shortened to tars.

Jacob's Ladder
This is the term for a boat ladder dropped over the side of a ship. It comes from the Book of Genesis, where a dream is described in which Jacob saw a ladder ascending from earth to Heaven. Realistically, the first time one climbs up the side of a ship at sea, with the height, pitching, rolling and the ladder swinging, it is easy to understand why this ladder is named after the one that is endless and reaches into the sky.

Jersey
This close-fitted wool sweater was named for the largest of the British Channel Islands, the island of Jersey. As a result of the sweater's popularity with seamen, its use spread rapidly throughout the world.

Junk
European sailors reached Java even before the 13th century and they were able to come in contact with the primitive boats that were being used in that part of the world. The Javanese boats were not only clumsy and slow, but their crews did not keep the vessels neat, orderly or shipshape. Old ropes and tattered sails were tangled and hanging from the timbers of many of these vessels. The Javanese word for boat is "dgong," and the seamen used it to describe the tattered ropes and sails as well as the vessel. Finding "djong" difficult to say correctly, it was pronounced "junk" by the English sailors. By the 15th century, it was common to use junk to describe useless and untidy odds and ends.

Kangaroo
Captain James Cook won an international reputation as an explorer before he was forty. He brought back to England many exotic objects and interesting stories from remote places throughout the world. Yet, in 1771 when he returned from Australia, he was branded a liar. The trouble started when he described a strange Australian animal that the natives called a kangaroo. Cook reported that the creature stood as tall as a man, had large ears, hopped around on two legs and had the equivalent of a pocket on the front part of his body. Many doubted Cook's honesty and sanity until a kangaroo was brought to the London Zoo years later.

· THE FIRST CHRONOMETER ·

The first chronometer was made and demonstrated aboard H.M.S. CENTURION in 1736. Sir Isaac Newton declared the making of an instrument of such precision to be impossible. But the CENTURION'S carpenter built one of wood..... and it actually worked successfully. From that time on, longitude could be reckoned accurately.

· VIKING ·

The correct pronunciation of this word is, "Veek-ing," and refers to those wild sea robbers who laid in wait for their victims in the viks (veeks) or bays of Norway.

·WHITE RATS ·

Slang term in the old Navy for men who would endeavor to curry favor with the officers by carrying tales aft.

· BOWSPRIT ·

While the jib-booms of yachts and other small craft are often called bowsprits, the term is lubberly, as the bowsprit is an integral part of a vessel's hull, to which the figurehead is secured.

Keelhaul

To be "keelhauled" today is merely to be given a severe reprimand for rule infraction. As late as the 19th century, however, it meant the extreme. It was a dire and often fatal torture employed to punish offenders of certain naval laws.

An offender was securely bound both hand and foot, and heavy weights were attached to his body. He was then lowered over the ship's side and slowly dragged along the vessel's hull. If he didn't drown, which was rare, barnacles usually ripped the sailor, causing him to bleed to death or later die from infection. All navies stopped this cruel and unusual punishment many years ago.

Keep Your Shirt On

This expression for "Don't get fighting mad" came to us from the Vikings. Advice was given by a peacemaker to calm down and avoid a fight.

Kickback

A word of seagoing origin in which the captain of a ship entered into collusion with the ship's storekeeper, for illustration, and made available a quantity of the ship's stores to a merchant at bargain prices. This resulted in a "kickback" of money to the captain and his cohort, and a loss of inventory for the shipowner. In the world of today, this is a practice that occurs on many levels in politics and industry.

Kids

In the old Navy, the shallow wooden or metal vessels used in carrying food from the galley to the mess table were called "kids." It was the job of boys aboard the ship to help the cook by waiting on the seamen at mealtime. The boys were kids in the vernacular of the day, and the trays were named after them.

The King Spoke

The "king spoke" is located on a ship's steering wheel. It is the one which, when standing vertically, indicates the rudder is amidships. The name comes from the old custom of decorating this spoke with a crown in honor of the king. Sometimes the king spoke is given a different shape so it can be detected in the dark.

With the advent of rudder angle indicators, "king spokes" are no longer necessary.

Knock-Off

To "knock-off" is to "quit work or stop what you are doing." When boats were rowed by galley slaves, a galley drummer beat time for them with a mallet and block of wood. The slaves rowed when he knocked the mallet on the block. They could stop rowing, or "knock-off," when he stopped knocking.

Knot

The term "knot," or nautical mile, is used worldwide to denote one's speed through water. Today, knots are measured with electronic devices, but in the 18th century, such devices were unknown. Ingenious mariners developed the log line, a reliable device for measuring speed. From this method we got the term knot. The log line was a length of twine marked at 47.33-foot intervals by colored knots. At one end a long chip was fastened. Shaped like the sector of a circle, the chip was weighted at the rounded end with lead.

When thrown over the stern, it would float pointing upward and would remain relatively stationary. The log line was allowed to run over the side for 28 seconds and then hauled on board. There was a count of the knots that had passed over the side. In this way, the ship's speed was measured.

Know the Ropes

When we say someone "knows the ropes," we infer he knows his way around the sea, and is quite capable of handling most nautical problems. Through the years, the meaning of the phrase has changed somewhat.

FIRST 'SUB' VICTIM

The first recorded victim of a submarine was the U.S.S. HOUSATONIA, attacked by the Confederates while off Charleston, S.C., on February 17th. 1864.

• BANIAN DAYS •

Years ago, when as a measure of economy, two meatless days per week for seamen were introduced, sailors sneered at them as "Banian Days", naming them for the Hindu Banians, a tribe whose religion prohibits any diet other than vegetarian.

• A 24 ~ CENT 'PEEVE'.

When King Manuel of Portugal refused to raise the famous Magellan's army pay from $2.25 to $2.49 per month, that irate officer forsook his military career and turned navigator.

• LATEEN SAIL •

This name for a triangular mains'l was originally LATIN sail, so called to designate the rig of Mediterraean type vessels.

Originally, the statement was printed on a seaman's discharge to indicate that he knew the names of the primary uses of the main ropes on board ship. In other words, "This man is a novice seaman and knows only the basics of seamanship." Learning these basics kept many a young sailor's stomach in knots.

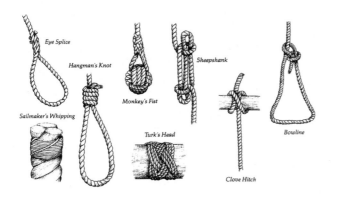

Know the Ropes

Scuttlebutt has it that if you gundeck your work and spend all of your time skylarking, instead of minding your Ps and Qs, then you'll end up in the horse latitudes and will never know the ropes.

Landlubber
It would appear that "landlubber" is one who "lubs" or "loves the land." However, lubber, even as far back as the 13th century was a clumsy oaf. In the following centuries, he was the one that sailors had to put up with aboard ship. At first, it was green seamen who, in contempt were called lubbers. Later, as landlubbers, it was applied with equal exasperation to passengers or others that did not know one rope from another.

Land of Big Feet
This South American country received its name when Portuguese sailors noted with amazement the huge feet of the natives. They nicknamed the Indians "Patagones" ("pata," feet) ("gones," big) and their country Patagonia. This area is now southern Argentina and southern Chile.

Lanyard
A "lanyard" is any line made fast to something for the purpose of securing it. It was originally spelled "land yard," and it meant a piece of rope with a length of three feet, equivalent to a land measure of one yard.

Larboard Side
The "larboard" is the old-time name for the "port," or left side of a vessel. Early ships were steered by a huge oar secured near the stern, on the starboard or right side. In order to keep the steering oar from being crushed against the side of the dock, ships tied up the left side fast to the wharf. As a result, the left-hand side of a ship was called the "lar" or "load-board" side.

Lateen Sails
Mainsails that were cut to a triangular shape were originally called "Latin sails" because they were copied from the rig of Mediterranean-type vessels. The pronunciation of "Latin" was corrupted to "lateen."

Latitude and Longitude
Latitude is the distance measured—north and south—from the equator to a point on the earth's surface as expressed in degrees. Longitude is the distance—east or west—from the meridian of a particular location on earth to the Prime Meridian at Greenwich, England, also expressed in degrees. Latitude and longitude are used by navigators at sea and in the air to determine their position. Arabian mathematicians and ship captains invented these critical navigational tools in the 15th century. However, it took two more centuries for a truly accurate measurement of longitude to be developed by a carpenter, John Harrison, who constructed a chronometer out of wood. Although longitude is measured from the Prime Meridian at Greenwich, England, in early times it was determined to be the distance from Paris, London, Madeira, Tenerife and other locations. As a result, charts with four different scales for longitude were common. (*Greenwich Time and Chronometers* story was chronicled on the History Channel in July 2000.)

Leatherneck
A United States Marine, as everyone knows, has the euphemistic title of "leatherneck." The 1812 Marine uniform included a leather-lined collar that looked military but was uncomfortable. It was abolished more than a hundred years ago, but the term is still used.

Lend a Hand
In sea-going parlance, this is a request for help. "Bare a hand" is a direct order.

Lime Juice and Limeys
British sailing ships as far back as 1795 were required by law to carry lime juice, and the seamen were ordered to drink it to avoid scurvy. Consequently, British sailors became known as "Limeys." No one in those days had heard of vitamin C, but that is what it was all about. Lime juice contained the vitamin and a pint a day helped keep the seamen well. Eventually the term

• OLD *STICK-IN-THE-MUD* •

This term, describing a person who is non-progressive or of no account, had a gruesome origin. It dates back to the days when pirates were hanged at the edge of the Thames tide-waters. When dead the felon was buried in the mud...... "so that forever none might find his foul body, nor account for his soul at the Ressurection."

•The BRASS MONKEY•

International nickname for the very dignified golden lion on the crimson field of the Cunard Steamship Co's handsome house-flag.

• SANTIAGO •

This well known South American city was named for the Portugese patron Saint Jago, but with the passing of time the name has been corrupted by illiterate seafarers, both in the spelling and pronunciation.

• ROVER •

While this name is now generally applied to buccaneers, it was originally the trade name for the hardworking brotherhood of riggers. These skilled men became known as ROVERS because they traveled from shipyard to shipyard as their jobs demanded, much as our modern fruit pickers seek work.

Limey was applied to all Englishmen and the word is now regarded as a friendly euphemism.

Listless
"Listless" has the meaning of being "dull" or "lifeless," and it was established as a word in the days of sail. A ship that is becalmed rides on an even keel, without the usual port or starboard list experienced under a good breeze. Therefore, a vessel that has no wind or list is "listless."

Liverpool Pennant
A lazy sailor would sometimes substitute a piece of string for a missing button on his uniform. But he would be punished if he were found with this "Liverpool pennant" during inspection.

Loaded to the Guards
This is another of many seamen's terms for one who had taken on more liquor than he could carry. It has reference to the load line, or Plimsoll marks, painted on all merchant ships to indicate the maximum load they can carry under various conditions.

Locker Stick
A mythical piece of equipment used by a sailor trying to jam all his gear into a tiny locker.

Log Book
Today, any bound record kept on a daily basis aboard ship is called a "log." Originally, records were kept on sailing ships by inscribing information on shingles cut from logs and hinged so they opened like books. When paper became more readily available, "log books" were manufactured from paper and bound. Shingles were relegated to naval museums, but the slang term stuck.

Log Book

Long Pig
Until the coming of the European Caucasians, the menu of natives in the Pacific islands consisted primarily of fish, fruit, roots and berries. The first explorers brought pigs, and they increased in numbers to such an extent that the word "pig" became a synonym for meat. Naturally, a human victim prepared for consumption became "long pig."

Long Shot
There is an old nautical term that has contributed to modern gambling terminology. Because ships' guns in early days were very inaccurate except at close quarters, it was only an extremely lucky shot that would hit the mark at any great distance. The chance of a hit decreased with distance and conditions. Hence the aspect of luck in the gambling term, whether in the casinos or at the race track.

Longshoreman
This is a contraction of "along-shore-man," a dockside worker who loads and unloads vessels. They are also called "stevedores" from the Spanish "estivador," one who packs things.

Love Apples
Tomatoes were native to South America and they were brought to Spain and Morocco shortly after Columbus discovered America. After the tomatoes reached Italy, they were known as "pomo dei Moro" (apple of the Moors). A Frenchman erroneously translated this to "pomme d'amour" (*love apple*), and a legend was born.

Lucky Bag
A locker aboard ship where lost articles of clothing or other personal gear were turned in was called the "lucky bag." Every so often, it was opened and those who could identify their property were able to reclaim it. But there was a catch, anyone claiming gear from the lucky bag got a few lashes with the cat-o'-nine tails to teach him not to lose anything again. "*Lucky Bag*" is the name of the annual yearbook prepared by midshipmen at the U.S. Naval Academy.

Lying On the Oars
In the days before boats had engines, the boat crew in the junior boat saluted the boat carrying a senior officer. The oarsmen did this by raising their oars parallel to the water as they passed.

Mae West
This actress was born in Brooklyn, New York in 1892 and was well-known and a highly popular veteran of burlesque, vaudeville, stage and screen. She was also the self-promoting possessor of an ample, curvaceous and hourglass figure. Early in World War II, an unidentified destroyer sailor put on one of the new type of kapok-filled life jackets and gleefully yelled to

The SHIP that CHANGED a RIVER'S NAME

The Oregon River's name was changed to that of Columbia River in honor of the U.S.S. Columbia, when that vessel called there in 1788 while on her famous voyage around the world.

THE JINX CAT

Page Hollywood, here's a new "Oscar". Oscar is the black cat which was rescued by British sailors when they sank the battleship "Bismarck". Later, Oscar was saved from the British destroyer "Cossack" when that vessel was torpedoed. Again Oscar was jerked from a watery grave when the plane-carrier "Ark Royal" was lost.
Oscar now lives at Gibraltar..... so keep your fingers crossed.

KNOW YOUR SPUDS

Contrary to popular belief, potatoes were not first introduced into Europe by Sir Walter Raleigh, but by that doughty seaman the great Admiral Drake.

TOUGH LUCK for "HARPIES"

There is now a bank in Glasgow, Scotland, which opens special accounts for seamen under a plan by which they may draw only enough each day for living expenses. This is to discourage waterfront women from reaping a harvest on sailor's pay days.

his shipmates one of Ms. West's famous film lines, "Why don't you come up and see me sometime?" By word of mouth, followed by wartime publicity, the jacket became universally known as the "Mae West."

Mainsail Haul
"Loot" or "booty" taken in a fight between ships was given this name.

Make the Starboard Side
The starboard side of a vessel is the traditional side to approach when making a visit by boat. This is because in ancient days ships were steered by a huge oar secured to that side. A shipmaster, whose equally traditional station was close to the helm, could thus easily see who was approaching his ship, and either welcome them or warn them off.

Marine Knotheads
During battles at sea in the 19th century, hand-to-hand combat took place between enemies. During a fight, American Marine sharpshooters were stationed in the rigging and their special duty was to shoot enemy officers on deck. Under these circumstances, it was difficult to distinguish friend from foe. To avoid hitting their own officers, they fashioned a green cloverleaf-shaped rope knot and sewed it to the officer's hat. It is because of this history that the modern marine officer's cap has crossed rope-like braid on top.

Marine Swords
Swords worn by present-day U.S. Marine officers are almost exact duplicates of one presented to William Eaton at the Bay of Tripoli during the Barbary conflict in 1804-05. Eaton helped lead a band of marines, sailors and tribesmen on camels across the desert from Alexandria to Tripoli, in North Africa. It was that expedition which gave the Marines the phrase, "to the shores of Tripoli," in the Marines," Hymn.

Marines
The first Marines were British, and were known as "The Duke of York and Albany's Maritime Regiment of Foot." In 1664, there were 1,200 of them. The first American Marines were enlisted at Tun Tavern in Philadelphia on November 10, 1775, before the U.S. Navy was officially organized. This day is celebrated as the birth date of the Marine Corps.

The Marines Have Landed
This news has made many headlines over the years. Richard Harding Davis, covering the Marine landing at Vera Cruz, Mexico, in 1914 originated the expres-

sion. His complete statement was, "The Marines have landed and the situation is well in hand!"

Martinet
A "martinet" is one who is a strict disciplinarian. It was the name of a Frenchman, the Marquis of Martinet, who served in France's army under Louis XIV, and he carried discipline to extremes. The French still call the cat-o'-nine-tails a martinet.

Master at Arms
The "Master at Arms" designation is by no means a modern innovation. Naval records show that these "sheriffs of the sea" were keeping order as early as the reign of Charles I of England. At that time, they were charged with keeping the swords, pistols and muskets in good working order as well as ensuring that the bandoleers were filled with fresh gunpowder before combat.

Besides being chiefs of police at sea, the sea corporals, as they were called in the British Navy, had to be qualified in close order fighting under arms and able to train seamen in hand-to-hand combat. In the days of sail, the sailors who held the MAA designation were truly "masters at arms." The master at arms in the U.S. Navy can trace the beginning of his rate to the Union Navy of the Civil War.

Master Mariners
There were no licensed masters in charge of ships until the year 1450. At that time, Charles the Fifth of Spain signed a law making it compulsory for a shipmaster to carry a certificate recording his qualifications for the job.

Mate
Whether First Mate in the Merchant Marine or Boatswain's Mate in the Navy, it is derived from the French "Matelot," meaning "sailor."

Mayday
The French word "m'aidez" is translated in English to "Help me!" Using the original French pronunciation, "Mayday" is a voice radio distress call for vessels and people in serious trouble at sea. It is also used as a rallying call for help from others in battles on land or sea, large or small.

Megaphone
Alexander the Great used this cone-shaped device for amplifying his voice in 335 B.C.

• GUN SALUTES •

Were first fired as an act of good faith. In the days when it took so long to reload a gun, it was a proof of friendly intention when ships' cannons were thus dis-charged upon entering a port.

WINDAS

HALF-MAST •

Flags flown at half-mast for mourn-ing, are a survival of the old custom which decreed that slovenliness was a mark of respect for the dead. Sails and rigging were slacked off, yards cock-billed, flags part lowered etc.; in fact, anything to give the ship a dejected appearance.

BOXING *the* COMPASS

Today meaning to tell off the points of the compass-card, it originally referred to the placing of the compass in a bittacle (small box). From this word "bittacle" we get our modern "binnacle."

• CAPTAIN •

This naval officer receives his title from the old word CAPUT (meaning Chief), a name of great honor among the ancient Thanes.

Merchant Marine: Our Critical Arm of Offense

The merchant marine was a major arm of both offense and defense. The 250,000 seamen who volunteered for Merchant Marine service during World War Two did a job that was sometimes forgotten, but was always indispensable. The ships they served on carried troops, munitions, food and other supplies across the oceans to the front lines in history's most far-flung conflict.

Soon after the government took over all U.S. flag merchant ships in February 1942, it embarked on a crash campaign of recruiting seamen and building cargo vessels. It settled on a single design called the Liberty ship, of which 2,770 were eventually mass-produced, as swiftly as one every 80 hours. The Liberty ship was 441 feet long, 57 feet wide, displaced 14,100 tons and could carry 10,000 tons of cargo. Later in the War, 534 Victory ships were also produced. These were faster than the Liberty, and could carry larger cargoes. The heavy output of ships was essential. The war's deadliest months were in May and July of 1942, when one U.S. merchant ship was sunk, on average, every 16 hours.

For American seamen, the Battle of the Atlantic was a cold, lonely and vicious campaign. Many men went down with their ships while others perished because of exposure or starvation in their lifeboats. From Pearl Harbor until V-J Day, 731 U.S. merchant ships were sunk, and 5,638 men of the Merchant Marine died as a result of enemy action. Also killed were 1,710 members of the U.S. Navy Armed Guard, whose job aboard the merchant ships was to man the guns. The Armed Guard suffered losses far out of proportion to its size; one out of every 185 men did not survive the war.

Mess

The Latin word "mensa" means table, as does the Spanish "mesa." "Mes" is the Gothic term for dish, and these words contributed to eating aboard ship, or "mess." Eating took place at the "messdeck."

Metal Men

"Metal men" is a good-natured expression for retired enlisted men recalled to active duty. Because most of them were past middle age, wore gold hash marks and were not as agile in their movements as younger men, it was humorously said of them that they had silver in their hair, gold on their arms, and lead in their pants.

Midshipmen

"Midshipmen" originally referred to the youngsters aboard British Navy vessels who were in training to become naval officers. Their primary duties included carrying orders from the officers in the stern, to the crew, quartered in the foc'sle. Their repeated scampering through the middle part of the ship earned them the name "midshipmen" and the nickname "middie."

Naval Academy students and Navy Reserve Officer Training Candidates are still called midshipmen because, just like their counterparts of old, they are training to become officers in the sea service. It is interesting to note that "mids" (the term middie is no longer in use), back in the days of sail, could begin their naval careers as early as age eight.

Midshipmen in the Old Royal Navy

During the Age of Nelson, between the 1790s and the 1830s, young boys who came from elite families would go to sea at age eight or nine. They were assigned to work as 'captain's servants' until about age 15, when they were eligible to become midshipmen. A ship-of-the-line might have as many as sixteen middies. Their function was to assist lieutenants, serve as aides to senior officers and to supervise gun crews during battle. The midshipmen received training from senior personnel, and might be appointed to the rank of acting lieutenant if a vacancy occurred while waiting for a commission. General regulations for a commission required the candidate to be 20 years of age, with six years at sea and two years as a midshipman or master's mate. Not everyone passed the rigorous oral test before an examining board and, surprisingly, midshipmen's messes had numbers of men ranging in age from twenty through the fifties.

· ABOVE BOARD ·

This slang-term for honesty, originated in the day when pirates would sometimes hide most of their crew behind the bulwarks, in order to lure some unsuspecting victim into thinking him an honest merchantman. In reverse, therefore, anyone who displayed all his crew openly on deck, was obviously an honest seaman.

· BETWEEN the DEVIL and the DEEP ·

In wooden ships, the "Devil" was the longest seam to be caulked, and called for a bos'un's chair in order to execute the job; thus a man was actually suspended between the "devil" and the water. This slang-term was coined to describe being in an awkward situation.

· KNOCK-OFF ·

Slang for quitting work. It arose from the custom aboard slave-galleys to have a man beat time for the rowers. While he kept knocking on the block with his mallet, they rowed; when he stopped, they could cease. .

· DAGO ·

A nickname which is at least 400 years old. It was bestowed by English sailors on the Portugese and Spanish seamen, who called loudly and often on their patron Saint Diego.

Mind Your Ps and Qs

There are few of us who have not at one time or another been admonished to "mind our Ps and Qs,"

or in other words, to behave our best. Oddly enough, "mind your Ps and Qs" had nautical beginnings as a method of keeping books on the waterfront. In the days of sail, when sailors were paid a pittance, seamen drank their ale in taverns where keepers were willing to extend credit until payday. Since many salts were illiterate, keepers kept a tally of pints and quarts consumed by each sailor on a chalkboard behind the bar. Next to each person's name, a mark was made for "P" for pint or "Q" for quart, whenever a seaman ordered another draught. On payday, each seaman was liable for each mark next to his name, so he was forced to "mind his Ps and Qs" or get into financial trouble. To ensure an accurate account by unscrupulous keepers, sailors had to keep their wits and remain somewhat sober. Sobriety usually ensured good behavior, hence today's meaning of mind your Ps and Qs.

Mine Warfare

This type of warfare reached its height in World War II when the warring nations laid hundreds of thousands of mines from surface ships, submarines and aircraft. Mines are not new; they had a beginning many years ago. During the siege of Antwerp in 1583, small boats called "infernals" or "fire ships," were filled with explosives and inflammables and were floated in among enemy ships. The torpedoes that Admiral Farragut so heartily damned at the Battle of Mobile Bay were a primitive form of mine. Decades after World War II ended, mines are still turning up and they can be dangerous. There is much truth in the say-ing: "Mines never surrender."

Miniature Salute

The U.S. Naval Academy owns a model of the French three-decker, *Ville de Paris,* which has a very historic and unique background. At Dresden in 1814, Alexander the First of Russia was given a 120-gun salute from the little brass cannon peeping from the model's gun ports.

Miracle in the North Atlantic.

Army Sergeant Cecil Davis was seasick in a sick bay bunk of his troopship, *Uruguay,* while the vessel pitched and rolled in the stormy night as part of a 1943 convoy to Britain. There was a sudden, loud noise and loss of lights and, before he blacked out, Davis felt as if he was floating in air.

When the sergeant awoke, he was wet, cold, bruised and bloodied. Lying on the deck with no knowledge as to how he got there, a dazed Davis rose to his feet and asked a passing seaman where the sick bay was. "Follow me," the sailor said.

A doctor treated the sergeant for cuts and bruises in the brightly-lit infirmary, and then the physician noticed his dog tags. The doctor looked at him and asked the question, "What are you doing on this ship, soldier?" Davis responded, "I came aboard this troopship with 5,000 other GIs!" The physician exclaimed, "This is not a troopship! This is the Navy tanker *Sallimonia,* and there are no Army troops on board!"

There was an answer to this ocean mystery. At 1:00 AM, the ships of the convoy were ordered to stop zigzagging and to go full speed ahead. It was dark, the *Sallimonia*'s steering gear jammed and she rammed her bow into the hull of the nearby *Uruguay. Sallimonia* withdrew, leaving a large hole in the hull of *Uruguay* and the bodies of 13 men on the decks of the troopship. Knocked out of his bunk, Davis fell through the now non-existent sick bay floor onto the tanker's deck. Therefore, when *Sallimonia* backed off, she had a new passenger who boarded in the middle of the North Atlantic.

Missed the Boat

A liberty boat works on a schedule to return sailors to their ship from shore leave. If they arrive at the dock too late, they have "missed the boat." The phrase is now used to describe a lost opportunity.

Mother Carey's Chickens

Stormy petrels are small birds that are often seen flitting over wave crests just before a storm. This alerted

· SEVEN BELLS ·

American sailors are quick to note the absence of the striking of "Seven Bells" in the second dog-watch aboard British ships. In 1797 "Seven Bells" was to be the signal for the navy mutiny at the Nore. The plot was discovered and the mutiny quelled. The Admiralty decreed that "Seven Bells in the second dog-watch" should never again be struck on British vessels.

· TATTOO ·

Tattooing was first used as a means of identification. In the days when most poor navy men could neither read nor write their names, it meant something to be able to prove identity by means of an anchor on one's arm, or a full-rigged ship on your manly chest.

·HARNESS CASK ·

Old navy slang for the "Salt Horse" barrel. Sailors swore that horse-meat was used instead of beef, and pointed out that the extra tough pieces were parts of the horses' harness.

· SIDE-LIGHTS ·

It was not until between 1825 and 1830 that RED and GREEN side-lights were introduced. Up until then all ships' running lights were WHITE, but the advent of speed called for the colored lights as a further aid to navigation. · ·

the crew to be careful and wary. The name of Mother Carey comes from "mata cara" (dear mother) and it refers to the saint who protects sailors at sea.

Mustang

A mustang is a commissioned officer who was formerly an enlisted man.

Mutiny

This is an ocean term first used between 1560 and 1570 to describe a rebellion against the constituted authority of a ship, specifically the vessel's commanding officer. One of most interesting instances of mutiny in the United States Navy occurred in 1842 and, because of the people involved and its impact, it deserves attention in this book.

Philip Spencer was the son of John C. Spencer, Secretary of War in the Cabinet of President Tyler. Young Spencer was appointed as an acting midshipman on the training ship, *USS North Carolina*, where he balked at Lieutenant William Craney's attempts to discipline him. Pressure was placed on Craney from several higher sources and he was eventually driven out of the Navy.

Spencer was transferred to the *Potomac* and then to the *John Adams*, where he was forced to resign. Political influence enabled him to be re-appointed as an acting midshipman and, in 1842, he was assigned to the 126-ton brig, *USS Somers*, which mounted ten guns and carried 120 officers and men.

On November 26, 1842, the purser's steward, Mr. Ward, informed Captain Alexander Slidell Mackenzie that Philip Spencer had twenty men pledged to mutiny. Spencer's possessions were searched and evidence showed that a mutiny was actually in the planning stage, and that the leaders of the rebellion were Spencer, Boatswain's Mate Samuel Cromwell and Gunner's Mate Elisha Small.

An investigation by officers of the ship over the next few days indicated that these men were plotting to take over the ship, throw the officers and loyal members of the crew overboard, and then to use *Somers* for piracy.

The ship's Court of Inquiry found the three men guilty and sentenced them to death by hanging with execution to begin ten minutes after announcement of the verdict. Before the hanging, Philip Spencer confessed that he also tried to incite mutiny on his former vessels, *Potomac* and *John Adams*. The colors were hoisted, the cannon fired and the drums rolled. At the Captain's command, the crew hauled on the ropes, and the three mutineers, with their heads wrapped in peajackets and hands manacled, swung from the mainyard.

There were no objections to the hanging of Cromwell or Small, but the execution of Spencer jolted Washington and the nation. The Secretary of War and his followers, including novelist James Fenimore Cooper, tried to discredit Captain Mackenzie. The Board of Inquiry exonerated Mackenzie for his action, but he was ruined financially.

The Spencer affair attracted so much attention that the whole nation was made aware of the demoralizing practice of appointing unqualified officer candidates through political connection. It aroused the need for stringent midshipmen selection criteria and the necessity for a strong-staffed, well-disciplined naval school with a strong curriculum. As a result of this case and other factors, impetus was given to the founding of the United States Naval Academy at Annapolis.

It is of interest to note that one of the officers who tried the mutineers was later killed while riding a horse, another died of alcoholism, a third committed suicide and the last was permanently institutionalized as a result of mental illness. The *Somers* herself, four years later, capsized off Vera Cruz, Mexico, and 40 of her crew drowned.

Navy Blue

Blue has not always been "navy blue." In fact, it wasn't until 1745 that the expression navy blue meant anything at all. In that year, several British officers petitioned the Admiralty for adoption of new uniforms for its officers. The first sea lord requested several officers to model various uniforms under consideration so he could select the best. He then selected uniforms of various styles and colors to King George II for the final decision.

King George, unable to decide on either style or color, finally chose a blue and white uniform because they were the favorite color combinations of the first lord's wife, Duchess of Bedford.

Navy Day

Once a year the Navy holds open house for the public. The Navy League of the United States inaugurated the day, known as "Navy Day," in 1922. The League chose October 27 because this was the birth date of former President Theodore Roosevelt, who strove to promote this country's modern Navy.

Navy Uniform Evolution

"Blue flat hats" were authorized in 1852 and their use was terminated on April 1, 1963, reportedly due to the lack of materials. Unit names were displayed on the front until January 1941.

· LADRONE ISLANDS ·

The Ladrones received their name from the Portugese word "Latro" (thief), and were so called because Magellan's sailors suffered so much loss of small arms and wearing apparel through pilfering by the natives.

· First NAVY BOARD ·

The first NAVY BOARD was inaugurated in the 16th. Century. Until that time, all naval strategy and fighting was directed by ARMY officers.

· The "HUSH-HUSH" FLEET ·

Nickname given the first British battle cruisers, because of the profound secrecy surrounding their building.

· SICK-BAY ·

Ship's hospitals were originally known as "Sick Berths", but as they were generally located in the rounded sterns of the old battle-wagons, their contours suggested a "bay," and the latter name was given them.

A "white cover" was added to the soft visorless blue hat in 1852, and a "white straw hat" was issued as an additional item in 1866. During the 1880s, the first "white sailor's hat" was authorized, and it had a low rolled brim, high dome and was constructed of canvas wedges. After replacing the canvas with cotton, the white hat was redesigned into the modern style.

The "jumper flap collar" originated as a protective cover for the jumper jacket in order to protect it from the grease or powder normally worn by seamen to hold their hair in place. The "black neckerchief" was first used as early as the 16th century for use as a sweatband and collar closer. Although the myth persists that the black color was selected as a sign of mourning for the death of Admiral Nelson, it was selected for practical reasons, as it did not readily show dirt or stains.

Naval War College
All navies have such an institution of one sort or another, in which officers receive advanced training. The first war college of record was established at Sagres, Portugal, in 1415 by Prince Henry the Navigator. The U.S. Naval War College was established at Newport, Rhode Island, on October 6, 1884 and the first superintendent was Commander Stephen B. Luce.

Nearer, My God, to Thee
Legend has it that the famous White Star liner *Titanic* went down while the ship's orchestra played the hymn, "Nearer, My God to Thee." According to research, the orchestra had been playing ragtime as the end approached. Their last number was the Anglican hymn, "Autumn."

Nelson's Blind Eye
Admiral Viscount Horatio Nelson, the great British sailor, was blind in his left eye. During the battle of Copenhagen on April 2, 1801, his senior officer ordered him to break off the action. Not wanting to quit, Nelson put his telescope to his blind eye and said, "I really do not see the signal." A statue of Nelson was placed in London's Trafalgar Square but it portrays him as blind in the right eye instead of the left.

Nelson's Blood
"Nelson's Blood" is rum. This has been a naval euphemism that became popular after the death of Admiral Horatio Nelson (1758-1895) at the Battle of Trafalgar. The Admiral's body was reportedly preserved in rum for shipment back to England, and Nelson's Blood has been a nautical term since.

No Holidays
When a bosun's mate bellows at the sailors on painting duty, "no holidays!" he is demanding that painting be carefully done without missed spots, or "holidays."

No Quarter
"No quarter" represents a determination to fight to the death without the sparing of life. It is the reverse of "giving quarter," another old custom by which officers, upon surrender, could ransom themselves by paying one quarter of their year's pay.

No Thank You
When Tahiti was discovered by the western world, the Tahitians had no word for "thank you." Their way of saying thank you was to show their appreciation by carrying loads, unpacking cargo, moving heavy gear—anything to help.

Officers in the Old Royal Navy
In the 1790s, most of the world's navies were very short of men who were qualified to operate a ship or effectively deal with the complex matters of command. This was not the case in Britain where Royal Navy officers were drawn from the class of "gentlemen." The titled and wealthy were welcomed to officer rank and the same path was even open to talented members of the growing middle class, provided they had enough good luck and backing. This atmosphere helped make the Royal Navy a career of choice for the aristocracy and the gifted children of more modest families. Regardless of his record or background, a commissioned officer in the King's Navy shared the aura of its prestige and reputation for invincibility.

Oil-Canning
"Oil-canning" is an effect seen on the hulls of very thin-skinned ships, such as destroyers and destroyer escorts, where the relatively thin plates are slightly dished in between frames.

Oil on Troubled Waters
This expression, meaning an "endeavor to pacify belligerents," comes from the old seagoing custom of discharging oil in rough seas around a disabled vessel. The oil tends to break the waves, making it safer for rescue craft.

Old Man
Captain, as applied to an officer in the Merchant Service, is a courtesy title only. His official rank is that of Master Mariner and he is generally called the "Old Man." In the Navy, the commanding officer of a ship

· WHISTLE *for the* WIND ·

In calm weather, Norsemen would whistle loudly, believing that Thor (the thunder god) would whistle in answer, thus creating a breeze which would enable the seamen to set their sail and save the arduos work of rowing. So tenacious has been this superstition, that to this day it is against regulations to whistle aboard sailing ships during a gale.

· BLACK · NECKERCHIEFS

Every time an American gob dons his neckerchief, he is unconsciously paying tribute to the death of Lord Nelson. This however, is only because the American uniform is patterned so closely after the British.

· SNUG HARBOR ·

A term used to describe the enviable position of a sailor who has saved enough during his service to retire and live in comfort ashore for the rest of his life.

· FEELING BLUE ·

If you are melancholy, and describe yourself as "feeling blue", you are using a phrase coined from a custom among many old deepwater ships, by which, if the vessel lost captain or officers during a voyage, she would fly blue flags and have a blue band painted along her entire hull, when returning to home port.

is called Captain, even though he may be only a lieutenant. Officers and men refer to him as the "Old Man," but not necessarily when he's around. During World War II, the average age of commanding officers on destroyer escorts was 27 and the rank of these CO's was mostly lieutenant commander, with lesser numbers as lieutenant senior grade.

Old Navy
The "Old Navy" is a period of time when things in the Navy were very different and much better than the present. Old timers will always talk about the "Old Navy" to anyone with less service time than they have and, of course, life as a sailor was much better then. As long as there are "Old Timers," there will always be an "Old Navy" as compared to the Modern Navy.

Old, Old Navy
King Minos of Crete is said to have established the first regularly organized navy in approximately 1400 BC.

Oldest Sea Story
The oldest known tale of the sea, dated 2500 BC, is housed in the British Museum. Written on papyrus, it recounts a horrifying struggle between a sailor and a sea serpent.

Overwhelmed
This expression that describes "being crushed, defeated or dismayed" emanates from the old Anglo-Saxon "whelman," which means to turn a vessel completely over.

Own Hook
The Grand Banks off the coast of Newfoundland proved to be a bonanza for catching codfish. Sea captains ordinarily hired crews for the season, but many fishermen would board the vessels as semi-independent operators. The fisherman would provide his own fishing gear, but he would give the captain a share of his catch in exchange for passage and meals. To keep count of his daily take, he cut out the tongue of each fish he caught and strung it on a wire. It then became customary to say that one who is "independent" or is "responsible for his actions" is "on his own hook."

Pacific Ocean
Portuguese Navigator Ferdinand Magellan's expedition was the first to circumnavigate the globe. After going through the stormy strait between the southern tip of South America and Tierra Del Fuego, he found the ocean so calm that he named it "Pacific" from the Latin "pacificus," meaning "peaceful."

Paddy Wester
"Paddy Wester" is an old British term for a seaman whose behavior, experience or background is really not the same as recorded on his official papers. In the 1880s, Paddy West was a boardinghouse keeper in Liverpool who made a great deal of his income by providing seamen for the completion of ocean sailing ship crews. Qualified seamen were difficult to obtain, so Paddy rounded up misfits and outcasts in the slums, fed and clothed them, and then turned them over to shipmasters for a fee. It is understood that he trained his men so that they would qualify as seamen. Reportedly, he had them walk around a pair of cow-horns so they could truthfully say they had been around the Horn. Then, with cleverly faked certificates showing them to be fully qualified able seamen, Paddy West got his payment and shipped these sailors out as soon as possible. Today, with the prolific counterfeiting of documents and licenses relative to college degrees, professions and employment history, it can be stated that the "spirit of Paddy West" lives on.

Paddy's Milestone
The island, Ailsa Craig, near the entrance to Glasgow harbor, became known as "Paddy's Milestone" because of the large number of Irishmen who crossed to Scotland. They gave it the affectionate nickname because they were cheered by the nearness of their goal when they sighted the island.

Paint Washers
This is what the old seadogs of square-rigger days called the young upstarts who served aboard the "new-fangled steamships," where there were no lines or sails to handle, and nothing to do but "wash paint."

Painter
This is the line fast at the bow of a boat. It is used either to secure it or tow it. It gets its name from the French "pentoir," meaning "rope."

Painting of Naval Vessels
U.S. Navy ships have been painted almost every color there is and battleship gray is only one of them. Black was standard until 1888, when the Navy changed to white to reduce heat in ships in tropical waters. White lasted until 1908, when gray became the standard. During World War II, camouflage was necessary and ships wore mixtures of gray, black, white, green and blue. Styles of camouflage were classified by the Measure

· GANGWAY ·

The gangway or gangplank received its name from the plank which extended midships from stem to stern on the old slave-galleys. Here paraded the whip-master who urged the slaves to continuous effort with triple-thonged lash.

· DITTY BOX ·

The ditty box (or bag) was first known as the "DITTO" bag, because of the fact that it contained TWO of everything; two spools of thread, two needles, two buttons, etc, etc.

· BELAY ·

Originally, this caution to cease hauling was "DE-lay", then followed the order "make fast". The word was later corrupted to the modern "be-lay."

· POUND and PINT~ERS·

Slang term for British ships when poor feeding aboard them caused Parliament to pass a law making it compulsory that every seaman be given ONE POUND of food and ONE PINT of tea or coffee at each meal.

System. In illustration, a destroyer with a dark blue hull and gray superstructure would be classified as Measure 22.

Pale Ale
Old Navy lingo for a plain drink of water from the scuttlebutt.

Panama Canal
The 50-mile canal across the Isthmus of Panama, completed in 1914, runs from Balboa on the Pacific side to Colon on the Atlantic side. Strangely enough, a ship moving from the Pacific to the Atlantic winds up farther west when it reaches Colon that it was at Balboa. This is because the canal runs in a northeast to southwest direction, and it is dramatically evident when you study a map of the Panama Canal and the isthmus. It is of interest to know that the Panama Canal cuts the distance from New York to San Francisco by roughly 60 percent. During World War II, a successful enemy attack on the canal would have been catastrophic, and it is for that reason this critical passageway was regarded as our "Achilles Heel."

Pango is Spelled Pago
People who hear sailors talk about "Pango Pango" will never find it on the charts of the Pacific; the place they are talking about is shown as "Pago Pago" in the American Samoan islands. According to legend, when a first printing plant was set up there by missionaries, they had to spell the name as "Pago Pago" because they lost the letter "n" from their type case. As a result, it is spelled "Pago Pago," but pronounced "Pango Pango" by the islanders.

With regard to American Samoa, Navy ships periodically docked in the harbor at Tutuila during World War II. The sailors were surprised to see members of the Navy and Marine Corps wearing skirts. Actually, these were native Samoans of the Fita Fita Guard who served with the two forces on the island. These men wore distinctive uniforms that included a skirt, tee shirt and a hat. However, the colors of the uniform for the two services were different.

Pay on the Cap
A tradition in the British Navy is that enlisted men receive their pay on their cap tops. This was originally done so that all could see the amount paid and any errors could be corrected.

Pea Coat
Sailors who have to endure pea-soup weather often don their "pea coats," but the coat's name isn't derived

from the weather. The heavy topcoat, worn in cold, miserable weather by seafaring men, was once tailored from pilot cloth—a heavy, course, stout kind of twilled blue cloth with the nap on one side. The cloth was sometimes called P-cloth for the initial letter of the word, and the garment made from it was called a pea coat. The term has been used since 1723 to denote coats made from that cloth.

Pelican
A sailor's jargon for a hearty eater, "a chow hound."

Pelorus
"Pelorus" is a navigational device for measuring in degrees the relative bearings of observed objects. It came into use about 1850. This instrument is named for Pelorus, the navigator who helped Hannibal evacuate his troops from Italy about 204 B.C.

Pigeons
Those cosmopolitan birds that spend much of their time sitting around in parks and perching on statues, once were "official" parts of the Navy. The birds were used before and during the Spanish-American War to provide one-way messenger service from ship to shore. A bird based at Mare Island, California, was turned loose from the steamer *Alameda* over 400 miles at sea in May 1897 and made it home. When seaplanes first operated, it was the practice to carry a pigeon on each flight. If the plane was forced down, the pilot sent it back to base with a note stating where he thought he was. When *USS Langley*, the first aircraft carrier, was fitting out at Norfolk, the pigeon sailor-handler sent his birds out every day to practice. Later the ship moved up the Chesapeake and when the birds were sent out, they failed to come home. When the ship returned to Norfolk, all the pigeons were sitting on the dock waiting for her.

Pilot
He is a person that is qualified to take a ship into or out of harbor, through a canal, or through difficult and hazardous waters. The word comes from the Dutch "loth" (to lead) and "peil" (to mark with pegs), which both join together to form "leadline."

• THE BOTTLE of WINE •

Christening a ship with a bottle of wine when launching her, is supposed to be a relic of the barbarous days when Norsemen were alleged to have broken the backs of prisoners across the bows of vessels being launched......this, as a peace offering to the gods.

• STERLING SILVER •

This modern term for genuine silver was originally called "Easterling Silver," and referred to a tribe on the Baltic who insisted on being paid in cash for their goods instead of by the then common system of barter. Seamen of that early date therefore carried money specially for that trade, and called it "Easterling money" or "Easterling Silver."

•BATTEN YOUR HATCH•

Old Navy slang meaning to "stop talking"; or in less polite and more modern language to "shut up."

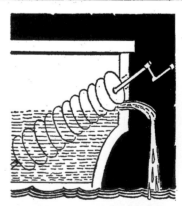

• FIRST SHIP'S PUMP •

The first known device for emptying a vessel's hold of water was invented by Archemides in the year 217 B.C.

Piping Aboard

Boatswains have been in charge of the deck force since the days of sail. Setting sails, heaving lines and hoisting anchors required coordinated team effort, and boatswains used whistle signals to order the coordinated actions. When visitors were hoisted aboard or over the side, the pipe was used to order "Hoist away!" In time, piping became a naval honor on shore as well as at sea.

Plankowner

In the old days when men slept on deck, many of them favored a particular spot where perhaps the planks were more comfortable, and some slept on such a spot until they felt they owned the plank. In the modern Navy, a crewmember who is aboard a ship at the time of a ship's commissioning is considered to be a "plankowner" of that vessel. It is now a custom to give each man who helped commission a ship either a plankowner's certificate or a small wooden plank with his or her name and ship inscribed on it.

Plimsoll Mark

The most important mark on the side of passenger and cargo vessels is the "Plimsoll Mark" or "Plimsoll Line." It is a circle with a horizontal line through it, located midship on both sides, and it marks the maximum depth to which a ship may be loaded. Until Parliament passed Samuel Plimsoll's bill in 1876, ship owners sent undermanned and overloaded ships to sea. Many were "coffin ships," purposely sent to sea to sink for the resulting insurance proceeds. The establishment of the Plimsoll Mark represented a major improvement in world shipping, and the marking was named in Plimsoll's honor. American ships also carry A.B.S. marks (American Bureau of Shipping), which designate the maximum load under four conditions: (1) fresh water-summer; (2) fresh water-winter; (3) salt water-summer; (4) salt water-winter.

Poop Deck

The after deck of a ship is known as the "poop deck." It received its name from the old Roman custom of carrying "pupi" (small images of their gods) in the stern of their ships for good luck.

Pork Barrel

In the sailing days before refrigeration, the Navy brought barrels of heavily salted fish, beef and pork aboard its ships. Each of the barrels contained about 250 pounds of these foods, and the U.S. government paid contractors by the pound for these supplies. When pork was being packed, many of the suppliers were able to make an even larger profit on the sale. They did this by including quantities of pork fat in the cask, and being paid for the fat on the basis of weight. The story did not end with contractors because on some vessels the ship's cook would scoop the fat from the bottom of the barrel and sell it to his shipmates as a palatable substitute for rancid butter. As the media constantly reminds us, "pork barreling" is alive and thriving today in many ways.

Port and Starboard

"Port" and "Starboard" are shipboard terms for left and right, respectively. Confusing those two could cause a shipwreck. In Old England, the starboard was the steering paddle or rudder, and ships were always steered from the right side on the back of the vessel. "Larboard" referred to the left side, the side on which the ship is loaded. So how did larboard become port? Shouted over the noise of the wind and waves, larboard and starboard sounded too much alike, so sailors eventually used the term "port" instead of "larboard" for that side of the ship.

Portholes

Sometimes, novice seamen will ask, "how come holes on the starboard side are called 'portholes' instead of starboardholes?" Many old salts are ready with explanations, but actually the name "porthole" has

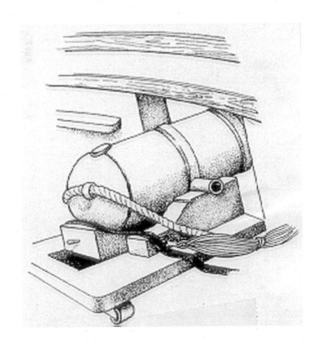

nothing to do with location. The word originated during the reign of Henry VI of England (1485). The king insisted on mounting guns too large for his ships and therefore the conventional methods of securing the weapons on the forecastle and aftercastle could

• The ROUND BATTLESHIP •

Invented by an Australian in the early 70's, the plans for a battleship with a circular hull were purchased by the Russian government, and such a vessel was actually built and launched in 1876.

• First Ship on GREAT LAKES •

The first ship to sail on the Great Lakes was a fighting ship, the GRIFFON, built and launched by La Salle in 1679

• LANYARD •

This word was originally spelled "Land Yard", and meant a piece of small stuff of a regulation length of three feet. In other words, a landsman's measure of one yard.

• GET OUT YOUR WEB FEET •

Old Navy slang, indicating that dirty weather was ahead. It was offered as advice to young seamen by A.B.'s, and suggested that they should get sou'westers and oilskins out of their seachests, as rain or snow was coming.

not be used.

A French shipbuilder named James Baker was commissioned to solve the problem. And solve it he did by piercing the ship's sides so the cannon could be mounted inside the fore- and aftercastles. Covers (gun ports) were fitted for heavy weather and when the cannon were not in use. The French word "porte," meaning door, was used to designate the revolutionary invention. "Porte" was Anglicized to "port" and later corrupted to "porthole." Eventually, it came to mean any opening in a ship's side, whether for cannon or not.

Posh

This word has come to mean "high-class," "stylish," "elegant" or "swanky," and it can be a person or place. At the height of the British Empire, the Peninsula and Oriental Steam Navigation Company (known as P&O) started in 1842 to transport passengers and mail between England and India. It was extremely hot during the journey through the Red Sea and the Indian Ocean because the vessel traveled almost parallel and to the right-hand side of the equator. As a result, passengers found it favorable to have a cabin on the cooler port side for the trip to England. The same was true on the starboard side for the return journey to the colonies. In order to get more comfortable bookings there was an additional cost for the tickets. As a result of the difference in accommodations, the word "POSH" came into use because of the acronym, "Port Out, Starboard Home." Contrary to popular legend, P&O never stamped POSH on the tickets or documents.

Posted at Lloyds

When a ship is wrecked, sinks, or disappears, this fact is stated on a bulletin board at Lloyds, the large marine insurance company in London.

Pound and Pinters

Poor feeding on board British merchant ships caused Parliament to pass a law making it compulsory that every seaman be given one pound of food and one pint of tea or coffee at every meal. Ships that complied with this requirement were called "pound and pinters."

Practice Makes Perfect

The aircraft carrier USS Lexington, operating as a training ship in the Gulf of Mexico, counted 350,000 arrested landings between 1955 and 1975.

Presidents at Sea

The President of the United States is the Commander-in-Chief of the Navy. However, some presidents were in the Navy long before they became Commander-in-Chief. During World War Two, the Navy had five officers on active duty who later became President. They were: Lieutenant John F. Kennedy, 35th President; Lieutenant Commander Lyndon B. Johnson, 36th President; Lieutenant Commander Richard M. Nixon, 37th President; Lieutenant Commander Gerald Ford, 38th President. The 39th President, James Earl Carter Jr., was an Annapolis graduate who served from June 1946 until October 1953, when he resigned his commission as a Lieutenant. The 41st President, George Bush, was a Navy combat pilot. President Kennedy was wounded in action aboard PT-109 and President Carter served on atomic submarines.

Press-Gang Pets

In the days when press-gangs operated, seamen engaged in dockyards or sail lofts were given papers exempting them from being pressed into service. Since press-gangs were naturally anxious to get ex-seamen rather than inexperienced landlubbers, a "press-gang pet" was anyone in the exempt classification who forgot to carry the necessary papers because, despite his protests, he could be shipped out for a cruise.

Propellers for Ships

In 1752, Frenchman Daniel Bernoulli first suggested the idea of a screw wheel. In 1785, Englishman Joseph Bramah patented a first propeller. John Ericsson made the first practical propeller in 1836. The British Argo was the first screw-propelled ship to go around the world. It took 121 days in 1853. The first screw steamship was the USS Princeton, launched in 1842. Twin screws were first used in 1888, and in 1905 and 1906, three and four screw propeller ships were respectively constructed.

Pump Ship

This is sailor's slang meaning "to urinate" or to "throw up." It was first used in the year of 1788, and by 1870 it had become a popular phrase on land. It draws upon both naval and plumbing terms, as does its vulgar equivalent, "to spring a leak."

Purser

The "purser" is the officer aboard a merchant ship who handles the accounts, and pays bills and wages. It originated from the Latin "bursa," or "bag." This is understandable since money aboard ship was carried in leather bags.

• OIL on TROUBLED WATERS •

When this popular term (meaning an endeavor to pacify belligerents) is used, it is borrowed from the old whaler's custom (now practised generally) of putting down a coating of oil on the rough seas around a sinking vessel in order to make a safer seaway for the rescuing boats.

• MAINS'L HAUL •

This old-time Navy order to "tack ship" was also a nickname for loot or booty taken in a fight.

• NAVY or MERCHANT SERVICE •

The rivalry between navy men and merchantmen is deep rooted. As far back as Ceasar's time, when it was against the law for government ships to put to sea between the months of September - April, the navy called the merchant seamen "an avaricious lot" because they were not content to stay ashore but continued their trading despite the laws and the adverse seasons.

• ARRIVE •

The good dictionary word "Arrive" was originally an exclusively nautical expression. It was derived from the Latin word "Arripare," and meant "To come to shore."

Quaker Guns

Many ships carried "Quaker guns" in the 17th century. They were fake wood guns which closely resembled real ones. The fakes were added to the battery to create an impression of being more heavily armed than they were for the purpose of discouraging pirates.

Quarantine

This term for medical confinement comes from the French "quarant," meaning "forty." The first known case of a ship being isolated to prevent spread of disease took place at Marseilles, and the ship was detained for forty days. Hence the name.

Quarterdeck Voice

Contrary to popular belief, a "quarterdeck voice" does not refer to the amount of noise an officer can make in giving orders. It is an old expression coined to describe the voice of authority. The term also carried the suggestion of the cultured or educated voice of an officer.

Rack

A sailor who is asleep in his "rack" or "bunk" is "racked out."

Radar

The acronym for "Radio Detecting and Ranging equipment" is "radar," which was used for the first time by the Navy in 1942. The American scientist, Albert Hoyt Taylor, is regarded as the inventor of radar. However, British scientist, Sir Robert Watson-Hall made radar practical for wartime use. The Royal Navy successfully introduced radar in their defeat of the Italian Navy in the Battle of Matapan. *Bismarck,* the German battleship, was the first to use this system for night battle.

Railroad Pants

Officer's dress trousers with stripes of gold braid down the outside seams.

Raise the Wind

This is a nautical term for raising funds for some specific purpose, and it dates back to the days when a shipmaster went to a witch or fortune-teller and

· RAISING THE WIND ·

paid her for assurances that fair winds would enable his vessel to make a successful voyage.

Red Bulwarks

In the 18th century, the gun decks and bulwarks of fighting ships were painted red. This was done so the sight of blood splattered around during battle would not dismay the sailors. It was on the same basis that some captains wore red or maroon uniforms in battle.

Red Duster

The Red Ensign is a flag flown by ships in the British Merchant Navy and it is referred to as the "Red Duster." It originated during the reign of Queen Anne (1702-1714), when it was called the "Union Jack."

Red Lead

This is an anti-fouling paint applied to the hull of a ship, and another sea term for it is "chromate." "Red lead" also serves as a sailor's nickname for catsup (ketchup).

Retread

A "retread" is an officer or enlisted sailor who has been recalled to active service from inactive duty in the reserves.

Reversed Ranks

There is a reversal of the precedence of rank at naval and military funerals. During these occasions, the seaman marches ahead of the commander, and the commander ahead of the admiral. This is a practical demonstration of the teachings of humility as a cardinal virtue. This was adopted from a paragraph in the Bible that states, "the first shall be last, and the last first."

Riding the Bear

This had nothing to do with a circus. The "bear" was a box-like frame filled with holystones, which seamen hauled back and forth along wooden decks for an extra slick-up.

Rocky Mountain Cruise

The first ship in the U.S. Navy to cross the Rocky Mountains was the destroyer escort *Brennan*. She was prefabricated at Denver, Colorado, then her hundreds of pieces were hauled to Mare Island, California, where she was assembled and launched. During World War II a dozen DE's and more than 200 landing craft were loaded, piece by piece, on long trains of flat cars and crossed the mountains from Denver to Mare Island, California. *USS Brennan* had the ship number of DE-13 and, for the

HAVEN FERRY N°1

WINDAS

• A FIGHTING FERRYBOAT •

When the Confederate ironclad ARKANSAS was making things miserable for the Federalists during the Civil War, Yankee genius rose to the occasion by commandeering an unfinished ferryboat and sheathing her in iron. This was the Essex, which met and sank the ARKANSAS after a hot fight.

• RIDING *the* BEAR •

Whenever you feel that you are overworked in Uncle Sam's modern battle-wagons, just remember that in the old Navy "riding the bear" was common practise. This consisted of filling a box-like frame with holystones and hauling it back and forth to give rough decks an extra slick-up.

•MAKING a HALF-BOARD•

In this modern era "mechanics" have almost driven "sail" into the discard, so it would be interesting to know how many of our young seamen could "make a half-board," i.e; Run a sailboat into the wind, hold her there until all way is lost, then fill again on the same tack moving forward to your goal.

• A "HUGH WILLIAMS" •

British slang term for a sole survivor of a sea tragedy. The term is based on the fact, that, over a period of some two hundred years, nearly forty 'sole survivors' have born the name Hugh Williams.

most part, was kept out of combat zones because of her unlucky number.

Room to Swing a Cat

This group of words was coined in an era when it was often customary to flog men in the ship's brig. If the brig was too small to allow full play for the "cat-o'-nine-tails," the culprit would be taken to ample space on deck and there punished for his misdeeds.

Rope Yarn Sunday

On the day the tailor boarded a sailing ship in port, the crew knocked off early, broke out rope yarn and mended clothes and hammocks. One afternoon per week at sea, usually a Wednesday, was reserved for mending. Since it was an afternoon for rest from the usual chores, much like Sunday, it was dubbed "rope yarn Sunday."

The Navy adhered to the custom through the 1970s. Men used Wednesday afternoon for personal errands like picking up their laundry and getting haircuts. Of course, they paid back the time by working a half-day on Saturdays.

Today, uniforms require less attention, so "rope yarn Sunday" has been turned to other purposes, mainly early liberty or a time for rest and sleep. Some, however, still adhere to tradition and break out the ditty bag for an afternoon of uniform personal clothing maintenance.

Round-Bottomed Chest

Old Navy description for a sailor's carryall, his "sea bag."

Round the World Cruises

The first American merchant ship to sail around the world was the *Columbia*, of Boston. She departed on September 30, 1787, and returned in August 1790. The first U.S. Navy vessel to circumnavigate the globe was the *USS Vincennes*, which left New York on August 31, 1826, and returned on June 8, 1830. In 1838, the Wilkes Expedition of six ships sailed from New York on a trip that covered over 85,000 miles. Only the flagship, *Vincennes*, completed the trip. It returned in June 1842. The American "Great White Fleet" of 16 battleships and auxiliaries made the next global trip by a group of vessels. They sailed from Hampton Roads, Virginia, on December 16, 1907, and returned on February 22, 1909.

In 1960, the Navy submarine *USS Triton* made a trip entirely around the globe while submerged. It followed in general the path of Magellan's ships. She completed the trip in 84 days. The first steam powered ship of the Navy to circumnavigate the globe was the *Ticonderoga*, which made the trip from Hampton Roads between December 7, 1878, and November 9, 1880.

The first group of ships ever to sail entirely around the world without refueling included the aircraft carrier *USS Enterprise*, guided missile cruiser *USS Long Beach* and frigate *USS Bainbridge*. All were nuclear powered and they made the 30,560 mile eastbound trip in 64 days.

Tourists began making round the world trips in the 1890s. They sailed on more than one ship and broke the cruise by taking a train across the United States from the Pacific to the Atlantic. In 1922, the Cunard liner *Laconia* made the first round the world trip in which passengers rode the same ship all the way.

Rover

"Rover" is another name for "buccaneers," and it was originally the trade name for ship riggers. They became known as rovers because they went from shipyard to shipyard, as their jobs required.

Row, Row, Row Your Boat

They probably didn't sing all the way, because the trip took two months, but in 1869 two Norwegians, Frank Samuelson and George Harbo, climbed into an 18-foot boat in New York and rowed across the Atlantic to the port of Le Havre in France.

Rudders

"Rudders" at the ship's stern first made their appearance in the 13th century. Prior to that time, they were fitted on the starboard quarter. In 1242, the *City of Elbing* was the first to use this new steering arrangement.

Running Her Easting Down

This old nautical colloquialism refers to sailing in a particular area of the globe between South Africa and Australia. Vessels bound south to Melbourne or Sydney would round the Cape of Good Hope and bear eastward on the long haul to the southwestern corner of the land down under. A ship's progress was hampered by the ever-prevailing trade winds in that quarter and sailors spoke of this as "running her easting down."

Sack

This is another sea term for "bed" or "bunk." A sailor "hits the sack" and is "sacked out" when asleep.

• FINANCING COLUMBUS •

Contrary to popular belief and most historians, Queen Isabella of Spain did not pawn her jewels nor advance one penny to finance the discovery of the New World. Luis de Santangel, keeper of the Ecclesiastic Revenues of Spain loaned Columbus the money for his famous voyage. Incidentally, it was fortunate for Santangel that Columbus was successful, otherwise little Luis would have been executed for misuse of the funds in his keeping.

• KNOW YOUR ENSIGN

Did you know that for 23 years, Old Glory carried 15 stripes? This was from 1795 until 1818, when the original 13 stripes were restored permanently.

•UNLUCKY NUMBER•

To those who claim that the number 13 is unlucky, it seems more than mere coincidence that the shell which blew up His Majesty's ship HOOD, traveled 13 miles.

• NOT SO HOT •

Germany "didn't do so good" in her last "shootin' war" with us. The only shell to strike U.S. soil was fired from a U-boat and landed on Cape Cod, Mass., in 1917.

Sail Training

Steam has replaced sail in the navies of the world, yet most naval officers still receive basic training in handling ships under sail. Midshipmen at the U.S. Naval Academy learn to handle knockabouts, yawls and go on to big ocean racing craft. The U.S. Coast Guard sends cadets to sea in the 294-foot barque *Eagle*. The Portuguese training ship *Sagres* was named for the city in Portugal where Prince Henry the Navigator established the first naval war college in the world in 1415. Other sail training ships include *Gorch Fock* (Germany), the 375-foot four-masted bark *Kruzenshtern* (Russia), *Danmark* (Denmark), *Dar Pomorza* (Poland), *Nippon Maru* (Japan), *Libertad* (Argentina), *Amerigo Vespucci* (Italy), *Mircea* (Romania), *Tovaristsch* (Russia), *Esmeralda* (Chile), and *Sorlandet* (Norway). The oldest ship still used in sail training is the ex-Portuguese *Gazela Primeiro,* built in 1883, and now operated by the Philadelphia Ship Preservation Guild.

Sailing Close to the Wind

A sinister meaning has crept into this innocent and harmless phrase. When a man is making money by shady or suspicious methods, it may be said, "He's making a fortune but—he's sailing awful close to the wind." In other words, he is "taking a chance." As a matter of fact, when a vessel is sailing "close to the wind," she is merely pointing her nose as nearly into the wind as will allow headway, and is sailing close-hauled. There is nothing dangerous in so doing, and why the sinister element has been injected in to the term is a mystery.

Sailing Under False Colors

This was a subterfuge of pirates who flew the flag of some friendly nation in order to lull prospective victims into a feeling of security. When ready to attack the ship would raise the *Jolly Roger* which bore the frightening symbol of the skull and crossbones.

St. Elmo's Fire

This is the display of luminescent electricity that occasionally occurs at the tip of a ship's mast. Even though regarded by some as patron of navigators, St. Elmo seems never to have existed by that name. However, it is believed that his name may have evolved from St. Anselm or St. Erasmus, the patron of Neapolitan seamen. It appears that this phrase goes back to the Greek "elene," meaning a torch.

Sally Ship

"Sally ship" was not a ship. Rather, it was a method of freeing a vessel from mud that was holding her fast. In the days before sophisticated navigation equipment, ships ran aground relatively often. A grounded ship could be freed with little or no hull damage if she could be rocked out of her muddy predicament.

To free her, the order was given to sally ship. The crew gathered in a line along one side and then ran athwartships from port to starboard, back and forth, until the vessel began to roll. Often the rolling broke the suction of the mud and she could be pulled free and gotten underway.

Salt Junk

Sailors in the Old Navy gave corned beef the nickname of "salt junk." Since junk was the product of unraveled old rope to be used in caulking seams, one has only to imagine the stringy quality of the corned beef. This meat was also called "salt horse" when a rumor circulated in the fleet that sailors found what might have been a piece of harness in a tub of the food.

Salute the Quarterdeck

When Rome ruled the seas, a pagan altar was placed aft and all men boarding a ship genuflected to it. Homage to these altars was made to appease the gods of the sea. Later, when early Christians went to sea, similar tribute was paid to the Shrine of the Virgin, which was set up in the same location. The flag of the sovereign later replaced the shrines. It could be a monarch, ruler and nation, or company ship owner. Today, the quarterdeck is saluted, whether or not a flag is flying.

Santiago

Argentina and many other places celebrate the name of the Portuguese "Saint Jago." The name of Santiago came about as a result of poor spelling and pronunciation over the years.

Schooner

This type of sailing vessel is one that has a foremast and mainmast, with or without other masts, and having fore-and-aft sails on all lower masts. It is a speedy shallow draft vessel which literally "schoons" or "skips" over the water. Nowadays, many persons only know a schooner as being a tall glass for the drinking of beer.

Scratch the Cat

After a couple of centuries of faithful service, Britain's seagoing pussycats were put out of work. The cats were brought to sea in 18th century wooden ships to combat the huge rats that infested them. Cats were used for this purpose to a lesser degree for two more centuries. Fear that cats might bring rabies into Britain from overseas led to a 1977 official order to ban cats from

• FIRECRACKERS •

Next time you are celebrating the Fourth of July, remember the days of your youth, and salute the memory of the United States ship GRAND TURK. This famous vessel was not only the first American ship to visit China... she was the first ever to bring home a load of firecrackers, thus fostering our tradition for pyro-technic display.

•PENNY ROYAL•

This famous oil, universally recognised as an anti-dote for mosquito bite, was misnamed by the illiterate seamen who discovered its beneficial use in Havana in early days. It is now known only as Penny Royal, but its real name is PENNER OIL.

• IRON SHIPS •

Remember, when you are slipping through the water in your mighty steel battlewagon, that only 12 decades ago seamen protested to Parliament against sending iron ships to sea on the grounds that "Everyone knows that metal cannot float."

ANNIE DOESN'T LIVE HERE ANYMORE!

The famous old school-ship "Annapolis (known to hundreds who served their cadet-ship in her as "Annie") has been retired and a steamship substituted in her place. Built in 1896 the "Annapolis" served in the Spanish-American War and also in the first World War

vessels.

Screws Versus Paddles

The first steamboats used paddlewheels. Similar wheels had been used long before that in water-powered mills on the banks and streams, and people could see and understand how they worked. However, a screw propeller, turning completely under water, was something new. In 1839 the British Admiralty ordered a tug-of-war between *HMS Alert* (a screw steamer) and *HMS Rattler* (a paddle wheeler). Made fast to each other stern to stern, the ships steamed in opposite directions. The *Alert* proved victorious.

Scrimshaw

"Scrimshaw" is the carving of whale ivory or backbone into art. It comes from a Dutch word meaning, "a lazy fellow." On long voyages there was little for a seaman to do in his spare time, so men worked out intricate designs. The earliest known examples of American scrimshaw are dated between 1821 and 1827.

Scurvy Trick

This commonly used phrase, which means "dirty trick" or "dirty deal" has a distinctly nautical origin. In the old days of sail and interminable voyages, lack of fresh vegetables and clean drinking water made scurvy one of the most dreaded diseases to beset the seamen. It was a loathsome condition marked by bleeding gums and livid spots on the skin, caused by a lack of vitamin C. So scurvy is certainly apt when it is used to describe a particularly "scurvy trick."

Scuttlebutt

The origin of the word "scuttlebutt," which is a nautical parlance for a "rumor," comes from a combination of "scuttle," to "make a hole in a ship's side causing her to sink," and "butt," a "cask" or "hogshead" used in the days of wooden ships to hold drinking water. Thus, the term "scuttlebutt" means a "cask with a hole in it." "Scuttle" describes what most rumors accomplish if not to the ship, at least to morale. "Butt" describes the "water cask" where men  naturally congregated, and that's where most rumors get started. The terms "galley yarns" and "messdeck

intelligence" also mean the "spreading of rumors" and many, of course, start on the messdeck.

Sea Chanties

"Sea Chanties" were songs sung in the days of sail by crews as they worked at heaving the lines or turning the capstan. The songs' rhythms caused everyone to push or pull simultaneously, hence causing a concerted effort and better results. Some believe that the term is a derivation of the French word "chanter" which means, "to sing." Others maintain that the spelling should be "shanties," claiming the name refers to the shanties along the Mobile, Alabama, waterfront where many of the tunes were learned by sailors.

Whatever the origin, chanties were divided into three distinct classes. "Short-drag chanties," used when a few strong pulls were needed; "long-drag chanties," which were longer songs to speed the work of long-haul jobs; and "heaving chanties," used for jobs requiring continuous action such as turning the capstan.

One man, the "chanty man," stood high above the working crew and sang the main lines while the rest of the crew added their voices strongly on the second line. On the last word, a combined pull made the ropes "come home." A good chanty man was highly prized by officers and crew alike. Although he had no official title or rate, he was usually relieved of all duties to compose new verses for "sea chanties."

Sea Dog

An "old timer" and an "old salt" in the old Navy were synonymous with "sea dog."

Seagoing Cow

After Gail Borden invented canned condensed milk in 1856, cows were no longer carried aboard ships. Borden's primary objective was to produce a suffi-

GEORGE WASHINGTON
almost A SAILORMAN ·

"The Father of his Country" was a land-lubber through no fault of his own. As a young man he was so determined to join the navy (in spite of parental objections) that he allowed himself to be taken in a waterfront saloon by the press-gang. However, he was doomed to disappointment, for the officer in charge of the press-gang recognised him as the son of an influential citizen and ordered him to go home ... much to George's chagrin.

· COFFIN SHIPS ·

This term is in no way descriptive of vessels loaded with wooden kimonas It is a maritime insurance designation and refers to the corrupt custom of over-insuring un-seaworthy hulls, and sending them on a voyage with the sinister purpose of deliberately losing them.

·FIRST NAVAL BATTLE·

The first historic naval battle was fought in 480 B.C., when 366 Greek ships outfought and overpowered 600 Persian vessels at the Battle of Salamis.

· ENSIGNS ·

Though today we look on ensign as a purely naval rank, as a matter of fact an ensign was originally the lowest commissioned officer in the <u>Army</u>.

cient and sanitary food supply for babies on sea voyages.

Seaman Pronunciations

Throughout history, because of the lack of written reference and variations in language and dialect, the old time seamen corrupted the original sound and spelling of words and phrases. In illustration, old-time merchant sailors pronounced the island of Diego Ramirez as "Dagger-rammer-rees." Hawaii was "Owyhee," delay became "belay" and Saint Diego ended up as "Dago." As illustrated in this book, the absorbing of foreign terms into the English language after nautical adoption provided interesting and sometimes humorous results.

Seven Bells

Seven bells are never struck in the second dogwatch aboard British naval vessels. In 1797, British sailors planned a mutiny and the striking of seven bells in the second dogwatch was to be the signal for action. The plot was discovered and the officers stopped the bells before they could strike the seven-ring mutiny signal. As a result of this episode, the Admiralty decreed that never again should seven bells be struck in the second dogwatch.

Seven Seas

It's a common expression to say that some old salt has sailed the "seven seas," but how many people can name them? And why stop at seven? The best known seas are the Mediterranean, Caribbean, Philippine, China, North, Red, Black, White, Yellow, and Adriatic Seas. But there are also the Aegean Sea, Ionian Sea, Sea of Marmara, Sea of Crete, Coral Sea, Arafura Sea, Java Sea, Sulu Sea, Celebes Sea, Barents Sea, Norwegian Sea, Caspian Sea, Sea of Japan, Chukchi Sea, Laptev Sea, Kara Sea, Arabian Sea, Tasman Sea, Timor Sea, and the Dead Sea. All in all, there are at least 77 bodies of water around the globe named as seas.

Shackle

"Shackles" are metal rings or fasteners that were used for securing equipment aboard ship. The word's use has been broadened to include the "inhibiting of movement," as with ankle shackles, or stopping the freedom of action. Shackle comes from the old English "sceacel," which has the meaning of "fetter."

Shanghai

To "shanghai" is to seize a man beyond his will and place him aboard a ship other than his own through the use of force, drugs or liquor. This occurred frequently during the sailing ship days of the 19th century when the fierce reputations of captains made it difficult to get full crews. Shipmasters would pay disreputable hustlers on the beach for each sailor they brought aboard. It is believed that "Shanghai" came from the Australian phrase, "Ship him to Shanghai," meaning "on a long journey."

Shape Up or Ship Out

Nautically, to "shape" is to determine a course for a vessel to sail. In its application to men at sea, the phrase demands that a sailor do his job in the right way. Otherwise, he would be replaced on the job, transferred, "shipped out."

Ship that Lit Up a Town

There was a severe drought in the Puget Sound area in 1929 and Tacoma, Washington, faced a power shortage. The Navy sent the big aircraft carrier *USS Lexington* to Tacoma where she tied up to a pier, spliced into the city electrical system and for one month supplied power for the entire city. During World War II, there were several instances similar to this when warships provided temporary electrical power to communities.

Ship With No Ends

An Australian inventor drew up plans for a battleship with a circular hull. The Russians purchased the plans, built and launched such a vessel in 1876. With no bow or stern, the only directions aboard such a craft would be outboard and inboard.

Shipbuilding Records

The monitor *Monadnock* was laid down in Vallejo, California by a private company in 1876. After seven years the Navy took over the unfinished hull and managed to complete it in another thirteen years. The ship finally went to sea in 1898. By contract, the Kaiser Shipbuilding Company laid the keel of the Liberty ship *Robert E. Peary* on November 8, 1942, and launched the completed ship four days and 15 hours later. She was sent to sea on November 15, 1942.

Ships by the Hundreds

Merchant ships mostly sail in convoys during wartime, but in peacetime they usually operate singly and congregate only in port. Contrary to what one might expect, the greatest assemblies of ships were not always in the big ports of the world. A great number of ships at one location took place in the 1840s, when as many as 400 ships would be anchored at one time, off the African island of Ichaboe, where they waited to load

A "CHEESEY" SEA-FIGHT

In 1841, when warships of Uruguay and Argentina battled for sea supremacy, the Uruguayan fleet, in one action, ran out of ammunition. Undaunted, they substituted hard round cheeses for cannon-balls and actually came out victorious in the engagement.

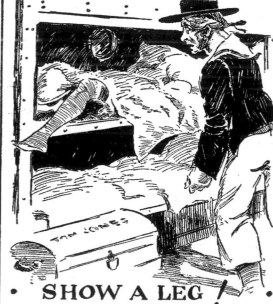

SHOW A LEG!

This slang term for ordering men to turn out, originated in King George Third's time when women were allowed to accompany sailors on long voyages. It was customary when ordering seamen from their bunks, for the bos'un to demand "Show a leg." If the leg was covered by a stocking he knew it belonged to a woman; otherwise the skulker would promptly be routed from his bunk.

AMIDSHIPS

Though there is a common tendency these days to misname the waist of a ship "midships," all good sailormen should know that "midships" is an imaginary deckline running parallel with the keel from stem to stern. Thus, the masts are stepped "amidships."

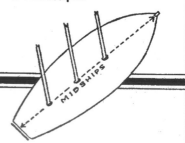

SQUARED AWAY

When you use this expression for putting yourself into a posture of offense or defense, you are borrowing a phrase which described a square-rigged ship bracing her yards to run away before the wind.

guano (bat dung). A few years later, there were even more ships in the harbor at San Francisco, but these were abandoned in the rush to get to the newly discovered gold fields. Entire crews deserted their ships, and in July 1849 there were 526 ships without captain or crew. In addition to these vessels, many more had been sunk or beached.

Ship's Husband

Sometimes when a ship is heading to the yards, an old salt says she is going to her husband. Used now, it causes novices to wonder what he's talking about. A "ship's husband" was once a widely used term that described the man in charge of the shipyard responsible for the repair of a particular ship. It was not uncommon to hear the sailors of creaky ships lament, "Ah, she's been a good ship, lads, but she's needing her husband now."

In the course of a ship's life, she may have had more than one husband but this had little bearing on her true affections. Tradition has it that her true love was saved solely for her sailors.

Ship's Master

The officer who commands a merchant ship is known as the "ship's master." It originated during the Punic Wars (268-202 BC) between Carthage and Rome, when such men were titled "magestis navis," Latin for "master of the ship."

Ships Named For a Family

A number of ships in the U.S. Navy have been named for several members of the same family. The *O'Brien* was named for five brothers who served during the Revolutionary War; the *Ellet* was named for five members of the Ellet family; and the *Nicholson* was named for five members of that family. *The Sullivans* was named for five brothers, killed at Guadalcanal aboard the same cruiser *USS Juneau*. Several ships, *John Rodgers, Hollister, Rogers, Gearing,* and *Barber* were named for three members of the same family.

Shore Patrol

As far back as the Vikings, attempts were made to protect the populace from seamen, and to protect seamen from other seamen. However, the first organized shore patrolmen were the Royal Marines of the 18th century. Being responsible for the discipline of sailors aboard the British warships, it was natural for them to be assigned the task of maintaining order in port. During World War II, the United States Navy instituted a shore patrol command. They were men with law enforcement experience for this permanent

duty specialty. Their jurisdiction, as with the Army's military police, extended to all military personnel. When ships came into port, sailors from a vessel were selected and assigned to temporary shore patrol duty. Outfitted with white leggings, an "SP" armband and club, they would cooperate with "SPs" from other vessels and with the local police force, if any. The purpose of the "SPs" was to maintain order, and they really were not as depicted in the above illustration.

Short Timer

A sailor whose term of Navy service is nearly completed is a "short timer."

Shot in the Locker

This expression means "something in reserve," and it comes from the days of sail when the British Admiralty advised captains to "keep always good reserve supplies in the shot-locker." Thus, in battle, there would always be enough ammunition on hand to serve the guns. In the present day, if one says, "I haven't a shot in the locker," he is saying he's out of food, liquor, money, or whatever.

Shove Off

This order is given to the coxswain of a small boat alongside a ship when it is ready to depart on a trip. In small boats, a sailor standing in the bow actually does "shove off" the bow by pushing against the ship with a pole called a bow hook. Any and all leave-takings or

SPINNING A YARN

This term for tale-telling, was coined in days when sailors would be given old ropes to unlove for the making of sennit and small stuff. As this was the only duty during which they could talk at will, the act of making yarn became synonomous for free and unrestricted conversation.

MATE

Bosun's Mate, Gunner's Mate, Mate of a ship, all derive their rating from the French word "Matelot" meaning sailor.

THREE COLLAR BRAIDS

The three white braids on the American sailor's collar really commemorate three big British naval victories, viz:- Battle of the Baltic, Battle of the Nile and Battle of Trafalgar; and this is because the American uniform is practically a duplicate of the British.

FIRST SHIP'S WHEEL

While history fails to record the exact date when wheels took the place of tillers for steering, it is generally conceded as somewhere between 1703-1747.

departures are termed as "shoving off," whether at sea or land.

Show a Leg
Many of our Navy's colorful expressions originated as practical means of communicating vital information. One such expression is "show a leg."

In the British Navy of King George III and earlier, many sailors wives accompanied them on long voyages. This practice caused a multitude of problems, but some ingenious bosun solved one that tended to make reveille a hazardous event: that of distinguishing which bunks held males and which held females.

To avoid dragging the wrong mate out of the rack, the bosun asked all to show a leg. If the leg shown was smooth and adorned with silk, the owner was allowed to continue sleeping. If the leg was muscled, hairy and tattooed, then the owner was forced to "turn to."

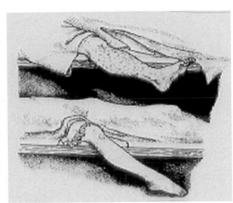

In today's Navy, "showing a leg" is a signal to the reveille petty officer that you have heard his call and that you are awake.

Shows His True Colors
Early warships often carried flags from many nations on board in order to elude or deceive the enemy. The rules of civilized warfare called for all ships to hoist their "true national ensigns" before firing a shot. However, more than one man-of-war and many pirate vessels flew a false flag, hoisting their own when getting into firing range. Doing so was a "demonstration of falsehood" through the "showing of true colors."

Sick Bay
In the modern Navy, "sick bay" is the place a modern sailor can receive medical attention. In the days of sail, there were few such places on shore designated specifically for ill seamen, but on board most ships there were "sick berths" located on the

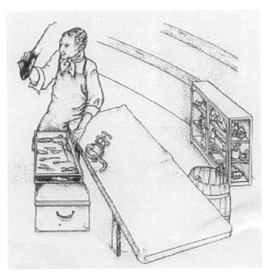

rounded stern. The contour of the stern suggested the shape of a bay and consequently sailors began calling the ancient dispensaries "sick bays."

Side Boys
The use of "side boys" is a custom inherited from the British Navy. In the days of sail, gangways were not frequently used, so sailors boarded ship by climbing the rope ladders. Important persons were granted the privilege of wrestling with the Jacob's ladder. Very important persons, many of whom were rather hefty or aged, were hoisted aboard on a bosun's chair.

The officer of the deck instructed the bosuns to rig a chair hoist from a yardarm and, with much heaving and hoeing, the VIP's were hoisted aboard much like casks of salt horse. The men who did the hoisting were called side boys. Today, sailors lined up in clean uniforms on the quarterdeck when visiting dignitaries embark, are still called side boys, preserving another naval tradition.

Sidelights
Lighting was white on both sides of ships until about 1830, when it became the practice to burn red on the port side and green on the starboard sides. Now, aircraft also carry distinguishing red and green sidelights on the same sides as vessels.

Sideways is Possible, Wilbur Wright
When the Wright brothers made their first flight at Kitty Hawk on December 17, 1903, the plane was airborne for 120 feet. Seventy years later they could have made several touch-and-go landings on the 1,100-foot flight deck of the carrier *USS Enterprise* or even landed athwartships, as the ship is 252 feet across at her widest point.

Sinbad, the Four-Legged Sailor
A famous old sea dog, "Sinbad," was honored with a grave, headstone, memorial service, taps and an 18-gun salute at Barnegat Light, New Jersey.

Sinbad was the mascot of *USS Campbell* (PG-32), a 327 foot Secretary Class Coast Guard cutter during its World War II duty in the Battle of the Atlantic. This dog was a 24-pound, brown, black and white mongrel that came aboard *Campbell* in Portugal in 1937. The salty sea dog stood watch with the crew and ate with them in their mess. He went on liberty with the enlisted men and only occasionally would associate

PLUM DUFF

Some bright sea-cook once decreed that if R-O-U-G-H spelled "ruff," and T-O-U-G-H spelled "tuff," then D-O-U-G-H must spell "duff." Thus ships' dessert received its traditional name.

CAPE HORN "FEVER"

Old navy slang for malingering when in the latitude of "Cape Stiff." Sailors developed the habit of acquiring sudden and mysterious maladies in order to avoid working on deck in these bitter regions. Needless to say, officers discouraged the habit.

BO'SUN

In the 17th. century, ships were required by law to carry THREE boats, and named respectively ① the BOAT ② the COCK ③ the SKIFF. The men in charge rated BOATSWAIN COCKSWAIN and SKIFFSWAIN. Swain meant lover or keeper.

THE PAINTER

The boat painter receives its name from the French word "Peyntours" meaning noose or bight.

with the officers.

He was given a service record, dog tags and was awarded the rate of Chief Dog, which he held until busted at a Captain's Mast. When in port, he raised hell like most sailors and, like them, sometimes went too far. In fact, due to his annoying the sheep, the government of Greenland issued an official edict forbidding him to set his foot on Greenland soil when *Campbell* was in port.

However, he was regarded as a true hero and welcome guest in Ireland. The newspapers regularly reported on his arrival and social activities on shore. Reportedly, Sinbad had acquired a taste for Irish whiskey.

When *Campbell* encountered a German submarine wolf pack in a 12-hour duel, ramming one of the subs and sinking it with gunfire on February 22, 1943, Sinbad remained on deck, witnessing the action. When most of the crew was transferred to another escort in order to lighten their vessel, Sinbad was chosen to stay aboard because the Captain said, "As long as Sinbad is aboard, *Campbell* will survive!"

LIFE Magazine, newspapers, other publications and the wire services carried features about Sinbad. In addition to having a book written about him, Sinbad was the subject of a 1947 film documentary, *Dog of the Seven Seas.*

After he aged, the dog lived with Coast Guard personnel at the Barnegat Lifeboat Station. He passed away and was buried at an unmarked site on the property.

Although his exact location remains unknown, a two-year search involving many Coast Guard personnel, *Campbell* veterans and civilians, determined that Sinbad's remains were within a 20' X 20' area at Barnegat Light. That is where a headstone was placed on September 15, 1989.

Siren

A ship "siren" is acoustical equipment that produces sound by means of a perforated, rotating disk that interrupts a jet of air or steam. This device gets its name from the Greek "sirenes." In Greek mythology, sirens were half women and half birds who used their beautiful and seductive singing to lure mariners to destruction. In the oldest sea story known, Ulysses escaped the sirens by having himself lashed to the mast of his ship, and having all his rowers plug their ears with wax so they could not hear the dangerous singing.

Skipper

The commanding officer of a ship is the "skipper." The title comes from the Dutch "schipper," which means the same thing.

Skull and Crossbones

Here's another belief gone by the board. The "skull and crossbones" was not the death flag of the pirates. When this insignia was flown it was to signify, "Deliver up all your cargo and you and your ship can go free." If total death and destruction were planned, pirates hoisted a red flag.

Skylarking

Originally, "skylarking" described the antics of young sailors who climbed up and down the mast shrouds for fun and races. Their swinging high among the backstays resembled birds flying among the limbs of a tree. Since the ancient Latin word "lac" means "to play" and the games started high in the masts, this lively activity was "skylacing." Later, corruption of the word changed it to skylarking.

In the days of wooden ships, skylarking was thought to be a good occupation of energetic sailors with free time on their hands. Skylarking on the weatherdeck was preferable to their engaging in disruptive or mutinous talk in a ship's dark corner. This word eventually took on the meaning of "joyful behavior by an individual or group that interferes with an assigned job." Otherwise referred to as "goofing off."

Sling it over

"Pass it to me," is the meaning of this nautical lingo. To seamen forever watching the loading or unloading of the ship's cargo by means of a sling, this became a phrase to embody in any type of request to another sailor, such as "sling me the salt," or "sling over my laundry."

· The THREE MILE LIMIT ·

In view of the current controversy over the gambling ships, it is of special interest to note that the reason for three miles being the distance over which a nation has jurisdiction regarding coastal waters, is because at the time this international law was established, three miles was the longest range of any nation's largest guns, and therefore the limit to which they could enforce their laws.

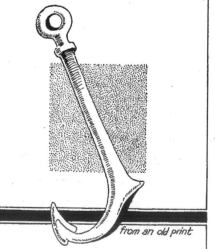

from an old print

· ANCHOR ·

Anchors received their name from the ancient Greek word meaning "crook or hook", and old Grecian anchors were actually in this crude form.

· COMMODORE ·

This title arose from a practised economy of the old Dutch Admiralty. In her war with England, Holland found herself short of admirals and distressingly short of cash. She solved her difficulty by creating a brand new rank of "Commodore", which carried with it all the responsibilities of an admiral ... but only HALF his pay.

· 'SHE-OAK' NET ·

A slang term from "Down Under," for the safety-net slung under gang-planks. The name is derived from a brand of potent Australian beer, which carried a picture of a she-oak tree on the bottle label. As the beer had an alcoholic content of some 15 or 20 per cent, one can very easily understand why the safety net was so nicknamed by "Aussie" sailors returning from a particularly hilarious shore leave.

Slipped his Cable

A sailor who dies is said to have "slipped his cable." This expression comes from the fact that only in great emergency, such as escaping an enemy in a hurry, does a vessel willingly leave cable and anchor on the sea floor when she departs her anchorage.

Slop Chest

This locker was carried on deep-sea ships. It contained clothing and other items the master of a vessel could sell to needy seamen during a long voyage at a very good profit. "Slop" is a corruption of the old English "sloppes," meaning "breeches" or "trousers." Today, a "slop chest" is a container that holds any number of items for possible future use.

Smoking Lamp

The exact date and origin of the "smoking lamp" has been lost. However, it probably came into use during the 16th century when seamen began smoking on board vessels. The smoking lamp was a safety measure. It was devised mainly to keep the fire hazard away from highly combustible woodwork and gunpowder. Most navies established regulations restricting smoking to certain areas. Usually, the lamp was located in the forecastle or the area directly surrounding the  galley, indicating that smoking was permitted in this area. Even after the invention of matches in the 1830s, the lamp was an item of convenience to the smoker. When particularly hazardous operations or work required that smoking be curtailed, the unlighted lamp relayed the message. "The smoking lamp is lit" or "The smoking lamp is out," were the expressions indicating that smoking was permitted or forbidden. The "smoking lamp" has survived only as a figure of speech. When the officer of the deck says "the smoking lamp is out" before drills, refueling or taking on ammunition, that is the Navy's way of saying, "Cease smoking!" With regard to smoking by its personnel, the Navy strongly discourages use of tobacco in any form because of proven health hazards.

Soldiering

Early Navy sailors gave this description to anyone "loafing on the job." This came from the times when soldiers or marines aboard ship did their share of fighting, but refused to have anything to do with working the vessel. Many of them believed that such labor was not their function and it was beneath their dignity as fighting men.

So Long

These words of good bye come from "salaam" of the East Indies, meaning "farewell."

Solo Sailor

Joshua Slocum, a retired sea captain, sailed from Boston in 1895 aboard the 33-foot *Spray*. Slocum embarked on a one-man voyage around the world, and he made it back to Newport in three years and two days.

Son of a Gun

This nautical expression comes from the days when British sailors were allowed to take women to live aboard ship. If a baby boy was born aboard ship, and there was some uncertainty as to who his father might be, he would be entered on the muster roll as "Son of a Gun."

SOS

The familiar radio signal for assistance by a ship in distress does not stand for "Save Our Ship." Early radio operators developed the signal because those particular letters were easy to identify. The signal consists of three dots, followed by three dashes and three dots.

Sparks

The traditional name for the "radio operator" aboard ship. This nickname came about during the early days of wireless, when there was a large spark jumping across the open arc of a set when transmitting.

Spic and Span

Centuries ago, the Dutch joined the other countries of Europe in the quest for exploration and colonization. The Dutch constructed large numbers of new ships, and they were so proud of the new vessels that they invented a new word to describe them. The word was "spiksplinternieuw," which meant that the ship was "new in every spike and splinter." The British anglicized it to "spick and spanew," and then it was Americanized to the "spic and span" that we know.

Spinning a Yarn

Salts and landlubbers alike delight in hearing a tall tale told with all the trimmings by someone with a talent for "spinning a yarn." While today "spinning a yarn" refers to an exaggerated story, in earlier times it was exclusively a nautical term understood by sailors

WINDAS

The CAPE of GOOD HOPE

Because U.S. seamen may be seeing a lot of the Cape in the near future, it is of interest to note that originally this promintory was known as the Cape of Torments. Thus it was called by Bartholomew Diaz who first braved its bitter dangers in adverse weather. But his king changed its name to that of Good Hope, saying "its discovery promises great and lively hopes of wealthy lands to add to the realms of Portugal."

• CONNING TOWER •

The control center got its name from a corruption of "Cunning", and literally referred to the cunning or cleverness of a sailing master in maneuvering his vessel.

• The SUN'S over the FOREYARD •

Old Navy slang for "It's time to have a drink." It derived its meaning in the days when drunkeness was common aboard ship, so the Admiralty ordered "no officer shall partake of liquor until the sun shall have risen well above the foreyard".

• FIRST AMERICAN ENSIGN •

The flag first raised by John Paul Jones was originally designed for the private use of the "Honorable John Company" (British East India Co.)

only.

Officers and mates in the old Navy were stern

disciplinarians who believed if sailors were allowed to congregate and tell sea stories, no work would be done. However, there was one job that required congregating on a weekly basis, unraveling the strands of old line.

On this day, the salts could talk to their heart's content and the period came to be known as the time for spinning yarns. Later, anyone telling a tale was said to be "spinning a yarn," a cherished naval tradition.

Splice the Main Brace
During sea battles in square-rigger days, a vessel's rigging was a favored target of an opponent. The first job following an engagement was to set up broken gear and repair sheets and braces. It was the custom, after the main braces were spliced, to serve grog to the entire crew. Today, the meaning of this old custom has been twisted into a general invitation, "to have a drink," or as the saying goes, "splice the main brace."

Spotted Cow
A British nickname for any German ships registered at Hamburg. The term was coined for Simon of Utrecht, Lord of Hamburg, whose banner bore the device of a dappled bull.

Spud Coxswain
A ship cook or helper who prepares vegetables for the galley carries this nickname with him. A "spud locker" is where potatoes and other vegetables were stored on deck.

Squared Away
If one is in a satisfactory position for whatever has to be done next, it is said that he is "squared away." When a square-rigged ship braced her yards right across the ship to run before the wind, she was "squared away."

Square Meal
One of the major advantages of being in our early Navy was that a sailor was assured of having enough to eat. The utensils that he used included a spoon, cup and a square board that served as a plate. The shape of the board and regularity of meals suggested, in combination, the concept of a "square meal." This held true even after the introduction of flat rudimentary receptacles and the compartmentalized aluminum trays of the early 20th century.

Starboard
The right side of a ship is known as "starboard." Since the Vikings located their "star," or "steering oar," on the right side of their vessels, and because they called the side of a ship its "board," the right-hand side of ships has been known as the "starboard" side.

Sterling Silver
"Sterling silver" was once called "easterling silver" because a certain tribe on the Baltic Sea insisted on being paid in cash or silver for their goods instead of by the usual system of barter. Seamen carried money especially for that trade, and called it "easterling money" or "easterling silver," from which sterling originated.

Stick in the Mud
When English pirates were hanged, their bodies were often buried in the mud of the Thames River so that no one would find them.

Stick to One's Guns
This phrase means "to maintain one's position despite powerful opposition." Of nautical origin, it dates to the time of battle between wood ships, when cannon balls would crash into the side of a vessel and send splinters and debris into the gun crews. With chaos and screams of pain, the blood flowed and the gun mates would yell for the men in the batteries to continue loading and firing, and not back off. The time and weapons have changed, but the updated battle scene continues even today.

Stork Ship
During 26 years of service on the North Atlantic run,

The WOMEN of FIDDLER'S GREEN

Just in case you didn't know it, calm weather and smooth seas are the result of the sweet songs of the women of Fiddler's Green, who sing to keep the waves in unison. Whenever they stop singing, the waves get restless, and bad weather ensues. Next time you're enjoying a pleasant voyage, remember that Davey Jones' glamour girls are really doing their stuff......for which be thankful.

SKYLARK

This perfectly good dictionary word was originally a slang term, used to describe the antics of lusty young navymen, who would slide down the backstays for fun. The latter half of the word is from the ancient "LAC," meaning "to play".

STEAMSHIP

Strangely enough, the inventor of the steamship was neither a sailor nor an engineer. Robert Fulton was a nationally recognised ARTIST, who forsook Art to devote his life to his wonderful invention.

SCHOONER on the ROCKS

In old Navy parlance, a "Schooner on the Rocks" was a roast of beef surrounded by baked potatoes.

the SS *Independence* had 1,500 babies born aboard ship while at sea. All of them were brought safely ashore.

Stow it Away
This expression means to "eat ravenously with a robust appetite," and it compared eating with the filling of the hold of a ship with cargo. This saying for eating immense quantities of food traces itself back to 1692 in England.

Strike-Me-Blind
This was an old Royal Navy nickname for "rice pudding with raisins." The inference was that one could go blind looking for the scarce number of raisins in the serving.

Submarines
The modern nuclear submarine had an inventive ancestor. Cornelius van Drebel, a Dutch scientist, built the first submersible in 1622. It was made of wood, propelled by six men using oars, and actually navigated, surfaced and submerged in London's Thames River.

Submarines: Our Terrors of the Deep
The United States Pacific Fleet suffered grave losses at Pearl Harbor, but our submarine force was left primarily intact. It is this group of vessels that immediately initiated an offense against Japan. They continued until Japanese ships were no longer safe in their own waters. The submarine force was the smallest offensive arm of the U.S. Navy, less than two percent of the total. Yet this small volunteer force destroyed more enemy shipping than all the rest of the allied forces combined.

More than 55 percent of enemy ships were sent to the bottom, including one battleship, four large carriers, four small carriers, three heavy cruisers, eight light cruisers, 43 destroyers, 23 large submarines and 1,113 cargo ships of greater than 500 tons. The subs did many jobs: laying mines, hauling ammunition, delivering troops, rescuing trapped "friendlies," transporting secret agents, guerrillas, coast watchers and rescuing 504 airmen, including future President George Bush. This was not done without a price: the submarine force suffered the highest loss ratio of naval personnel. One of three men was lost and one out of five submarines failed to return to port.

Suez Canal
The first attempt to link the Mediterranean and the Red Sea was made by an Egyptian Pharaoh about 1800 BC. The present canal was completed in 1869 by the French engineer Ferdinand de Lesseps. The canal is 107 miles long and ranges from 500 to 700 feet wide. Ships take about 15 hours to transit it. The first ship of the U.S. Navy to make the passage was *USS Palos*, on August 13, 1870.

Suit
"Suit" is a nautical term dating from the early 1600s, meaning the "outfit of sails" used by a ship. The term was revived after World War II, when a Navy ship's complement of electronics could be referred to as an "electronics suit" and its total armament might be called the "weapons suit." The word is sometimes incorrectly spelled "suite."

Sunday to Saturday
If a ship has only one mast, it is called the mainmast. Most sailing ships had three masts: fore, main and mizzen. In the late 1800s there were a few schooners with four masts, some with five or six, and one—the *Thomas W. Lawson*—with seven masts. Technically, her masts were, from forward aft: fore, main, mizzen, jigger, driver, pusher and spanker. But many people could not remember the order, so the masts were also named for the days of the week. Sunday was formost; Saturday was all the way aft.

Sundowner
A "sundowner" is a "harsh disciplinarian," a "martinet." The term came from the early days when strict captains ordered all officers and men to be aboard by sunset.

Sun's Over the Foreyard
"It's time for a drink," is the meaning of these words. In days when drunkenness was common aboard ships, the British Admiralty ordered that "no officer shall partake of liquor until the sun shall have risen well above the foreyard." The order failed to specify what to do on cloudy days.

Sure Cure for Seasickness
According to old salts, the best way to get rid of seasickness is to lie under a palm tree. Of course, by the time one gets ashore to a palm tree, he is no longer seasick. Perhaps the worst case of seasickness on record was that which afflicted a woman living in Cape Town, South Africa, who sailed to visit Europe just before World War I began in 1914. She was so sick on the trip that she spent the rest of her life, 32 years, in Europe, rather than go aboard a ship again.

Swallowed the Anchor
When a seaman uses this expression, he means he has

· CRAFT TO INVADE ENGLAND ·

The barges which were to carry Napoleon's troops across the English Channel when the Corsican planned to invade England, were powered by windmills, which in turn drove huge side paddles. However, they were never used, for Napoleon, like Hitler, got cold feet.

· A "SUNDOWNER" ·

Nickname for those tough Old Navy martinets who insisted that the entire crew be aboard "by sun-down prior to the day we sail."

·BRAZIL·

This South American republic was named for a wood found by early navigators. The wood was known as "BRAZA", meaning a live coal.

·FIRST LIQUID COMPASS·

The first liquid compass was invented and used by Arabs in the year of Our Lord 1242.

permanently quit the sea to take up a shore job, or to retire.

Sweating the Glass
This was an old scheme by which the sand in the hourglass was hurried down by shaking it in order to shorten the time of a watch. At a later time, the hands of the clock were put forward for the same reason, and this was called "flogging the clock."

Swiss Navy
Though it is a traditional joke among sailors that "I served my first hitch in the Navy of Switzerland," such a navy actually existed in 1799. That year, English Captain Williams commanded a fleet of small vessels on Lake Zurich in operations against the French.

Sword-Hilt Cross
In medieval days, every Christian knight had a cross embossed on the hilt of his sword as a solemn token that he would keep the faith. To this day, the dirk worn by British midshipmen carries on its hilt the emblem of religious faithfulness.

Sword Salute
The first movement of a modern "sword salute" is a survival of the ancient custom of kissing the cross, which was emblazoned on the hilt of every sword carried by a Christian.

Taffrail
The rail at the stern of a vessel is the "taffrail." Some historians maintain that taffrail is a combination of three words: "the after rail." Others claim it is a misspelling of the Dutch word "tafareel," which means "painting on the stern."

Tailor-Mades and Glad Rags
Often, one of the first things that a Navy sailor did after completing boot camp was to get a "tailor-made" uniform to wear on leave. These uniforms were sold at specialty shops that surrounded most shipyards and bases. They were lighter, held a crease longer, and had a zipper in the blouse to make it form fitting. As a result of buying his "glad rags," it was possible for a recruit to look like a real salt in three months or less. And, of course, one of the first stops made by a sailor in an Oriental port was a tailor shop where it was possible to have colorful silk dragons sewn on the interior cuffs of a dress jumper. In minutes, one could be transformed into an "old China hand."

Taken Aback
When a sailing ship was "taken aback" by reason of sudden squalls or faulty steering, she was momentarily helpless, "in a position of great peril." With her sails blown back against the masts, she was in grave danger of losing her mast and only the smartest action by skilled seamen could save her. In modern language, taken aback, describes the feelings of a person jolted by unpleasant news. He is "taken aback." His mental state is upset and, for a moment, he is unable to act effectively.

Taking a Sight
Yes, they did it in the Old Navy, too. This is "thumbing one's nose," or "cocking a snoot," at an officer behind his back. Sighting is related to use of a sextant.

Tampon
A cotton dressing used to stop the flow of blood from a wound and, perhaps more commonly, a woman's sanitary device. Of nautical derivation, it comes from the French "tompion" or "tampion," which was a wooden plug or similar item placed in a cannon muzzle to close it from sea water.

Taps
The 24-note melancholy bugle call known as "taps" evolved from a French bugle signal called "tattoo," a word that derived from the Dutch "taptoe." The last five measures of "tattoo" resembled taps. It notified soldiers to return to their barracks. The notes were sounded an hour before the final bugle signal, "L'Extinction des feux," which called for the "extinguishing of fires and lights."

Union General Daniel Adams Butterfield headed a brigade camped near Richmond, Virginia. He decided that the French "lights out" bugle call, which the Federal army then used, was too formal to signal the day's end. In July 1862, Butterfield recalled the tattoo music and hummed a version of it to an aide who wrote it down in music form. The general then asked the brigade bugler, Oliver W. Norton, to play the notes while he modified them, yet keeping the original melody.

General Butterfield ordered Norton to play this call at the end of the day thereafter instead of the regulation signal. The music was heard and appreciated by other brigades and adopted by them — as well as by the Confederate buglers. The music was made the official Army bugle call after the War, but was not called taps until 1874.

The first time that taps was played at a military funeral was not long after Butterfield composed it.

· PRESS-GANG "PETS" ·

In old press-gang days, seamen engaged in dockyards or canvas-lofts were given papers exempting them from "pressed" service. As press-gangs were naturally anxious to get ex-seamen rather than landsmen with no experience, a press-gang "PET" was anybody in the "exempt" classification who forgot to carry the necessary papers on his person, for then, despite his protests, he could be carried off to serve.

· HORN-PIPE ·

This sailor's dance was named for the two instruments which constituted about <u>all</u> of the orchestra usually found aboard old deepwatermen.

· SCRIMSHAW ·

How many modern seamen go in for Scrimshaw, i.e. the art of carving models etc., from bone or other material? In old days a sailorman who wasn't handy with his knife wasn't worth his salt. Just out of curiosity we'd like to get some answers in reply to the above question.

· STEEL MASTS and RIGGING ·

The first ship to have steel masts and rigging was the SEAFORTH, built in 1863.

Union Captain John Tindal, head of an artillery battery, ordered it played for the burial of a cannoneer killed in action. Not wanting to reveal the battery's position in the woods to the enemy nearby, Tindal substituted taps for the traditional three volleys fired over the grave. Taps was also played at the funeral of Confederate General Stonewall Jackson ten months after it was composed. It is now played by United States military forces at burial and memorial services, to accompany the lowering of the flag and to signal the "lights out" command at the end of a day.

Tarpaulin Muster
A "tarpaulin muster" was a method for helping a shipmate in distress. A tarpaulin was rigged as a catch net and the crew would file past, contributing whatever they could spare to help their financially needy comrade.

Tattoo
A "tattoo" on the drums just before taps was sounded was one form of warning for sailors and soldiers to return to quarters. In the mid-1600s the English spelled it "taptoo," from the Dutch "taptoe" which means, "the tap is closed." In other words, tattoo originally meant that it was time to close the bars. English navigators, however, introduced the new meaning of body decoration after visiting various Pacific Islands where the natives used this type of art. Tattooing was later adopted by seamen as a means of identification and body art. After becoming popular with many sailors, a unique art form developed. At one time "tattoos" were in vogue for many of the most elite members of society. Tattoos are again popular in certain segments of our population.

Tell it to the Marines
The Royal Marines were quartered aboard English warships. They were responsible for discipline of the sailors and preparation for battle, but with no sailing duties. The ship's crew had a general dislike for the marines, and the tars considered them to be stupid, naive and gullible about seafaring life. They even referred to empty bottles as "marines." As a result, any tall tale told to a sailor was likely to be met with the response, "Tell it to the Marines!"

Thief Islands
The Ladrone islands in the western Pacific, now known as the Marianas, were so named when Magellan's sailors discovered that the natives pilfered weapons, clothing, and anything else they could carry off. "Ladrone" is from the Portuguese "latro," meaning "thief." The

Marianas were the scene of one of the fiercest air battles of World War II, which took place June 19, 1944. Naval history records it as the "Marianas Turkey Shoot."

Three Mile Limit
Three miles, by international agreement, is the distance over which a nation has jurisdiction of its coastal waters. At the time that this limit was established, three miles was the longest range of any guns; beyond that no nation could enforce its laws. The "three-mile limit" has been replaced, in many instances, by a twelve-mile limit. Some nations also enforce a 200-mile limit to prevent fishing in their waters.

Through the Hawse Hole
In the merchant marine, a sailor who advances from the rank of ordinary seaman to master or captain is described as having "come in through the hawse hole." (As described previously, a "hawsehole" is an opening in the bow for the anchor cable.) On the other hand, if he starts as a cadet, trains as an officer, and reaches captain's rank, he is said to have "come aboard through the cabin portholes."

Tie that Binds
It is believed that this phrase originated with the short chain that secures the main and fore yards to their respective masts. It has come to mean an expression of sentiment regarding a blood relationship or similarity of ideals, which holds people in a common bond.

Tin Can Sailor
A destroyer sailor.

Toasts While Seated
British naval officers have the privilege of remaining seated when drinking a toast to the King or Queen. This custom came about as the result of a Royal accident.

When Charles the Second of England rose to drink a toast while dining aboard ship, he bumped his head on a low beam. He then decreed that from that time on, officers drinking the royal toast could remain seated without incurring regal displeasure.

To Lose One's Bearings
Originally, "to lose one's bearings" meant "to sail at an angle at which a ship did not have is best stability." Later, it came to mean "to lose knowledge of one's ship's position." On land, the phrase is used to describe

· FLOATING MINES ·

These implements of naval warfare are by no means new. As far back as 1583 at the siege of Antwerp, boats were filled with explosives and floated against the enemies ships. They were given the very appropriate name of INFERNALS.

Can't you alter your handwriting a little bit, Bill? Those signatures look awful SIMILAR

·a "WIDOW'S MAN"·

A form of graft very popular in the early part of last century, when imaginary sailor's names were used to "pad the payroll" at unscrupulous navy hospitals.

PUBLIC REMINDER Nº 1 (for BOOTS)

Remember! You serve IN a ship... not ON her!

· "TURNPIKE SAILOR" ·

Slang term for beggars who bum a hand-out on the false assertion that they are old seamen in distress.

confusion, geographically or otherwise.

Tonnage

Today, "tonnage" refers to a ship's displacement in the water or the gross tons of cargo it is capable of carrying. Tonnage was spelled "tunnage" and referred to the number of "tuns" a ship could carry. A tun was a barrel normally used for transporting wine, and tunnage specified the number of barrels that would fit into the ship's hold.

Tons of Treasure

In February 1942 the U.S. submarine *Trout* was preparing to depart from Corregidor in the Philippines while the invading Japanese Army pushed back the ill-equipped American forces on Bataan. *Trout* needed ballast but no sandbags could be spared. Instead, the submarine skipper was given 20 tons of gold and silver to serve as ballast and received orders to deliver this treasure to U.S. authorities in Hawaii. In 1944 the Liberty Ship *John Barry* sailed for Russia with silver bullion worth $26 million (at that time) in her cargo. A German submarine torpedoed her in the Arabian Sea. The silver is still there two miles below.

Took the Wind Out of His Sails

Often we use "took the wind out of his sails" to describe beating an opponent in an argument. It simply means that one noble adversary presented such a sound argument that his worthy opponent was unable to continue the verbal fighting. Originally, the term described a battle maneuver of sailing vessels. One ship would pass close to windward, usually ahead of another, and thereby blanket or rob the breeze from the enemy's canvas, causing him to lose headway.

Topsail Buster

There probably is no better name for a howling gale than "topsail buster."

Torpedo Juice

During World War II, daring sailors aboard destroyers and destroyer escorts sometimes drained alcohol from Navy torpedoes, mixed it with juice and drank a strong concoction that was called "torpedo juice." This brew soon lent its name to any raw homemade whisky with formidable and dangerous power.

Torpedo Junction

The area of the sea off Guadalcanal in the Solomon Islands was known as "Torpedo Junction." Fierce battles between American and Japanese forces in the early part of World War II sent many ships to the bottom. Because so many ships were sunk there, it was also called "Ironbottom Bay" and "Ironbottom Sound."

Touching the Stars

This sentimental custom started when Annapolis midshipmen were making training cruises to Europe. French and Scandinavian girls would "touch the stars" on the midshipman's dress uniforms with the hope that they would bring themselves good luck.

Nowadays the underlying thought has changed. When a woman (wife, mother, sister or girl friend) is bidding farewell to her departing sailor, she touches the stars on his uniform as a silent wish for his well keeping and safe return.

Transatlantic Cat

The first cat to cross the Atlantic by air was "Whoops," a mascot of the Royal Navy. He rode the dirigible *R34*, which left Scotland on July 2, 1919, and landed in New York four days later. After four days at Mineola in Long Island, New York, the *R34*, her crew of 31, two homing pigeons and the cat all flew back to England.

Trim the Dish

These are orders by a coxswain to the occupants of a small boat to move their bodies about in order to balance the vessel so it can ride on an even keel.

Tumblehome

The use of sloping sides in a ship's construction provided an extra measure of strength or seaworthiness. Actually, "tumblehome construction," as it was called, was first invented to beat Suez Canal toll charges. These costs were based on a formula that multiplied length by depth by half the deck beam. Since the deck beam was reduced by at least twenty-five percent in tumblehome construction, the ship owner saved much in toll expenses until the Suez formula was revised.

Two of a Kind

USS Shaw, operating off the British Isles in World War I, collided with another ship and lost her bow. The skipper turned her around and sailed her to port back-

• AURORA BOREALIS •

Just in case you didn't know it, the Aurora Borealis, or Northern Lights, are the reflection of the engine-room fires from all the steam-propelled ships ever sunk. Their furnaces are kept going by Admirals, Captains, and all others of the useless Deck-gang, while worthy members of the Black-gang (engineers, tenders, et al.) loll around doing no work whatever, enjoying themselves with champagne, music and beauteous females.

• LOBSCOUSE •

If you're inclined to grumble at the menu aboard your battle-wagon, just recollect that "dad" was fed "lobscouse" as a regular diet. It was a concoction of broken ship-biscuit, chopped up potatoes and left-over meat ends.

• JACOB'S LADDER •

This name for a boat ladder is borrowed from the dream of the famous Biblical character, Jacob. In his dream, he saw a ladder ascending from earth to heaven, and because most of us can remember what an awful long climb it seemed, our first time aboard ship via this route, one can readily appreciate the significance of the nickname.

• TONNAGE •

Originally this word had nothing to do with the weight or displacement of a vessel. It merely denoted the size of a ship by the number of TUNS (barrels) of wine which she could stow in her hold.

wards, where another bow was fitted. The second ship named *Shaw* was wrecked during the Japanese attack on Pearl Harbor on December 7, 1941. Her bow was blown off. The photograph of that explosion is one of the most famous of the War. A temporary bow was fitted; she sailed back to the United States for repairs and fought successfully all through World War II.

In May of 1944, the Coast Guard-manned destroyer escort, *USS Menges* lost the after third of her 306 feet to a U-boat in the Mediterranean. By coincidence, the Navy destroyer escort *USS Holder* was the victim of a German aircraft torpedo, losing her forward section. Both ships were brought to Brooklyn Navy Yard where the stern of *Holder* was successfully joined to the forward section of *Menges* to form a new *Menges*. The name of *Menges* was continued on the joined vessel because *Menges'* portion was the larger part of the ship's hull.

Typhoon

A "typhoon" is a severe tropical storm or cyclone in the Pacific. The name comes from the Chinese "tai fung." A similar storm in the Atlantic is called a hurricane, from the Spanish "huracan."

Uncle Sam

During the War of 1812, a meat packer in Troy, New York, by the name of Ebenezer Wilson, worked with his uncle Samuel Wilson marking meat for government use. Because Samuel Wilson was known as "Uncle Sam," the two men stamped meat cases with "EW" and "US." People who knew them referred to such meat as being packed by "Uncle Sam." The US stamping soon took the meaning, "United States." Artists started to draw Uncle Sam in patriotic clothing and President Abraham Lincoln was characterized in this role.

Under the Weather

In wooden ships, ill seamen would be relocated from their cramped quarters and be given a chance to obtain fresh air by having their hammocks strung between the main deck and a partial weather deck above it. Being sick and where he was, the seaman would be described by his mates as being "under the weather." Evolving from this, the phrase was applied to one who is "drunk, incapable and under the weather."

Nautical analogies for drunkenness, like this weather expression, are extremely common because sailors had a reputation for heavy drinking. With this in mind, consider "a full cargo," "three sheets to the wind," "half seas over" and "decks awash." There even are phrases for holding one's liquor well and not showing it: "keeping one's sails up," "not heeling over" and "sailing a clear sea."

Uniforms

Official clothing for naval men was pretty much a hit-or-miss affair until 1747, when King George II of England ordered "uniforms" to be worn by all navy personnel. He did this as a means of boosting sailors' morale and improving their appearance. The first uniforms for the U.S. Navy, authorized on September 5, 1776, specified outfits for officers. These included a blue coat, blue breeches and a red waistcoat with narrow lace. Enlisted uniforms were first authorized in September 1817. The winter uniform included a black hat, blue jacket, blue trousers and a red vest, all with yellow buttons. Rating badges for enlisted men were first worn in 1885.

Union Jack

This flag is the blue and white starred portion of the Stars and Stripes. It is flown between 0800 and sunset on the jackstaff of a Navy ship at anchor. It takes its name from a British flag. The British called their flag the "Union" because its two crosses of St. George and St. Andrew symbolize the union of England and Scotland. They also added "Jack" because Jacques was the nickname of King James II, who authorized the flag. The American Navy acquired the name "Union Jack" with other British flag terminology.

Unlucky Friday

The reluctance of seamen to sail on Friday became so common that many years ago the British government decided to take strong measures to prove the fallacy of the superstition. They laid the keel of a new vessel on Friday, named her *HMS Friday* and launched her on Friday. Then they placed her in command of one Captain Friday, and sent her to sea on Friday. The scheme had only one drawback....neither ship nor crew was ever heard of again.

Unsinkable Cat

When the German battleship *Bismarck* was sunk early

CLOSE QUARTERS

This term, today indicative of hand to hand fighting, was originally "CLOSED Quarters" and referred specifically to special deck-houses to which the crew could retire if boarded by superior numbers. The doors were barred and loopholed, so that a deadly fire could be poured into the enemy.

MOORINGS

A contribution to our nautical vocabulary from the Netherlands. It is from the Dutch "Marren", meaning to tie.

TAKING A SIGHT

Old Navy slang for thumbing one's nose (discreetly and behind his back, of course) at an officer.

AMAZON RIVER

The Amazon River got its name when Admiral Orellana reported his crew attacked there by the huge native women. These female warriors were never heard of before (nor since) but the river's name stands pat.

in World War II, British sailors rescued the ship's mascot, a black cat, and named him Tom Bismarck. When his new ship, the *Cossack*, was torpedoed, the cat was one of the survivors. Transferred to the *Ark Royal,* the cat got sunk again when she was sent down, but again he was rescued. Eventually, the British put Tom on permanent shore duty because he was having too many ships sunk under him.

Unsinkable Island
Kahoolawe is a small Hawaiian island with a length of nine miles and it is located about 90 miles southeast of Oahu. This island served as a target during World War II and for two years after the end of the war. Between 1943 and 1947, more than 800 warships, in addition to the American air forces, used it as a target for bombing and gunnery practice.

USS The Sullivans
The destroyer, *USS The Sullivans*, was named in honor of five brothers of the Sullivan family who were lost when *USS Juneau* was sunk off Guadalcanal on November 13, 1942. George Thomas, Francis Henry, Joseph Eugene, Madison Abel and Albert Leo Sullivan had all enlisted at Waterloo, Iowa, on January 3, 1942, and their request for service aboard the same ship was granted. Following this tragedy, the Navy banned members of the same family from serving aboard the same warship during wartime or emergencies.

When President Roosevelt heard of the unfortunate loss of five men from the same family, he directed that the next destroyer to be commissioned be named after the Sullivan brothers —*USS The Sullivans* (DD-537), **not** USS Sullivan. The new destroyer joined the fleet in 1943 and distinguished herself in Pacific combat. Decommissioned in 1947, she was recalled to active duty in 1951 for the Korean War and, again decommissioned in 1965. This vessel now serves as a memorial to all destroyer sailors at the Naval and Serviceman's Park in Buffalo, NY.

Albert Sullivan Loughren, granddaughter of Albert Sullivan christened the second *USS The Sullivans* (DDG-68), on August 12, 1995. This ship is a guided missile destroyer of the *Arleigh Burke* Class.

Victory Parade
The smart gestures and prancing gait of modern drum majors and majorettes are a relic of the days when seamen went ashore after a naval victory. The seamen were encouraged to march through town shouting, waving their arms and side arms, leaping into the air to express exuberance and to work up public enthusiasm for their government's war efforts.

Viking
"Vikings" were Scandinavians who from the late 8th to 11th centuries engaged in raiding, trade and colonization throughout Europe and the islands of the North Atlantic.

Wallop
This word is of nautical origin and it is synonymous with "a forceful blow, punch and thrashing." When the French burned the town of Brighton, England, in the 1500s, Henry VIII sent Admiral Wallop to teach the French a lesson. He so thoroughly wrecked the French coasts that ever since; any devastating blow is referred to as a "wallop."

War at Sea
The earliest recorded naval battle took place in 480 BC off the Greek port of Salamis, near the present city of Athens. A Greek fleet defeated a Persian invasion force of 600 ships.

Wardroom
Aboard the 18th century British ships there was a compartment called the "wardrobe." It was used for storing booty taken at sea. The officers' mess and stateroom were situated nearby, so when the wardrobe was empty they congregated there to take their meals and pass the time. When the days of swashbuckling and pirating had ended, the wardrobe was used exclusively as a mess and lounge for officers. Having been elevated from a closet to a room, it was called the "wardroom."

Water Bewitched
"Water bewitched" was an old time sea-going way of describing "weak tea." It went along with "shadow soup," which the cook made by allegedly letting the shadow of a beef bone fall on a kettle of hot water.

What-the-Hell Pennant
A most unofficial pennant, but one that many captains and yachtsmen have used with all types of emotions. Over a speed flag, it means, "What the hell is your speed?" Over a course flag, it means, "What the hell is your course?" By itself, it just means, "What the hell?"

When My Ship Comes In
The phrase, "When I make my fortune," comes from the days when merchants sent ships out in search of rich cargoes. To finance such a venture, they borrowed from moneylenders. Since it was difficult to set an ex-

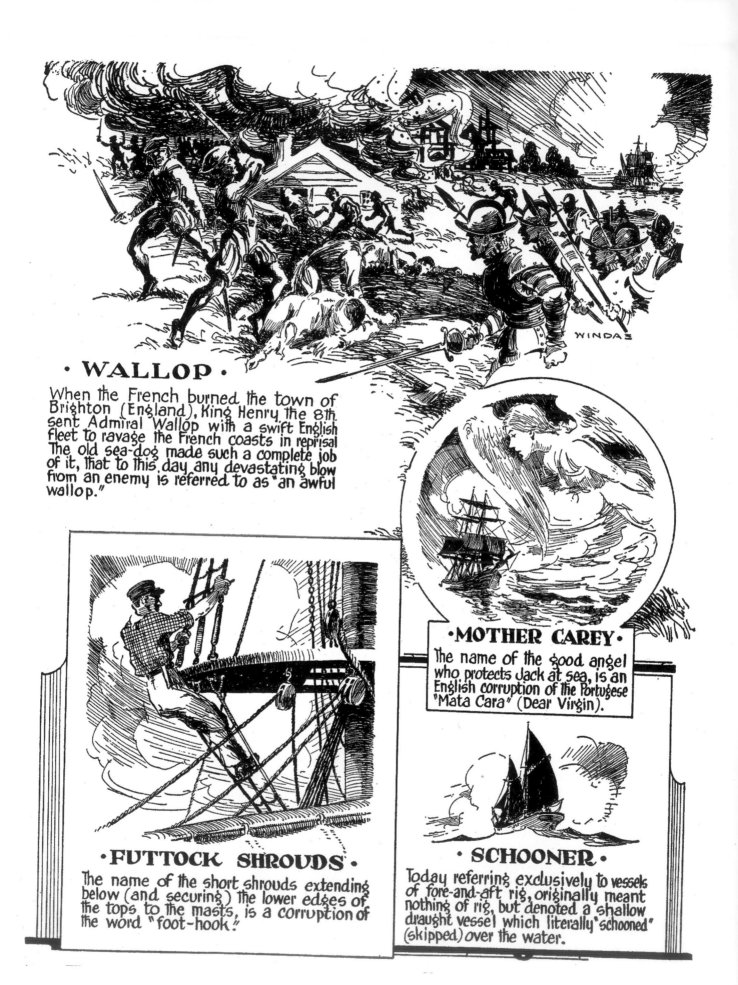

· WALLOP ·

When the French burned the town of Brighton (England), King Henry the 8th. sent Admiral Wallop with a swift English fleet to ravage the French coasts in reprisal. The old sea-dog made such a complete job of it, that to this day any devastating blow from an enemy is referred to as "an awful wallop."

· MOTHER CAREY ·

The name of the good angel who protects Jack at sea, is an English corruption of the Portugese "Mata Cara" (Dear Virgin).

· FUTTOCK SHROUDS ·

The name of the short shrouds extending below (and securing) the lower edges of the tops to the masts, is a corruption of the word "foot-hook."

· SCHOONER ·

Today referring exclusively to vessels of fore-and-aft rig, originally meant nothing of rig, but denoted a shallow draught vessel which literally "schooned" (skipped) over the water.

act date when they would repay the loan, they would sign documents promising to pay "when my ship comes in." Shakespeare refers to this in *The Merchant of Venice:* "Three of your argosies are richly come to harbour suddenly."

White Rats

In the Old Navy, men who tried to curry favor with the officers by telling them what was going on among the enlisted men were known as "white rats." This was also a World War II name for American POW's suspected of collaborating with or giving information to enemy guards.

Windfall

Of major importance to the construction of a sailing vessel was the availability of tall, strong trees to be used for the construction of masts. The British government reserved these trees in the forests of England and the northern American colonies, marking them with three slashes to represent the "king's broad arrow." Although the citizens were able to use lesser trees, they were forbidden to cut down any of the reserved trees. If, however, a broad arrow tree fell over as a result of a storm or other natural causes, the woodsmen would have access to the fallen tree. Getting this unexpected gift of a prize fallen tree became known as a "windfall."

Women at Sea

The British Navy permitted women on board its ships during long cruises. A woman named Ann Johnson served as a member of a gun crew and was killed during the Battle of Copenhagen in April 1801. American clipper ship captains used to carry their wives on board. The hospital at the U.S. Maritime Academy at Kings Point, New York, is named for the wife of a clipper master officer. This woman was Mary Patten and she was 19-years-old when her husband became ill on a trip from the East Coast in 1856. She took command and navigated the ship around the Horn and into San Francisco in 120 days. During World War II many women served aboard merchant ships.

Today, women serve in the U.S. Navy, Coast Guard, Marine Corps, Army and Air Force. There is a steady stream of female graduates from the four service and maritime academies. Women have commanded Navy and Coast Guard vessels and many ships have mixed crews. Female pilots flew combat missions in the Iraq conflict in 1998. The role of women in the armed forces and merchant marine was a major component of the equal opportunity movement of the late 20th century.

Yacht

A "yacht" is described as any vessel used for pleasure or recreation, whether it is a 30-foot day sailer or a 250-ton diesel-driven, air-conditioned, seagoing palace with a swimming pool. "Yacht" comes from the Dutch "gate," which was short for "jaghtschip" meaning ship for chasing. The English first used "yacht" as a name for pleasure craft about 1660. The first "yacht" built in America was *Cleopatra's Barge.* She took to the water at Salem, Massachusetts in 1816.

Yankee

Americans have many nicknames throughout the world, but the most widely used is "Yankee." There are several stories about the word's origins, but it is believed that the nickname started with the early Dutch. Early American sea captains were known, but not revered, for their ability to drive a hard bargain. Dutchmen, also regarded as extremely frugal, jokingly referred to the hard-to-please Americans as "wranglers." Mispronounced and corrupted to "Yankees," the name persists to this day.

· U.S.S. ALFRED ·

Strangely enough, the flagship of the Revolutionary Navy was named in honor of King Alfred, and yet was commissioned to fight against the British Navy which was originally founded by that old-time English monarch.

· MAGNETIC COMPASS ·

The Chinese also invented the magetic compass some sixty years B.C., by floating a magnetized needle on a piece of cork in a bowl of water.

·ANCHORS ·

The anchors invented by the Chinese nearly 4,000 years ago, were remarkably similar to the more modern Admiralty anchor.

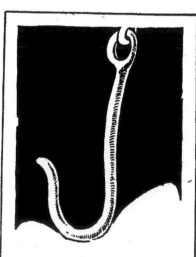

· GADGETS ·

This well known word was originally the nautical name for hooks, and derives from the French "Gâche".

CROW'S NEST

The ship's lookout station was named for the cage which housed the ravens carried by Norsemen at their mastheads. When these sea-warriors lost sight of land, they would release one of the birds, and as it headed for the nearest shore, they would follow its flight. A crude method of navigation, but, within limits, both efficient and practical.

AMERICAN INDIAN

The original American race received its name because of a great sailorman's mistake. When Colombus discovered America, he actually thought he had won through to India, and naturally enough he named the natives "Indians."

HARRIET LANE

Slang term on British ships for canned mutton. The name refers to an Australian victim of a particularly brutal homicide, who was chopped into small pieces by her murderer. British sailors swear that the pieces were then _ _ _ _ but we won't go into that.

HE KNOWS THE ROPES

Today a phrase indicating that a man is expert, it originally meant exactly the reverse. In very early days, when "He knows the ropes" was written on a seaman's discharge, it meant that he was only a novice, but knew the names and uses of the principal ropes.

· HAMMOCKS ·

Swinging beds for sailors were first used by Colombus, who discovered their practical use from natives in the West Indies.

· HOLYSTONE ·

The sandstone formerly used for scouring ships' decks, got its nickname from some witty sailor who declared that as its use always brought a man to his knees, it sure must be "HOLY"

· GROG ·

Admiral Vernon wore his cloak of groggam (mixed silk and wool) so habitually, that his men nicknamed him "Old Grog". When this officer suggested that the Government could save money by diluting the Navy rum-ration with 50% water, and a law was passed to that effect, sailors, jeering, called the new ration "GROG", and the name stuck to this day.

· BUTTONS on SLEEVES ·

Midshipmens' sleeve buttons are sewed on thwartwise because in Admiral Nelson's time midshipmen had no pockets in their uniforms and therefore no place to carry handkerchiefs. To discourage the bad habit of wiping noses on sleeves, Nelson ordered buttons sewed in such position that offending noses would be hurt. ·

• HUNKY-DORY •

This term, meaning everything is O.K., was coined from a street named Honki-Dori in Yokohama. As the inhabitants of this street catered to the pleasures of sailors, one can readily understand why the street's name became synonymous for anything that is enjoyable or satisfactory.

• NORMANDY •

This French province was named for the fierce sea-raiders who drove south along its coasts, and having conquered it, settled there; namely the Norsemen.

•RUDDERS at STERN•

Until the 13th. century, rudders were always affixed at the starboard quarter. In 1242 however, the ship "City of Elbing" was fitted with a rudder secured at her stern.

• DECKS PAINTED RED •

In John Paul Jones' day, decks, bulwarks and gun-ports were all painted bright red. This was not for decoration, but so that ..."a new hand, unused to scenes of strife, might not grow faint at the sight of blood splashed nearby."

• THE ACCIDENT WHICH PRODUCED A BOOK •

In 1839, a stage coach accident was directly responsible for the publishing of "Maury's Sailing Directions." Badly hurt in the accident, Captain Matthew Fountaine Maury utilized the time he was compelled to stay in bed, by compiling his wonderful book on sailing directions and sea geography.

• SOLDIER ~ ING •

This term for loafing on a job is derived from very early times. Soldiers aboard ships would do their full share of fighting, but refused to have anything to do with the working of the vessel, feeling that it was beneath their dignity.

•FISH THAT COST A KING HIS HEAD •

Because Charles First put huge taxes on the great herring industry of England, it stirred up strife which finally resulted in Civil War...which in turn resulted in the beheading of Charles.

•PROVIDER ... on a BIG SCALE•

According to Irish law in the 13th. century, no commander of an Irish ship could put to sea without first having made sufficient provision for the wives and families of his seamen.

WINDAS

· BUCCANEER'S ARTICLES ·

The first Workman's Compensation Insurance were articles signed by the buccaneers. These articles provided that in the event of wounds received in service, the victim should be compensated "For the loss of One Eye $500; for the loss of Right Leg $500"... and so on through a list ranging approximately from $25 to $1,000.

· FURL ·

The word "Furl" (as in, furl the sail) is derived from the old English "Fardle", meaning to make a bundle.

· PEA-JACKET ·

This short coat or jacket was originally made of Pilot-cloth (material similar to Melton cloth) and was named for the initial letter of the word. Thus it was first spelled P-jacket, not Pea-jacket.

· SALT-JUNK ·

Junk being a tough stringy fiber from which rope is made, one can readily understand and appreciate the nickname "Salt Junk", as applied to the beef supplied to the old Navy.

· QUAKER GUNS ·

This was a name given to wooden guns in the 17th century. Most ships carried a number of these dummy guns in addition to their regular batteries, in order to create an impression of being heavily armed, and thus discourage attacks by pirates.

· ARMY DIRECTED SEA-FIGHTS ·

Until 1546, the supervision of a sea-fight was not entrusted to sea-faring men, but was under the direct control of some general or other army officer. Seamen were hired only to work the ship.

· the 'INDIA RUBBER' MAN ·

Old Navy slang for the ship's physical instructor _ _ _ _ obviously, because this trained athlete could twist, bend or stretch in any direction.

· QUARTER~DECK ·

The quarter-deck received its name in the days when decks were in tiers. The "Half-deck" was half the length of the ship, and the "Quarter-deck" was half the length of the half-deck.

WINDAS

· JUNKS ·

These Oriental vessels got their name from English seamen's mispronunciation of the Chinese word "Cheung." On close inspection, the hulls of these little ships will be found to still adhere in almost every detail to the great Magellan's craft, from which they were copied. Even the sail plan is obviously a crude attempt to imitate the sails of the famous Portugese exploration ships.

· MARTINET ·

This term for any strict disciplinarian was named for a French officer in Louis XIV's reign, who carried discipline to the nth. degree of harshness.

· 1st. NAVIGATION BOOK ·

The first book on navigation written in English was William Bourne's "Register of the Seas," published in 1573.

YE REGISTER of YE SEAS
—WILLIAM BOURNE HIS BOOK

· CREW ·

The members of a ship's company derive their name from the old Norse word "ACRUE." From this also comes our word "Recruit."

WINDAS

GALLEY WEST

"Knocked Galley West," meaning knocked cold or stiff, was a term coined with reference to an old Norse custom of placing the corpse of a Viking chief in the sepulchral chamber aboard his galley, and sailing her, afire, towards the setting sun. The significance of the "cold" or "stiff" is of course the corpse itself.

BELL-BOTTOM TROUSERS

Of all the reasons given for the extreme width of sailors' trousers at the bottoms, the obvious and practical one remains the best :- They were easy to roll to the knees when the owner was swabbing decks.

The FIRST COMPASSES

The first compasses known were the crude though clever contrivances which masters of Arab dhows showed to the sceptical Crusaders in 1190 A.D.

FLAMBOROUGH

This English coastal town was originally named "Flame-borough," because on the headland nearby the city kept a beacon perpetually burning to warn mariners away from the dangerous shores.

WINDAS

• DRINKING A TOAST •

This term for drinking to one's health, or in one's honor, was coined in early days along the waterfronts, when it was customary to place a small piece of toast in the hot toddy and the mulled wine so popular with seamen of the day.

• AYE ! AYE ! •

This seagoing affirmative was originally 'Yea ! Yea !', but Cockney tongues twisted it to 'Yi ! Yi !' and eventually to its present form, Aye ! Aye !

• BUM~BOAT •

A peddler's boat, filled with assorted merchandise. Its name is a corruption of "Boom-Boat", because these small craft were permitted to moor to a ship's boat-booms while disposing of their wares.

• KING~SPOKE •

The spoke of a ship's wheel, which when perpendicular, indicates that the rudder is dead fore and aft, received its name from the old custom of decorating that spoke with a crown in honor of the king. . . . .

• GONE WEST •

This old term, referring to men killed in action, dates back to an ancient Viking custom of burial. When a Viking chief died, his body was placed in the sepulchral chamber aboard his ship. Then, with sail set, and steering oar lashed to keep her on her course, the vessel was set afire and pushed off into the west, toward the setting sun.

• PELORUS •

The navigation instrument for taking bearings is named for Hannibal's famous pilot, Pelorus, who made such a wonderful job of evacuating the noted Carthaginian general's troops from Italy after it became imperative to return to the defence of their own country......

• BLUNDER~BUSS •

A clumsy weapon, with trumpet-shaped muzzle, it received its name from the old Dutch naval "DUN-DER (Thunder) GUN." Notorious for inaccuracy, its name of "DUNDER" was changed to "BLUNDER." The "BUSS" is evidently a corruption of "BESS," after the English weapon of the period, "Brown Bess."

• **ANCHORS AWEIGH** • The word "Aweigh" is from the old English "Woeg" to raise.

WINDAS

· TAPS ·

The Last Call got its name from the Dutch word TAP-TOE, meaning to turn off all beer spigots (or taps) and to put out all lights in waterfront taverns. From this same word we get also the corrupted term "Tat-too".

·HE GETS *the* POINT·

Following a courtmartial a British officer knows if he has been found guilty by the position of his sword which is placed on a table before him. If the point faces him he is guilty; if the hilt is nearest, he is innocent.

·SWORD SALUTE·

The first movement of the modern sword salute is a survival of the ancient custom of kissing the cross which was emblazoned on the hilt of every Christian's sword.

· WOMEN SPONSORS

Until 1846, it was thought 'un-ladylike' for the fair sex to smash bottles of wine against ships' noses. However, in October of that year, Miss Watson of Philadelphia established a precedent by sponsoring the launching of the U.S.S. Germantown, and ever since then our fighting craft have been christened by the ladies.

• FATHOM •

This well-known nautical word comes from the old English "FAETM" meaning to embrace. Parliament decided that, since an embrace involved the distance between a man's hands when placed around his sweetheart, and as that distance averaged about six feet, it should be established as a standard measure.

The • 'CAT' FLEET •

A nickname for those British squadrons or fleets, led by a ship of the "LION" or "TIGER" class, during the World War.

• AHOY •

This old traditional greeting for hailing other boats, was originally a Viking battle-cry.

• SHIP-SHAPE •

Just in case you think this is a term of recent origin, please note that Xenophone coined this phrase while chatting with his boy friend Socrates.

• SHANGHAIED •

Just in case you didn't know it, the term "Shanghaied" originated in the Chinese port of Shanghai. Here, masters of American tea-clippers delayed for want of crews, would pay the Chinese owners of dives where drunken sailors were carousing, to slip drugs into the seamen's drinking glasses and hustle the unconscious sailors aboard the waiting ships.

•CLIPPER BOWS •

The "Clipper" bow receives its name from the old English word "Clip" meaning "to be able to run at a fast pace."

• The LUCKY BAG •

The Naval Academy's Year Book is named for certain lockers on old-time ships, wherein were placed all lost articles. Once a month it was a seaman's privilege to re-claim from said lockers such articles as he had lost during that period.

• YACHTS •

Now that so many yachts are being turned over to the Government by patriotic owners, it is worthy of note to discover that the first yachts were built by the Dutch. They were named for the Dutch word "Jagan" (to hunt) and were the equivalent of our modern coast-guard vessels.

• WHEN MY SHIP COMES IN •

This phrase, meaning "If and when I make my fortune," was coined in the days when seafaring adventurers would send their fleets along the Mediterranean and African coasts in search of rich cargoes. First they would have to go to the money-lenders, in order to finance the venture. As it was impossible to set an exact date for the fleet's return, they would sign documents promising to repay the loans "When my ships come in."

MEDIEVAL NAVAL ARTILLERY

In strange contrast to the monster rifles in our modern turrets, is this medieval naval gun, which operated on the principle of a windmill. It was used to throw huge stones onto the enemy's decks.

• SAILOR'S PANTS • EXEMPT

You will be glad to know that a seaman's pants (and indeed his coat also) cannot be held for rent arrears. As late as 1938 a San Francisco landlord was haled into court and fined for breaking this law.

RECEIVE PAY • on CAPS •

A tradition of the British Navy is that enlisted men receive their pay on their cap tops. This was originally done so that all could see the amount paid, and any errors could be readily rectified.

BLOCKADE~RUNNER "EDINA"

Southerners please note! The old s.s. Edina, famous blockade-runner which dodged so many Union warships during the Civil War, is still afloat and in service. As a boy, the illustrator of this page sailed in her on many a cruise between Port Melbourne and Geelong, Australia. Like Johnny Walker she is "still going strong!"

What! NO KISSES?

Because they might possibly be used as code words, the traditional little crosses which every sailorman has used in his love letters, must now be eliminated by British seamen, according to Admiralty orders.

· ENSIGN ·

This title dates back to when privileged squires carried the banners of their lords and masters into battle. Later, these squires became known by the name of the banner (the ensign) itself.

· SPIRITUAL and PHYSICAL LIGHT·

The Cordovan Lighthouse near Bordeaux, France, was once a church. It is reputedly the oldest maritime light in existence.

The Drawings of Cedic W. Windas
Part II
1943-1948

WINDAS 1941.

. OLD GLORY'S .
FIRST WORLD VOYAGE

The ship "Columbia", Captain Gray, was the first vessel ever to carry the American flag clear around the world. This was when Gray circumnavigated the globe in the years 1787-1790.

. REAR ADMIRAL .

The title of Rear Admiral was first given to divisional commanders of reserve fleets. Hence the inference of Reserve, or "In the Rear."

. CRETE .

In view of the recent occupation of the Island of Crete by British forces, it is of interest to note that King Minos of Crete was the first to establish naval power which he did in 1460 B.C.

NOTICE

. PANTS OPTIONAL .

Fair warning is hereby given to all that the EMPLOYEES CO-OPERATIVE RESTAURANT at Norfolk Navy Yard has definitely "gone formal". They have posted a bulletin giving notice that no one will be served unless wearing a shirt.

WINDAS 1941

• SKULL and CROSSBONES •

Here's another boyish belief gone by the board; it appears now that the Skull and Crossbones was NOT the death-flag of the pirates. When this insignia was flown it meant that if you would deliver up all your cargo, you and your ship could go free. When total death and destruction was planned the corsairs would hoist the RED flag. (Page Mr Stalin).

• KISSED by MOTHER CAREY •

Just another way of saying, "Once a sailor, always a sailor." It is an old superstition that all boys who go to sea were kissed in their infancy by the sailorman's guardian angel 'Mata Cara , (Mother Carey).

BLOW the MAN DOWN •

Just a "down-East" way of saying "Knock him down".

• YEOMEN •

This rating dates back to the old Anglo-Saxon days, when it meant that a yeoman was one who was a freeman and had volunteered his services. Others not freemen were forced to fight in their lord's service.

WINDAS 1943

∘ COCONUTS ∘

The coconut was so named when Spanish seamen exploring the West Indies discovered the nut, and thought the hairy shell resembled a monkey's face. Coco is Spanish for monkey.

∘ROYAL NAVY∘ SHIPBUILDING

In the past ten years, ninety per cent of Britain's warships have been constructed in private shipyards.

'n' listen, swab! I just don't want NO competition

∘WHISTLING ABOARD SHIP∘

Ho, hum! everything changes. In our sailing Navy they would'nt let you whistle aboard for fear you would create storms or head-winds. In our steam Navy they ban all whistling for fear of confusion with the bo'sun's pipe.

∘CANADA'S "ANNAPOLIS"∘

The Canadian Naval College was officially dedicated and opened at Halifax in 1911.

FEELING A·I·

When you are in tip-top health, and express yourself as feeling "A·I," you are really borrowing a marine insurance classification term.

It all started in a little coffee shop operated by one Lloyd of London. Here merchants and master-mariners gathered to discuss freights and risks, over a friendly cup of Java.

Later, Lloyds grew to be the mightiest marine insurance company in the world, and classified first class ships as A·I· risks.

Hence came the popular term for feeling in first class health.

·CLIMBED IN *through* the HAWSEHOLE·

Old Navy slang for an officer who has been promoted from a seaman's rating.

·SOU' SPAINER·

More old Navy slang, designating a seaman serving with the Mediterranean squadron.

· DIVE ·

Seagoing term given to unsavory waterfront barrooms. Since these places were almost invariably below street level, one had to "dive" down the steps to the entrance. So was coined this slang term for the place itself.

WINDAS 1943

A NAME IMMORTAL

In four of her major wars, the United States has always had a ship named LEXINGTON to carry the fight to the enemy.

THE SAILOR COLLAR

The collar on a bluejacket's blouse was originally a utility rather than an ornament. It was designed to keep the oil used to grease a seaman's que from staining his jacket.

SEA-GOING TRADESMEN · About 80 per cent of U.S. Navy personnel complete trade-school courses sometime during their service.

NEPTUNE'S "FAVORITES"

The wild horses on Sable Island, Nova Scotia are descendants of a shipload of French horses wrecked on that island in 1659.

WINDAS 1943

· TAKEN ABACK ·

When you are surprised and embarrassed,
And express yourself s "taken aback," you
Are borrowing the nautical term which describes the dangerous position of a square-
rigged vessel, which by reason of sudden
squalls or faulty steering (or both), has had
her sails blown back against the masts and
is in peril of being thrown on her beam ends.

· JERSEY ·

The sweater you wear was
originally called a "Jersey."
It is still called that in some
Countries. This type of
garment was first used by
the seafaring inhabitants of
the Island of Jersey in the
English Channel group.

· GULLIBLE ·

This good dictionary word is
said to have been coined when
some idle seamen amused
themselves during a dog-watch
by throwing odds and ends
of small stuff etc., to hungry
sea-gulls wheeling around the
ship. "Look at 'em," laughed
one of the sailors " they think
it's food. Anything fools 'em."
Webster defines the word 'Gullible'
as "capable of being easily
deceived."

· TARRY BREEKS ·

This is very old Navy slang for
a deepwater sailor. It was coined
because of a common practise
among seamen of early days, to
actually give their nether garments
a coating of tar, in an attempt to
make them waterproof against
dirty weather.

WINDAS 1943

FIRST U.S. MARINES WERE MERCHANT SEAMEN

When John Paul Jones wanted riflemen to man his fighting-tops and pick men off the enemy's decks below them, he feared that soldiers, unused to the rolling of ships, might well become seasick and unfit for duty. So he gathered a mob of rip-roaring merchant seamen and trained them in the use of arms.

They were short on discipline; they handled their muskets like capstan bars, and their drill on parade was a nightmare to self-respecting officers.

But they were good patriots and first class fightingmen, and they built a lasting reputation which is a tradition among the modern gents who always "have the situation well in hand."

· HOUSE FLAGS ·

Merchant Service house flags, denoting the company to which the ship belongs, are a relic of the days when crusading knights carried banners bearing the device of their house and lineage.

· THEY'RE AT LOGGERHEADS · ·

A modern term inferring that two parties are really at outs with each other. It derives its meaning from an old shipboard tool used for spreading hot pitch in deck seams. The tool was called a 'logger head' and consisted of a long wooden handle secured to a blade something like an adze. Any fight in which these tools were used was a 'knock-'em down, drag-'em-out' affair; hence the deadliness of the suggestion contained in the modern slang term.

· JAPAN'S MIDGET SUBS ·

In response to repeated requests, here is how a 50 foot 2-man Japanese submarine looks. Her destructive equipment comprises two 18inch torpedoes. She carries also a 300 lb. demolition charge, which is a 'suicide device' used as a last resource to blow up target, sub, crew 'n'everything.

NOTE

THE FAN-LIKE PROPELLER

THE HOOP GUARDS PROTECTING BOW.

· LARGEST SILVER CARGO.

Eclipsing even the fabled cargoes of Spain's treasure-ships, the s.s. President Garfield established an 'all time high' when she once brought silver bullion valued at $10,000,000 into Los Angeles from China.

° SOUSSE °

The ancient port of Sousse, Tunisia was so named for the Susa, a moth-like insect found there in swarms by early seamen.

HEART OF OAK

Old sailors never die, and neither do the grand old ships. Admiral Nelson's famous VICTORY is still in service. Nearly 150 years have passed since this immortal vessel gained undying fame at Trafalgar. Today she serves .... as headquarters for British ratings studying for commissions in the Royal Navy.

· COMMODORE ·

In view of the recent Act of Congress reviving the rank of Commodore, it is of interest to note that this rank was first created by the Dutch during a war with England. The Netherlands was short of admirals and short also in their war-chest. So they created the rank of Commodore, whereby they obtained an officer who knew as much as an Admiral.... but received only *half* his pay.

· GIBSON GIRL ···· 1943 ·

"Gibson Girl", the nickname given a newly developed portable radio because of its hour-glass shape. The aerial is held aloft by a balloon, and with it distress signals can be sent over 100,000 sq. miles of ocean.

DRY~DOCK

The first part of this word is from the Old Norse *draugr*, meaning a dry log.
The latter part is from the Middle Dutch *docke*, referring to a ship's basin or berth.

PLUCKY PADDLE STEAMER

One of the most illustrious merchant ships of this war is the little paddle steamer ROYAL EAGLE, which used to carry Londoners on holiday trips.
ROYAL EAGLE made three crossings at Dunkerque, rescued 3,000 troops. She was 'dive-bombed' 48 times, and has been in action against aircraft 52 times. She has destroyed 2 enemy ships and is still in service.

HEADACHE for "SUBS"

The helicopter should prove an ideal weapon against enemy submarines. It can maneuver straight up or down, forwards or backwards, and needs no take-off or landing run.

MASTS for MEN-O'-WAR

In the tiny town of Maples, Maine, a small grove of stately pine trees grow. Some of them still show a trace of "broad arrow" markings put there by the Royal Navy in pre-Revolution days. The marks indicated that the trees were to be reserved as masts for His Majesty's ships.

The $64 QUESTION

Which has the greater number of ships, the Army or Navy? Sailor, you're WRONG! The Army has far the greater number. In 1942 the Army built 2,200 vessels; and in 1943, 3,900 of 'em.

• UMBRELLA DE LUXE •

To help guard the vast armada carrying troops and supplies to the North African invasion, planes of the R.A.F. flew a total mileage equivalent to FIFTY TIMES AROUND THE WORLD.

•and STILL they come!•

The one-thousandth Liberty ship was launched May 25th, 1943, at New Orleans.

•BUSY LITTLE WORKERS•

The average tug boat hauls about 4,000,000 tons annually.

•CHICKENS and PIGS•

In the Old Navy days, when comparatively few seamen could swim, many a sailor had a chicken tattooed on one foot, and a pig tattooed on the other. This was because of an old superstition that in the event of danger by drowning, patron-saints of birds and animals would see the emblems on the sailor's feet, and knowing that neither chickens nor pigs could swim, would exert their saintly powers to save the sailor and his tattoos from a watery grave.

· BLIMP "BUMPED OFF " *by* SUB ·

For the first time in history, a lighter-than-air craft has been destroyed by a submarine.
Theoretically, upon sighting a blimp, submarines should crash-dive, but this one fooled us by remaining surfaced and bringing the U.S. K-74 down with gunfire.

·*Reserved* AIR LANES ·

All navigable air in the U.S. above 17,000 feet altitude, is now reserved for military traffic.

·*Clothes Rationing* PAYS ·

With money saved by the rationing of clothes, economists estimate that Britain can build an extra navy of 15 battleships 50 cruisers, 130 destroyers and 8 aircraft carriers.

· REPAIR SHIPS ·

Just in case you didn't know it, repair ships of the U.S. Navy are named for characters in Roman and Greek mythology.

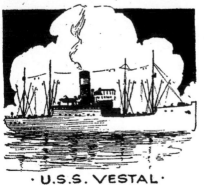

· U.S.S. VESTAL ·

WINDAS 1944

•MAHOGANY....and HEARTS of OAK•

Here's to the little P.T. boats and to the mahogany trees from which they are built.
As far back as 200 years ago, navy men praised mahogany for its durability and its capability for absorbing shot without splintering.
These sterling qualities, plus the "hearts of oak" who man the P.T.'s, is probably why the Germs and the Japs don't like 'em.

• INVASION FLEETS

In 1588, the number of ships in the Spanish Armada, which was to invade England, was 1500 vessels of all sizes. In 1943, in the invasion of Sicily the Allied forces used approximately 3000 ships.

•DRIVING POWER•

The first electrically driven warship in the United States Navy, was the U.S.S. LANGLEY.

•MARU•

Although the word "Maru" is used to designate Japanese merchant ships, its real meaning is of a certain mystic circle at the bottom of the sea.
Well, that's O.K. by us. We won't be angry when all "Maru's" are at the bottom of the sea.

WINDAS 1944.

• CERTIFIED CAPTAINS •

Until 1450 A.D., anybody, qualified or not, could take a vessel to sea. In that year however, King Charles the Fifth of Spain passed a law making it compulsory for every shipmaster to have a certificate showing his qualifications. Other nations promptly adopted this wise law.

• TIGHT •

This modern slang, describing an inebriates condition, gathers its meaning from an old Navy expression. When a sail was properly set and trimmed it was described as being "full and tight." In other words, like the drunk, it had all it could hold.

• AMIDSHIPS •

Once again a reader has requested clarification of the term "Amidships." He asks " Is the waist of the ship amidships?" Decidedly not. Amidships is an imaginary line running fore and aft along the deck and parallel to the keel.

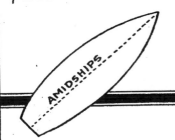

AMIDSHIPS

• TIN CANS •

This name for destroyers seems even more appropriate than ever now that W.P.B informs us that 13,000 pounds of tin actually goes into the construction of a modern destroyer.

KEEL HAULING

A brutal punishment, usually reserved for mutineers, which was abolished in the U.S. Navy about 1800. It consisted of securing a line around the victim's chest, another around his ankles. The lines were passed outboard, port and starboard, and the victim lowered into the sea, to be dragged under the keel from forefoot to sternpost. This punishment was virtually a death sentence, for if the victim did not drown, he would be practically cut to pieces by the barnacles on the ship's bottom.

A "BARNEY FOKKE" PASSAGE

Old Navy slang for a long drawn out voyage. It had reference to Bernard Fokke the "Flying Dutchman", who, for his sins, beats eternally back and forth off the Cape of Good Hope.

MAGELLAN'S CLOUD

A constellation discovered by the navigator as he hauled through the straits which bear his name near the southern tip of South America.

The LEAF that SOOTHES

Tobacco received its name through a misunderstanding of the famous seaman Columbus. When he first saw an Indian smoking he pointed and asked "What do you call that?" The Indian, thinking that Columbus referred to the pipe itself answered "Tobago" (the native word for tube or pipe).

WINDAS 1944

WHY SEAMEN PASS TO LOO'ARD

Why sailors should never pass to windward of an officer is a very old tradition indeed. It dates back to early days when cleanliness of person was not regarded as an important factor. Thus, since the officer kept to windward, he was not subjected to the unpleasant smell of the seamen as they passed.

GLORY HOLE

That special section reserved in Davey Jones' locker for the eternal peace and happiness of all good ships' engineers who are buried at sea.

BACKING and FILLING

Old Navy slang descriptive of a person nervously beating about the bush instead of coming straight to the point and stating his case. The term got its meaning from the actions of sailing ships which would maintain a temporary position at sea by backing their yards and drifting away, then filling the sails and running back to the original position.

QUEEN MARY BIRTHPLACE

Because there were no yards big enough to accomodate her keel, the huge luxury liner Queen Mary, which is doing such yeoman service in this war as a troopship, was built in the middle of a corn field.

WINDAS 1944

•WAR-DOGS *for* 'DEVIL-DOGS' •

The first Americans to use trained dogs of war in combat, were the U.S. Marines when they invaded Bougainville in the Solomons.

• TONS *of* TIN •

A battleship requires approximately 76 tons of tin in her construction; a submarine about 3 tons.

•1st. NAVAL FLIER•

The first airplane takeoff from a ship's deck was made by Eugene Ely flying a biplane in Nov. 1910.

•NICE TRIBUTE *from* BRITAIN•

The British Ministry of War Shipping has chosen a very courteous system for naming vessels built for them in the United States.
The first letters of the name honor "Uncle Sam;" the remaining letters denote some English river or lake, thus :-
Sam-Avon, Sam-Kendal, etc., etc.

HE LOST THE NUMBER OF HIS MESS

An Old Navy term meaning killed in action. Originally the term was "lost from the number of his mess". It was coined because of the old method of hiring stewards under contract to feed so many men per day at so much per head. By this arrangement, if the number of men decreased, so did the steward's pay. The original meaning of the term therefore, embraced seamen who left the vessel for any reason whatsoever, and not only those killed in the line of duty.

SEAMAN of the SEVEN SEAS

The first American to circumnavigate the globe was Captain Robert Gray, sailing out of Boston Town in 1787.

NOTE for HOMEFOLK

Next time you write your aunt Matilda, sailor, remind her that if she'll save 5,500 tin cans, she'll have enough cans to manufacture ONE torpedo.

LIFE SAVER

To drifting survivors of a sea disaster, the worst possible torture is that of thirst. To overcome this danger, science has contributed some wonderful aids, among which are synthetic resins. One pound of resin will treat six pints of sea water, making it drinkable.

• BLACK ~ BIRDERS •

This name was given to the little South Sea island schooners which carried governmental recruited native labor to the banana plantations in Queensland, Australia. When certain unscrupulous ship masters took to stealing the natives instead of hiring them, the recruiting business degenerated into sheer slavery. The schooners became known as slavers or "black-birders", and the Australian navy had a long hard job putting an end to their lawlessness.

• MAIRSY DOATES.... *RUSSIAN VERSION* •

Russian sailors use mare's milk to manufacture their alcoholic drinks.

•GAS RATIONING JUSTIFIED •

Half of the supplies shipped overseas to our boys and to our allies are petroleum products.

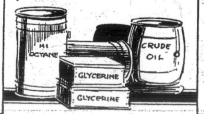

•BEATING THE SUB MENACE •

In 1942, twelve out of every 100 U.S. ships sailing for Europe were sunk by Axis submarines. 1943 showed an appreciable decline in sinkings to One out of every 100. In 1944 the percentage has been even less.

• SHOW A LEG •

This traditional 'turn out' call originated in the days when seamen were privileged to carry their wives with them on long voyages. When the bos'un ordered "show a leg," and a limb encased in a stocking was exhibited from an occupied bunk, he assumed its owner was a woman, as sailors wore no stockings. The woman was left to rest. If, however, the leg was bare, its owner was promptly rousted out.

• POPEYE *the* GREAT •

Affectionately known as 'Pop-eye', George Sanderson 84 years young, is the oldest man serving in the U.S. Navy. Good luck, sailor!

PLYWOOD *for* DEEP SEA SHIPS •

About 10,000 feet of plywood goes into construction of a Liberty ship.

• FIRST SEA FIGHT •

The first sea battle of historic record was between the Corinthians and the Corcyreans, about 665 B.C.

WINDAS 1944

• GRATITUDE •

As a reward for his discovery of America, Christopher Colombus was presented with a purse of approximately 320 dollars.

CAN'T I EVEN TAKE A SHOT AT THE ADMIRAL ?

• OMIGOSH ! •

Don't ever let the Marines know it, sailor, or there'll be no living with 'em, but the first duty of the original U.S. Marines was "to restrain seamen from any act of mutiny."

•INVASION CRAFT•

Landing craft for the invasion of Europe were delivered to Britain in sections, packed with bolts, gear and engines. Seamen put each one together in 9 days, a job which formerly had taken 53 days.

• GOLDEN DRAGONS •

No, Boots. The Golden Dragons are not a Chinese Secret Society. All you have to do to join, is to cross the International Date Line and the Equator at one and the same time, and you're IT.... providing you survive the Barber, the Bear et al.

WINDAS 1944

° CAMOUFLAGE °

Though all navies of the world now use camouflage as a protection for their fighting ships, France must be credited as the first nation to use this deceptive art. France officially enlisted painters for this work in 1914.

° A FIGHTING NAME °

The U.S. destroyer O'BRIEN was named for Wm O'Brien, who fought the first sea-fight of the Am. Revolution.

PRECIOUS *Stones* for PRECIOUS *SHIPS*

Uncle Sam uses garnets in making non-skid mats for battle ship's decks; mats that prevent slipping accidents.

I wish they'd use GARNETS in apartment house BATH MATS

° THEY ALSO SERVE °

During this World War II, the increase in Navy shipyard personel has been tremendous. From a total of 443,000 in January 1942, it has now grown to the unprecedented number of 1,049,000 workers.

WINDAS 1944

° FIRST IRONCLAD °

To Korea goes the honor of having built the first ironclad ship of war.... back in 1590. This was the TORTOISE BOAT, commanded by Admiral Yi Sun Sin, an intrepid Korean often compared to Lord Nelson as a naval strategist. The TORTOISE BOAT was whale-backed with iron plates, making her impervious to stones, fire-pots and arrows.

°WEIGHTY *Argument* °

During a month of fighting at Bougainville, one Marine artillery unit fired 35,000 rounds, weighing well over HALF A MILLION pounds.

°ARMED *Merchantmen*°

Answering Seaman E.J. Norton's enquiry :– Congress repealed the Neutrality Act of 1939, on Nov. 17th, 1941, thereby permitting U.S. merchant ships to be armed, and to proceed to belligerent ports anywhere.

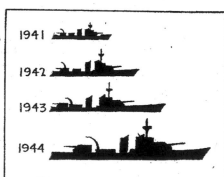

1941
1942
1943
1944

° SOME *Growth* °

Despite our losses at Pearl Harbor and in the Pacific, the tonnage of U.S. fighting ships has grown from barely 1,000,000 tons in 1941 to nearly 3,000,000 tons in 1944.

—WINDAE 1944

∘ QUARTER-DECK VOICE ∘

A very old term meaning literally "the voice of authority."
Even when for any reason the speaker was unseen, his speech and tone would command respect and obedience.

∘ FIGURE-HEADS ∘

In modern times, figure-heads were designed for beauty. Originally they were created to inspire terror, and were carved in the likeness of supernatural beasts of prey.

∘ Other FISH to FRY ∘

During this war over 50 per cent of Boston's off-shore fishing fleet has been converted to naval duty.

THIS MAKES IT REAL NICE FOR US!

∘ CAPE HORNER ∘

In Old Navy parlance, this term indicated that a seaman had served in the South Pacific. A "Sou'-Spainer" was one with Mediterranean service. A "Flying-Fish sailor" had served in the Orient.

WINDAS 1944

° PADDY WESTER °

Old Navy term of reproach for an in-
efficient seaman. The term originated from
the rascally scheme of a Liverpool board-
ing-house keeper named Patrick West.
This shyster kept an old ship's wheel in his
back yard, and a cow's horn nailed to a
post. He taught his lodgers the merest
rudiments of steering, and walked them
around the post. His wife sat on the fence
and threw buckets of salty water over them
to give them a weather-beaten look.
At the end of this "tuition" Paddy sold his
lodgers fake discharges which stated that
the bearers were expert helmsmen and had
been "around the horn" several times.

° CAT-HEADS °

Heavy timbers projecting from port and starboard bow, used
in dropping or weighing anchor. They went into disuse about
1890, but had been standard equipment for centuries. The name
derived from ancient Egyptian ships whereon these timbers
were fashioned in the image of cats, which were held sacred.

°SHIP~SHAPE *and* BRISTOL FASHION°

An old naval term indicating
the ultimate in ship construction.
It was coined and used universally because of the seaworthiness, efficiency and smart appearance of ships out of Bristol.

° HAND - ME - DOWNS °

This old sea-going term for ready-to-wear clothes originated in the days when uniforms were not G.I..... each man bought his own. Waterfront stores invariably hung their merchandise high on hooks to safeguard them from grab-and-run theives. The store owner would climb a ladder and hand down a suit for a customer's inspection. Hence the term.

° HOOKERS °

This disparaging name for ships dates back many years, when smart navymen looked with disdain on the slovenly vessels and nondescript seamen trading out of the Hook of Holland.

°DISCOVERED....TWICE °

Wake Island was discovered by the British in 1796. Then lately the Japs discovered it was too hot to hold from Uncle Sam's avenging hand.

°STRIKE UP the BAND °

The U.S Marine Corps band became known as the "President's Own", when President Adams ordered its appearance at all official functions.

· POSTED AT LLOYDS ·

Meaning "lost at sea". The term originated from an old custom of Lloyds of London.

When a ship was long overdue they would post a bulletin outside their offices, informing relatives that the vessel named must be presumed to have been lost with all hands.

· DINKUM BLOKES ·

Australian navymen's endearing term for American sailors. It means "they're swell shipmates."

· A BONZER SKIRT ·

More Australian sea-going slang..... this time for a good looking dame.

· LOBLOLLY BOY ·

This title was first bestowed on boys in the British Navy who assisted in the care of sick and wounded. The first official use of the term in the U.S. Navy appeared in Navy Regulations of 1814, wherein it stated that "The loblolly boy shall serve the surgeon or surgeon's mate."

WINDAS 1945—

· QUARTER ·

The term 'quarter' (or mercy for prisoners) was coined because of an early custom by which a conquered man could save his life by paying to his captor "the sum of one quarter of his yearly wage"

· SPLICED ROPES ·

A term in the old Navy for friends who have quarreled bitterly but decided to be friends again. The term was coined because a spliced rope never runs so smoothly through a block.... in other words, it is never quite the same.

· FOREIGN TALENT ·

Musicians of our first Navy bands were instrumentalists picked up in random ports. They were surprisingly good bands, despite the fact that the individuals were ignorant of everything American, including the language.

D'ya vant a goot corn-.... cello- obo- viol ...fabriken Ya? No?

· INAUGURATION of NURSES CORPS ·

The Nurses Corps was established as an integral part of the Medical Dept in 1908. Nurses were designated neither as enlisted personnel nor officers, but were given recognised military status.

· NAVAL LAW ·

If you think that Navy laws are very strict today, just stop and consider the severity of Old Navy punishment for transgressors. One rule reads " If any seaman shall draw a knife against a shipmate, the culprit's hand shall be cut off."

·NORSE COMMANDOS....earlyModel·

Because of our victories on Normandy's beaches, it is of timely interest to note that this portion of France is named for the old Norse sea-raiders who stormed ashore in medieval days and kept the country for themselves.

· FAREWELL to SAIL·

It was not until 1869, that sail was finally abandoned as the principal means of propulsion for ships of war.

·SLOP CHEST ·

Old ships carried a special locker from which the captain would sell replacements of clothes to the crew. It was called the "slop" chest, the name being a corruption of the old English word "sloppe", meaning breeches.

WINDAS 1946

· LAUNCHING STERN-FIRST ·

Originally, ships were launched stern-first for superstitious reasons.... to keep sea-witches and other evil spirits from clambering over the vessel's bow and doing her harm while she was still incomplete and unable to ward them off.

· DOCTOR-DISCHARGE ·

Old Navy slang for a fake discharge purporting to show that some "greenhorn" was a fully qualified seaman.

· CANADIAN CONTRIBUTION ·

Life jackets for Allied seamen are now filled with Canadian-grown milk-weed floss.

· THEY SURE GET AROUND ·

Navy nurses serve EVERYWHERE! When Manilla fell to the Japs, one nurse escaped from Corregidor to Australia aboard a submarine.

• MOUNT VERNON •

George Washington's home was named in honor of Admiral Vernon, the British seaman who advocated the watery dilution of the Navy's rum ration. Now the Admiral's nickname was "Old Grog", because he always wore a heavy cape made of groggam. When the sailors tasted the weak ration of rum and water, they sneeringly referred to it as "Grog", a name which has stuck to that drink ever since.

WINDAS 1945

•A LONG WAY FROM HOME•

24 Canadian "Lake Freighters" were sunk during the "Battle of the Atlantic", some in or near the Mediterranean, others in icy Artic water on the run to Murmansk.

•ROPE for the NAVY•

The abaca plant, source of manilla hemp was first brought to America for experimental planting by an American naval officer in the early '80's.

•FIRST AMERICAN-BUILT SHIP•

The first vessel built in America was the sixty foot VIRGINIA, launched in the Kennebec River in the year 1607.

Drawn from a photograph taken off Lauderdale, Florida.

WINDAS 1945

• *from* MONITOR *to* HOUSING PROJECT •

The Civil War monitor AMPHITRITE has had a varied career. In 1866 she was stationed at Annapolis. In 1898 she was towed to Cuba and helped bombard San Juan. In 1917-18 she was a government training ship. Then, sold to some enterprising promoters, she was converted into a floating hotel for Florida speculators. World War II finds her at Elizabeth City N.C., solving the housing shortage problem for aircraft workers.

• HI, JO! •

JO, as a Navy nickname for coffee, derives from a series of breakdowns through JAMAICA (where lots of coffee comes from) to JAMAKE, JAMOKE, and finally to the very abbreviated JO.

•SUB-SURFACE CRAFT•

Though it is not generally known, submarines as vessels of war, date back to 1620 A.D.

• SHIPYARD DOLDRUMS •

From 1922 to 1937 only two freighters were built in U.S. shipyards.

WINDAS 1945

· THE OLD VETERAN ·

They may de-commission the battlewagon NEVADA,
but they cannot dim her glory. Grounded during the Honolulu sneak attack, she was refloated. Served in the Aleutians
and on Atlantic convoy duty. Supported landings in Normandy;
bombarded Toulon and Marseilles in the Southern France
invasion. She thumbed her nose at Jap kamikazas
although they stove in her main deck. Quickly repaired,
she knocked hell out of dangerous shore batteries on
Okinawa, and never quit fighting till Hirohito sobbed "hon Uncle!"

· CODE SIGNALS ·

Captain Marryat, famous
seaman and author, introduced the first practical
code for flag signals in 1817.

· ENSIGNS

Which country's naval ensign,
still in use, is the oldest in the
world... ?   No! sailor,
you guessed wrong. It's Turkey,
and dates back to 339 B.C.

· SIDE LIGHTS ·

It was not until 1848 that
the Admiralty ruled it was
compulsory to show RED for
port lights, GREEN for starboard.
Up until that time, the
captain of a vessel just about
pleased himself.

WINDAS 1945

• THE OATH •

The custom of raising the right hand before giving evidence under oath, or swearing allegiance, originated in the days when criminals were branded on the palm of the hand. As it was illegal for a criminal to testify, the act of raising the hand showed that it's owner, if unbranded, was presumably an honest man.

• OLD FACTOR RETURNS •

With the disappearance of sail, wind as a factor in battle tactics lost importance. With the advent of plane-carriers, however, it regained its old prestige, for these vessels must bear up into the wind in order that their planes can take off, and land again.

• RUDDER •

This word is derived from the Anglo-Saxon "Rother," that which guides.

• SHIPYARDS ACTIVE ...and HOW •

In 1939, 22 shipyards were engaged in Navy work. By 1945 the number increased to 375.

· AS GOOD AS NEW ·

Decks white and brightwork gleaming the USS CONSTITUTION is as shipshape as the day she was launched nearly 150 years ago.

Recommissioned in August 1940, she is the oldest US warship in service.

May her glory never fade from the minds and hearts of American seamen.

·FIRST ADMIRAL·

Up until 1296, the highest ranking officers in the British Navy were known as "Justices, Keepers, or Governors." In March of that year, however, William de Leybourne was given the title of Admiral, the first to be so honored.

WHAT THA HECK'S A GUY SUPPOSED TO DO WITH THESE THINGS?

Yes! WE HAVE NO PAJAMAS ·

Several times the Navy Department endeavored to convince enlisted men to wear pajamas to bed. But the boys preferred to sleep in the raw or in skivvies. As a result, the Department gave up the fight In 1915 and ordered its clothing depots to dispose of all the pajamas.

· BULKHEADS ·

Bulkheads were first called "co-bridge heads", and were strong barricades pierced for small guns and muskets to repel or drive away boarders.

• COPPER BOTTOMS •

Although he gained far more acclaim for his famous ride, Paul Revere's most valuable contribution to his country was his processing of copper for ships' bottoms. In the early 1800's, England was the only nation equipped to sheath her vessels with copper, sheathing which prevented fouling, and gave her ships great advantage in speed over all others. Britain kept her process secret, but Paul Revere devised his own method for rolling copper into sheets, and thus contributed greatly to the superior sailing qualities of American ships in 1812.

• PAINTER •

Boats' painters are so named by a corruption of the French word "peyntor". It means loop or noose.

• HARD-BOILED "EGGS" •

Throughout the years of World War II, British mine-layers carried out operations every 2½ days.

WINDAS 1945

The BEAUTIFUL and the BRAVE

Rallying to the call of the United States, nearly 2,100 yachts of various types served in hazardous Coast Guard operations during the late unpleasantness with the Axis.

This must be the original "DEEP SIX"

Native pearl divers of Ceylon, without any mechanical aids, have been known to remain submerged for **SIX** minutes.

INSURANCE

The earliest known form of insurance was a guarantee of reimbursement in case of mishap and loss at sea.

U.S. NAVAL UNIFORMS

First regulations governing naval officers' uniforms were passed by Congress in 1797.

KEEPER of the KEYS

The custom of giving the keys of the powder magazine to the captain each night for safe keeping, dates back to John Paul Jones.

BOARDING PIKES

These steel-pointed weapons were standard equipment aboard American ships of war until about the middle of the last century.

Some "BRAKES"

If you could drive an automobile 1,000 miles an hour, and bring it to a dead stop in TWO feet, you would have a pretty close idea of what the RECOIL SYSTEM has to do each time a turret gun is fired.

Durable DERELICT

The schooner Alma Cummings, abandoned in an Atlantic gale, actually remained a floating menace for about 16 months, and traveled over 5,000 miles.

· FROZEN FLATTIE ·

Conceived by the British; christened "Habakkuk" by Winston Churchill; OKed by the combined naval chiefs of staff; developed by U.S. and British scientists......an aircraft carrier built of ICE. She was to have been 2,000 feet long, 300 feet beam, 200 feet deep; with accomodations for 200 planes, crew of 3,600. The war ended before she was completed.
Note! *The small ship illustrates comparative size of average carrier with proposed "Habakkuk."*

· SMALL BUT GALLANT BAND ·

On the voyage in which he discovered America, Colombus had with him only 120 men all told

Another LONG "DRIFT"

The sketch below, from a photo, shows lifebelt from s.s. Stanley Dollar, which drifted 10,000 miles in SIX years.... from Japan, around No. America to the Shetland Islands.

GOSH! are admirals only 80 years old? they always ACT TWICE as old as that!

· 80th. ANNIVERSARY ·

In 1866, Congress created the the grades of Admiral and Vice-Admiral.

WINDAS 1947

HEARTS of OAK

Commander Perry's flagship, LAWRENCE, and most of his fleet in The battle of Lake Erie (1813) were built of green lumber by house carpenters. Reason: the fleet was needed in a hurry and there was no time to season lumber, or to bring experienced shipbuilders from Maine or Massachusetts. Perry used the only carpenters that he could get, and they were house carpenters. They did a great job and they played an important role in history.

"Pull yer keelts doon Jock, yer skiva's showin'"

SKIVIES

This traditional sailor slang for underwear derives from the old Scottish "skiva clothes" which were tight-fitting short breeks worn under the kilts.

HERRINGS wrote HISTORY

King Charles I. of England taxed British fishing fleets so heavily (to finance the building of a big navy) that the "ship tolls" started the Civil War.... and Charles lost his head.

They'd orta call it PHOENIX Island. It always rises again from its own ashes!

JACK-in-the-BOX

Falcon Island of the Tonga Group has disappeared again. Several times, during the last century it sank, only to rise again due to volcanic pressure.

WINDAS 1947

· SHE SAILS FOR 'SNUG HARBOR' ·

The JOSEPH CONRAD (100 foot square-rigged ship, ex-GEORG STAGE, frigate, of the Danish Navy) has finally ended her wanderings after 65 years of service. Launched in 1882, she has in turn been frigate, training ship, grain carrier, and 'yacht' for wealthy adventurers. Allan Villiers, Australian author, sailed her for several world voyages, sold her to the U.S. Maritime Commission as a training ship. Her last port will be Mystic, Connecticut, where she will dock permanently as a marine museum.

· A COLD 'ROOST' ·

The ivory gull, found in Lat. 85 N., lives less than 350 miles from the Pole, the most northern habitat of any bird.

Br-rr-rr-r'- I'm gonna quit and go south to California

N. POLE

· A LOT of BUNTING ·

Most American warships carry more than 40 foreign flags for ceremonial purposes.

· FLOUR SAVES SAILOR ·

An Australian seaman who left the service to turn pearl diver, had his leg seized by a shark. He gouged the shark's eyes, forcing it to let go. The diver was bleeding to death when he was hauled aboard his boat. He yelled for a sack of flour and thrust his bitten leg into it. Dough formed and it stopped the bleeding until he reached port at Thursday Island. Doctors successfully treated him.

· ANCIENT "FIRE-PROOFING" ·

As far back as the days of the Roman Empire, ships' sails were woven with a mixture of asbestos to help prevent the effects of fire. This gave them an immense advantage over enemy vessels which were not so equipped.

· ATTENTION....NAVY WIVES ·

If you are running short on sugar coupons, read this item and weep; "In 1319, Venetian seamen took 100,000 lbs. of sugar to England in exchange for wool."

·COMBINED OPERATION·

The Duke of Marlborough is called the 'father of combined operations' because he placed the Army under the Navy's command to capture Gibralter from Spain in 1704.

· CRADLE ROBBERS ·

Before the turn of the century youngsters of twelve years of age could join the U.S. Marine Corps band as drummer boys.

• MISNOMER

The Solomon Islands were discovered and so named in 1567 by the Spanish naval commader Mendana.
He believed that the gold of which Solomon's Temple was built in Biblical days, had been obtained in this Pacific island group.

INSURANCE POLICY

• GAMBLING *against the* SEA •

Insuring vessels against risks of shipwreck dates back to the time of Ancient Greece.
Records exist which show that Athenian bankers underwrote many such policies.

• THAT'S A LOT *of* CHARTS •

In three months, Navy's Hydrographic Office printed and distributed 12,900,000 charts.

and if you don't believe me.... COUNT 'em !

• PARATROOPS •

U.S. Marines received parachute training as early as 1922.

FIRST U.S. NAVAL ENSIGN

Here is the U.S. ensign as hoist to the peak by John Paul Jones in 1775. It had an azure canton bearing the red cross of St. George and the white cross of St. Andrew. The field was of 13 alternate red and white stripes.

OYSTERS GROW on TREES

I don't believe it

U.S. seamen visiting Montego Bay, Jamaica, were dubious until they actually saw oysters there attached to tree roots growing in the water.

FAREWELL to SAILS

The SS METEOR, built in 1892, is said to be the first steamship ever to put to sea without sails as auxiliary power.

SPANISH TERRITORY

'AT'S MINE. I SAW IT FIRST!

WASHINGTON OREGON

Although not generally known, Washington and Oregon once belonged to Spain. Spanish seamen were the first to explore our Northwest coasts.

WINDAS 1947

SEMPER PARATUS

During the years 1797-1801, in the undeclared war against France, U.S. Coast Guard cutters operated in conjuction with the Navy.
They actually captured more enemy ships than did the Navy, accounting for 18 out of the total 22 taken.

GLOBE TROTTER

During the Great War, Britain's luxury liner QUEEN ELIZABETH sailed for six years in Navy gray war paint. She traveled 500,000 miles, carried almost 800,000 servicemen.

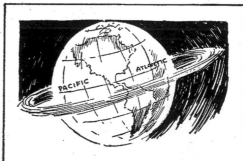

PIONEER

The U.S. frigate ESSEX was the first warship to fly the American flag in the Pacific, January 26th. 1813.

OLD PHRASE

The phrase "Seven Seas" is an old one indeed, being used in turn by ancient Hindus, Chinese and Romans. In each case they referred to different bodies of water. Today the term includes the Atlantic, Pacific, Artic, Antartic, Indian Oceans, Mediterranean and North Sea.

WINDAS 1947

· GALLANT VESSEL ·

While Americans in general know that the MAYFLOWER brought the Pilgrim Fathers to these shores, American Navymen in particular feel a thrill of pride remembering she was also a warship of renown. She was one of the immortal little fleet that scattered the huge Spanish Armada in 1588.

· SAILOR'S LUCK ·

Adams Dori in Tokyo, was named for John Adams, seaman, who was shipwrecked there in the 16th century. Strangely enough, though it customary in Japan at that time to enslave or kill foreigners, Adams was honored, feted, became like a patron saint.

GOLDEN DAY for · GOLDEN STATE

News of California's admission as a State was announced by the booming guns of the mail ship OREGON as she entered the Golden Gate in 1850.

Ah !!! Nineteen bucks. Now I'll be able to buy a square meal

· OH, MIGOSH !

In 1833, a United States midshipman's pay was NINETEEN dollars monthly, and ONE RATION per day.

• ATLANTIC PACKETS •

Those emigrant-carrying ships of the early 1800s, were built to serve a double purpose: ① Their heavy, full-rounded lines made them comfortable vessels in which to transport future citizens to the United States. ② They could be almost instantly converted into frigates as an invaluable addition to the navy.

•TRIBUTE TO BENEFACTOR•

Captain Cook, Britain's famous navigator, was held in such high international esteem, that even during American Revolution, all U.S. ships of war were ordered not to stop his vessel, nor to molest the captain on the high seas.

• TIE-ROPE •

The ship's hawser derived its name from the word "halter", the rope used in leading or holding a horse.

I think I'll have that red light on the starboard side for a change. I'm sick 'n tired of seeing it on the port side

•NAVIGATION LIGHTS•

It was not until 1848 that an official ruling decreed RED for PORT, GREEN for STARBOARD lights. Until then, RED was displayed on either port or starboard, at the option of the captain.

· ANCHOR WATCH ·

Anchor watch was originally stood only when the ship was tied up in dock and her anchors stowed on deck. Then a watch was posted, "Lest," says the serious chronicler of early days, "some miscreants from ye other ships about, steal ye anchyrs while theye (the crew) sleepe."

· KIDS ·

The shallow wooden (or metal) vessels used in carrying food from the galley to the mess table, received their name from the boys whose job it was to help the cook aboard old time ships by waiting on the seamen at mealtime. The boys were "kids" in the venacular of the day, and the wooden trays were named after them.

· DIFFERENT SHIPS... DIFFERENT LONG SPLICES ·

An Old Navy colloquialism meaning there is more than one side to an argument and more than one way of doing a shipshape job.

· CHIPPING .....
with a RUBBER HAMMER ·

This was an old-time superstition regarding eternal punishment for wicked seamen, and which pictured the souls of the evil ones forever hopelessly chipping.... with a hammer made of rubber

• COPENHAGEN ~ ED •

A naval term meaning to destroy an enemy fleet in port before it can up anchor and put to sea. Admiral Nelson used this strategy to wipe out the Danish fleet at Copenhagen, hence the term. The Japanese pulled the same disastrous trick on us at Pearl Harbor. Which is a good reason why we should determine to keep our ships in such strength and readiness that never again will any foreign power "Copenhagen" an American fleet.

Well, I helped cook many an enemies' goose, so this job oughta be a cinch

• OH, COOKIE •

Just in case you are inclined to grumble at the grub served aboard your particular battle-wagon, remember what the seamen of '76 had to swallow. In those days the galley was a "soft spot" for any deserving sailor who had lost an eye or a leg in battle. His qualifications as a cook were rarely questioned.

°CONSERVATIVE ... eh, wot !

As late as 1814, U.S. Navy Regulations were practically identical with those of British Admiralty publications of 1772.

Ye REGULATIONS AND INSTRUCTIONS Relating to HIS MAJESTY'S SERVICE AT SEA A.D. 1772

• TO BOOT •

The United States once owned a Russian warship. When we purchased Alaska from Russia in 1867, the Czar's government big-heartedly "threw in" the old gunboat POLITOFSKY for good measure.

· HEAVY WEATHER ·

The Cape of Good Hope was first named "Cape of Storms" because of the foul weather experienced by early Portugese navigators trying to beat up around the mountainous point for far-off India.

·SIGNAL SUCCESS·

Ship-to-shore radio was pioneered by the Coast Guard in 1904.

·WHAT'S *in a* NAME ?·

.... and then there were the two Navy recruits, George Sparr and Jo Yeoman.

· EXEMPT ·

Even as far back as 1639, ships were considered so essential in this country, that shipbuilders were protected by law from press-gangs seeking seamen.

Images of the Navy
Serious Stuff

OLD IRONSIDES

U. S. Frigate Constitution

Anatomy of a Ship
USS Constitution

USS Constitution

The frigate *USS Constitution*, also referred to as "Old Ironsides," was launched in 1797, carrying over 50 guns and a crew of 450 men. The vessel was never defeated in battle, and remains a commissioned vessel of the U.S. Navy.

*I*magine her over 150 years ago-heeled over and running free-with great clouds of sail booming in the breeze, her bow knifing the North Atlantic swells, throwing sheets of spray along her spar deck. Along her rigging a watch team of barefoot seamen from Nantucket, New Bedford and other New England areas dance precariously on her yardarm, while from the top of her foremast a lookout scans the North Atlantic for the first flash of white canvas on the horizon.

Named for the written commitment of the United States Government and designed by the noted Joshua Humphreys, *USS Constitution* was constructed under the supervision of George Claghorn, incorporating the best features of the French and English ships.

Her design, a large ship of 44 guns, was boldly conceived to be more than a match for her enemies. Building was started in 1794 and the document approving her construction was signed by George Washington.

At that early period she was an expensive ship and money for her construction was granted reluctantly. When she slid down the ways, *Constitution* had cost the American people a reported $302,718.84, including her guns and equipment.

Stem to stern she was hand-fashioned by craftsmen devoted to their task and their nations purpose. From the Boston shop of Paul Revere came the bolts that fastened her heavy timbers as well as the copper for her solid oak sides and bottom. The timbers themselves, consisting of live oak, red cedar, white oak, pitch pine and locust, came from states ranging from Maine to South Carolina.

As construction progressed, *Constitution* became a noble ship, proudly built with the tallest spars that had ever been raised on a vessel of her class. Just over 200 feet long, she required a crew of more than 400 men whose duties were as specialized then as those who served the Navy today. *USS Constitution* was never to taste defeat.

During one battle with the British ship *Guerriere* in the War of 1812, a legend resulted. On August 19th the sleek *Constitution* sighted *Guerriere*, a larger ship, and Captain Isaac Hull waited amidst the Britisher's shots until point blank range. The sight of shot bouncing off the *Constitution*'s side prompted a *Guerriere* sailor to shout, "Huzza, her sides are made of iron!"

And thus, *Constitution* was christened with the renowned title, *"Old Ironsides."* Oliver Wendell Holmes wrote about her in 1830, and his stirring poem helped save her for posterity.

The battle with *Guerriere*, which lasted only 30 minutes, fired our young nation with confidence and courage. *Guerriere* was a larger ship with more guns, but *"Old Ironsides"* was more maneuverable, and this historic battle left the Britisher a helpless hulk that had to be destroyed. So many of these battles were repeated by *Constitution* that the British finally had to order its ships not to attack these new frigates on a one-to-one basis.

She is a proud old warrior with an impressive record. Nearly all of her battles have been the basis for which the United States has become "a first-class power on the high seas." As the product of men not machines, her decks were never trod by an enemy. No flag but the Stars and Stripes ever flew from her halyards. Honor and triumph marked all her encounters.

After many years of battles and victory after victory, the old veteran gave way to progress during the Civil War when the sailing frigate made room for the steam-propelled *Monitor*.

With her battle days over, *Constitution* was used as a training ship, carrying goods from the United States to the Universal Exposition in Paris, touring important seaports and finally earning her well-deserved rest.

Today the black-hulled, 2,250-ton *USS Constitution* stands alone at Pier One in the Boston Naval Shipyard, a mile from where she was launched over 150 years ago.

The tall spars and sleek Yankee lines of *"Old Ironsides"* cast morning shadows on the water, while later in the day the bright noon day sun shines on her spotless decks and taut rigging. She welcomes the close of day when the sun drops below the horizon and signals time for the late visitor, representative of some 500,000 people who visit her yearly, to leave the ship. Finally, except for her tall spars, she is cloaked in darkness, silhouetted against Boston's glowing sky.

She carries America back in spirit to a time when, alone, she uplifted the hearts of Americans and stirred them into renewed belief in their cause and the secure future of the Nation.

THE CAPTAIN

ABLE SEAMAN

THE MARINE

THE SAILING MASTER

A SENIOR WARRANT OFFICER RESPONSIBLE FOR NAVIGATION

THE MASTER AT ARMS

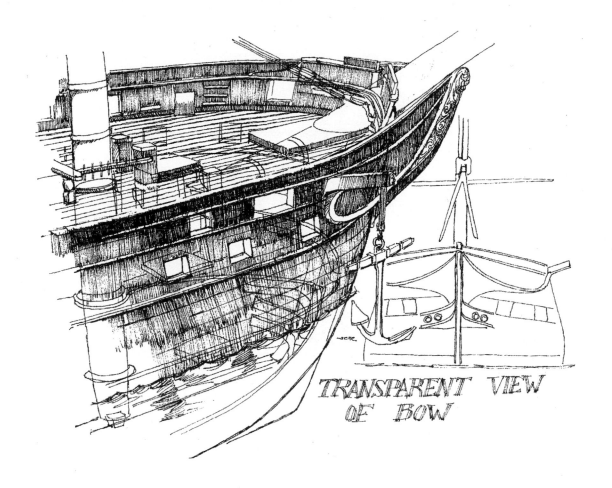

TRANSPARENT VIEW
OF BOW

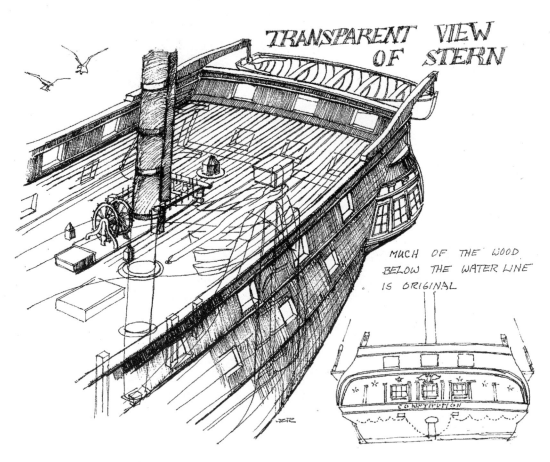

TRANSPARENT VIEW
OF STERN

MUCH OF THE WOOD
BELOW THE WATER LINE
IS ORIGINAL

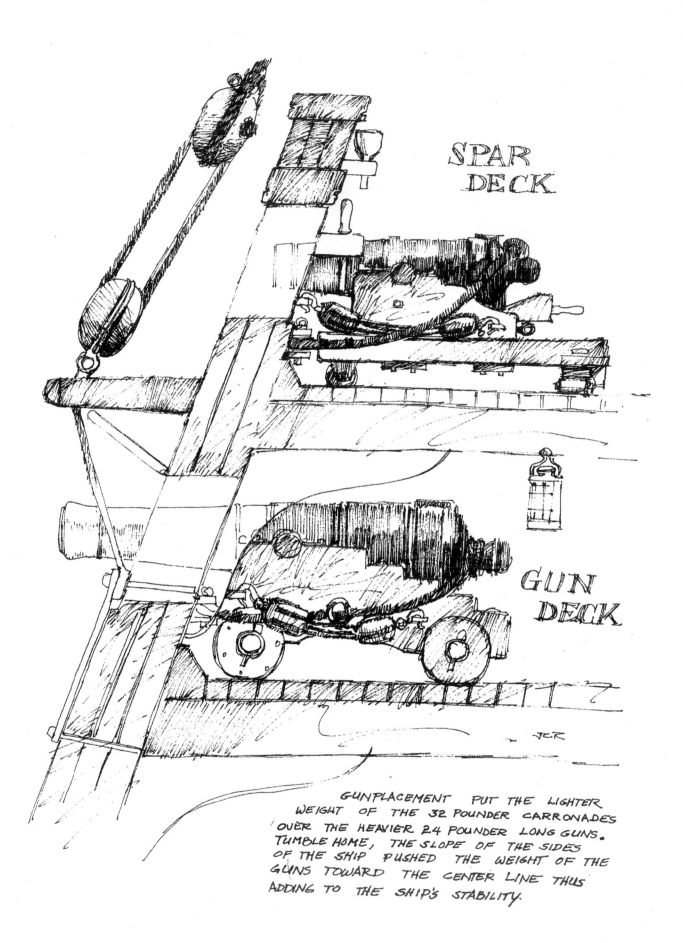

SPAR
DECK

GUN
DECK

GUNPLACEMENT PUT THE LIGHTER
WEIGHT OF THE 32 POUNDER CARRONADES
OVER THE HEAVIER 24 POUNDER LONG GUNS.
TUMBLE HOME, THE SLOPE OF THE SIDES
OF THE SHIP PUSHED THE WEIGHT OF THE
GUNS TOWARD THE CENTER LINE THUS
ADDING TO THE SHIP'S STABILITY.

SPAR DECK

AMERICAN 24-POUNDER GUN

WEIGHT, ABOUT 6,500 POUNDS
POWDER CHARGE, 8 LBS.
MAXIMUM RANGE, ABOUT 1,500 YARDS
(ACCURATE TO 300-400 YARDS)

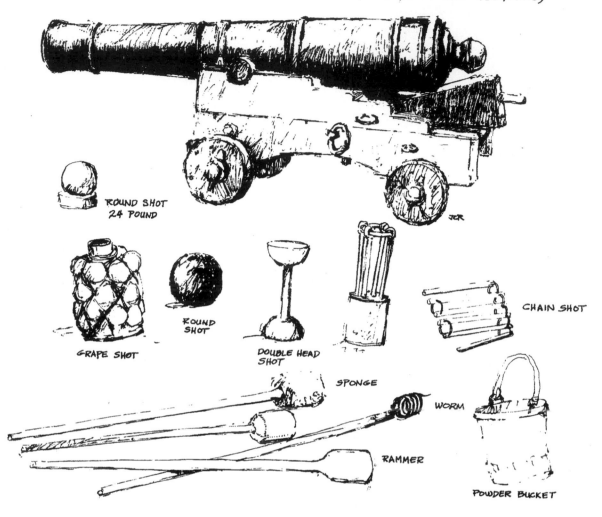

ROUND SHOT
24 POUND

GRAPE SHOT

ROUND
SHOT

DOUBLE HEAD
SHOT

CHAIN SHOT

SPONGE

WORM

RAMMER

POWDER BUCKET

SLOW MATCH TO IGNITE THE POWDER TRAIN
WAS MADE FROM SMALL LINE, SOAKED IN LYE
SOLUTION OR BOILED IN THE DRESS OF WINE.
THE LINSTOCK WAS A STICK, ABOUT 2 FEET LONG,
WITH A CLEFT END INTO WHICH A PIECE OF
MATCH WAS WEDGED.

MAGAZINES WERE DEEP IN THE SHIP BELOW THE WATERLINE.
THE GUN POWDER WAS STORED IN WOODEN CASKS. YOUNG LADS
RUSHED POWDER CHARGES TO THE GUNS ABOVE DECKS.
THESE YOUNG BOYS WERE CALLED POWDER MONKEYS.

HEATING POTS
HUNG THROUGHOUT
THE SHIP. THE SOURCE
OF HEAT WAS EITHER
CHARCOAL OR A CANNON
BALL HEATED TO A RED
HOT ON THE GALLEY
RANGE.

24 POUNDER

CONSTITUTION CARRIED 30 24-POUNDER LONG GUNS. THIS GUN COULD FIRE A 24 POUND SOLID SHOT ABOUT 1200 YARDS, AND COULD PENETRATE AT A LESSER RANGE OF 1000 YARDS A SHOT COULD PENETRATE ABOUT 20 INCHES OF HARD WOOD EACH GUN WEIGHS MORE THAN 3 TONS AND REQUIRED A GUN CREW OF FROM 9 TO 14 MEN THESE CREWS GAVE THEIR GUNS NAMES SUCH AS "REVENGE" OR "DEFIANCE". OF THE 30 24-POUNDERS ONBOARD THE SHIP 18 GUNS ARE OF BRITISH MANUFACTURE, BOUGHT FROM ENGLAND BECAUSE OF THIS COUNTRYS INABILITY TO MANUFACTURE ENOUGH CANNONS QUICKLY TO SUPPLY THE BUILDING OF OUR NAVY.

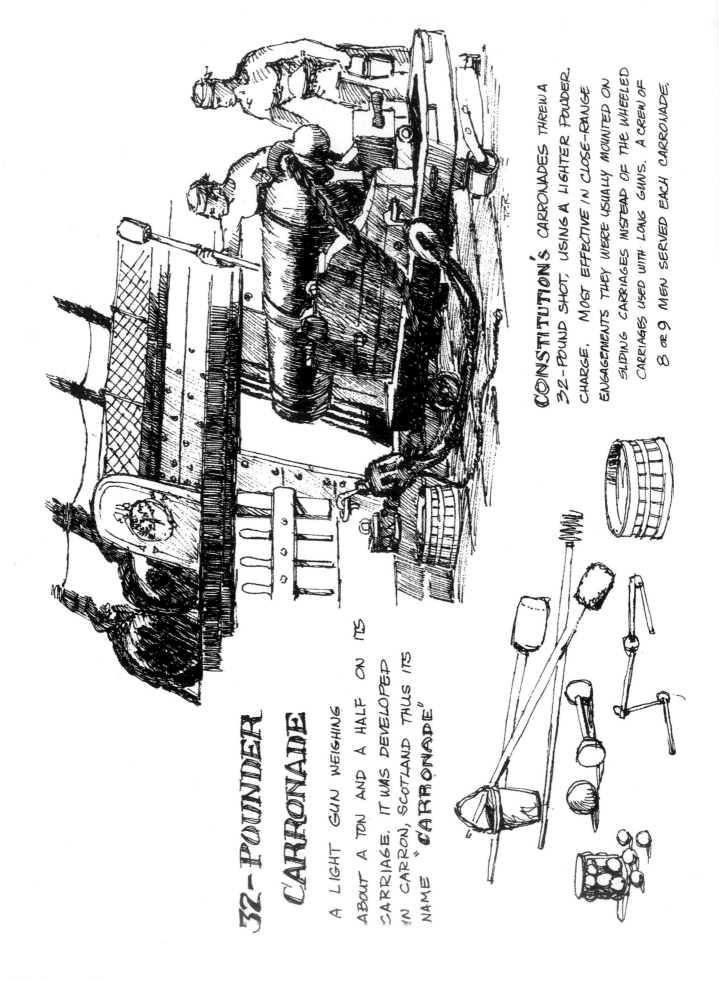

32-POUNDER CARRONADE

A LIGHT GUN WEIGHING ABOUT A TON AND A HALF ON ITS CARRIAGE. IT WAS DEVELOPED IN CARRON, SCOTLAND THUS ITS NAME "CARRONADE"

CONSTITUTION'S CARRONADES THREW A 32-POUND SHOT, USING A LIGHTER POWDER CHARGE. MOST EFFECTIVE IN CLOSE-RANGE ENGAGEMENTS THEY WERE USUALLY MOUNTED ON SLIDING CARRIAGES INSTEAD OF THE WHEELED CARRIAGES USED WITH LONG GUNS. A CREW OF 8 OR 9 MEN SERVED EACH CARRONADE,

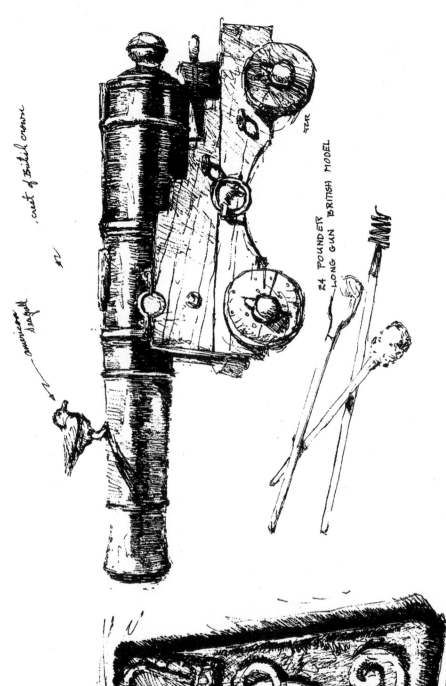

.crest of British crown

american seagull

24 POUNDER
LONG GUN BRITISH MODEL

MUCH OF THE ARMAMENT CARRIED ON BOARD CONSTITUTION WAS MANUFACTURED IN ENGLAND AND SOLD TO THE UNITED STATES DURING A MORE FRIENDLY PERIOD. DURING THE WAR OF 1812 THESE GUNS HAD TELLING EFFECT ON THEIR MAKERS.

TO FIRE A GUN REQUIRED THE SPONGE TO KILL ANY HOT SPARKS LODGED INSIDE THE BARREL. NEXT A CHARGE OF POWDER, IN ITS CLOTH BAG, WAS RAMMED IN, THE SHOT AND WAD FOLLOWED. A PRIMING TUBE--A LENGTH OF QUILL, FILLED WITH FINE POWDER AND TOPPED BY A BIT OF QUICKMATCH-- WAS INSERTED IN THE VENT HOLE. TOUCHED BY A BURNING SLOW MATCH, IT IGNITED AND SET OFF THE POWDER CHARGE. IN CASE OF MISFIRE, THE SHOT WAS ALLOWED TO ROLL OUT THE MUZZLE, AND THE WORM WAS USED TO PULL OUT THE POWDER BAG, A DANGEROUS TASK IF THE GUN WAS ALREADY VERY HOT.

ROYAL CREST CAST INTO BRITISH MADE GUNS USED ON THE FRIGATE CONSTITUTION

BRITISH GUNS
ON CONSTITUTION

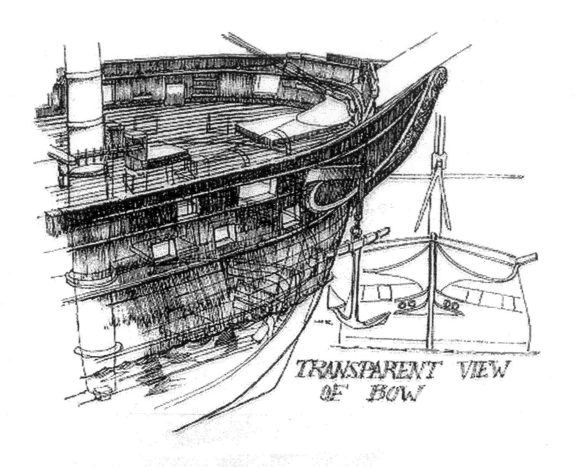

TRANSPARENT VIEW
OF BOW

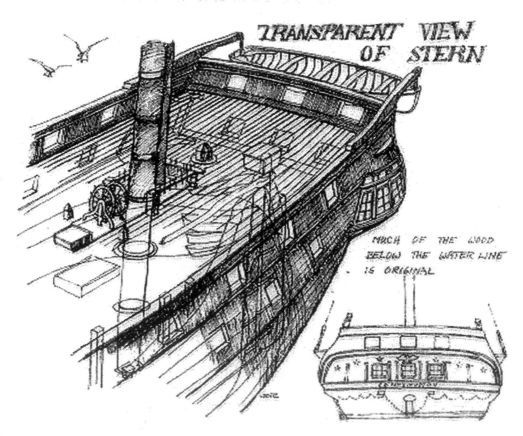

TRANSPARENT VIEW
OF STERN

MUCH OF THE WOOD
BELOW THE WATER LINE
IS ORIGINAL

GROG & SCUTTLEBUTT ON THE GUN DECK

WATER BARREL AND GROG TUB

GROG, A MIXTURE OF RUM OR WHISKEY & WATER SERVED TO THE CREW TWICE A DAY.

SCUTTLEBUTT, THE BUTT IS A KIND OF BARREL AND THE SCUTTLE IS A SMALL HATCH THROUGH WHICH SOMETHING IS PASSED. THE AREA ABOUT THE SCUTTLEBUTT, THE CREW'S SOURCE OF DRINKING WATER, WAS A NATURAL GATHERING PLACE FOR THE CREW TO JOKE AND EXCHANGE RUMORS AND GOSSIP, THUS SUCH TALK BECAME KNOWN AS SCUTTLEBUTT. THE TERM IS STILL USED IN THE MODERN NAVY IN THIS SENSE, AS WELL AS TO REFER TO DRINKING FOUNTAINS.

CAPTAIN'S DAY CABIN &
AFTER CABIN CONSTITUTION OFTEN SERVED AS A FLAGSHIP.
SMALLER CABINS TO EACH SIDE OF THIS ONE WERE FOR THE COMMODORE
AND CAPTAIN. THE DESK SEEN HERE BELONGED TO CHARLES STEWART
WHO COMMANDED CONSTITUTION WHEN SHE DEFEATED THE BRITISH
WARSHIPS CYANE AND LEVANT 6'N FEBRUARY 20TH, 1815.

QUARTER DECK WATCH
OFFICERS AND MEN AT THEIR
STATIONS BY THE SHIP'S HELM IS THE SAILING MASTER, A
STAFF OFFICER, RESPONSIBLE FOR TAKING THE
SHIP WHEREVER THE CAPTAIN ORDERS. ON THE HIGH SIDE
OR WINDWARD THE SENIOR HELMSMAN WOULD STAND ASSISTED
BY ANOTHER MAN ON THE OTHER SIDE. THE COMPASSES ARE IN
TWO BINNACLES FORWARD OF THE SHIPS WHEEL.

OFFICER COUNTRY

OFFICERS' STATEROOMS

THE ABOVE STATEROOMS WERE FOR THE WARRANT OFFICERS, BOATSWAIN, GUNNER, CARPENTER ETC.

THESE MEN WERE THE WORKING TECHNICAL EXPERTS RESPONSIBLE FOR THE MATERIAL WELL BEING OF THE SHIP. THE STATEROOM WITH THE OPEN DOOR IS THE SUPPLY OFFICE, WHERE THE PURSER DID HIS PAPER WORK ON A STANDUP DESK. BY FOLDING OUT THE TOP A BUNK WAS FORMED.

THIS IS AN EXAMPLE OF THE COMMISSIONED OFFICERS' STATEROOMS. HEAT WAS PROVIDED BY A PRE HEATED CANNON BALL HUNG IN A BUCKET FROM THE OVER HEAD.

OFFICER'S PANTRY

THE SQUARE HATCH IN THE PANTRY LEADS TO THE BREAD LOCKER BELOW.

ABOVE IS THE RUDDER TILLER WHICH ONE HAD TO DUCK WHILE WORKING IN THIS SPACE. THE BUCKET HELD A HEATED CANNON BALL USED TO TAKE THE CHILL OUT OF THE AIR

WARDROOM

EXCEPT FOR THE COMMODORE & THE CAPTAIN ALL OFFICERS TOOK THEIR MEALS IN THE WARDROOM AREA. IT'S A RATHER DARK AND CLOSE SPACE SO MOST OFTEN AFTER MEALS THE OFFICERS WOULD RETIRE TO THE OPENNESS OF THE GUNDECK ABOVE.

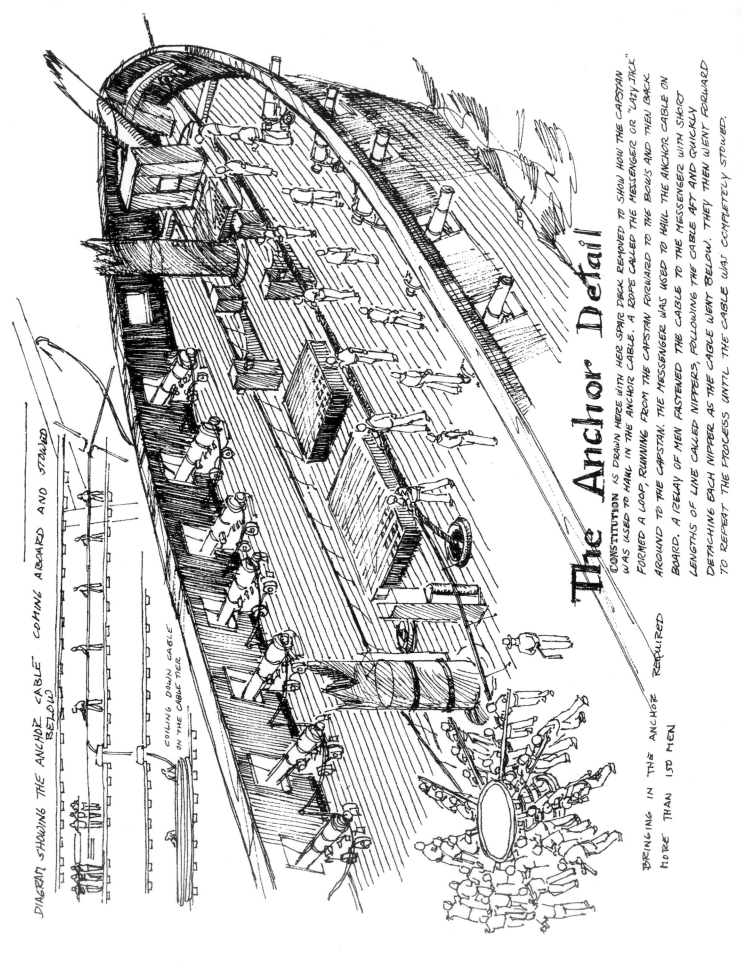

The Anchor Detail

CONSTITUTION IS DRAWN HERE WITH HER SPAR DECK REMOVED TO SHOW HOW THE CAPSTAN WAS USED TO HAUL IN THE ANCHOR CABLE. A ROPE CALLED THE MESSENGER OR "LAZY-JACK" FORMED A LOOP, RUNNING FROM THE CAPSTAN FORWARD TO THE BOWS AND THEN BACK AROUND TO THE CAPSTAN. THE MESSENGER WAS USED TO HAUL THE ANCHOR CABLE ON BOARD. A RELAY OF MEN FASTENED THE CABLE TO THE MESSENGER WITH SHORT LENGTHS OF LINE CALLED NIPPERS, FOLLOWING THE CABLE AFT AND QUICKLY DETACHING EACH NIPPER AS THE CABLE WENT BELOW. THEY THEN WENT FORWARD TO REPEAT THE PROCESS UNTIL THE CABLE WAS COMPLETELY STOWED.

BRINGING IN THE ANCHOR REQUIRED MORE THAN 150 MEN

DIAGRAM SHOWING THE ANCHOR CABLE COMING ABOARD AND STOWED BELOW

COILING DOWN CABLE ON THE CABLE TIER

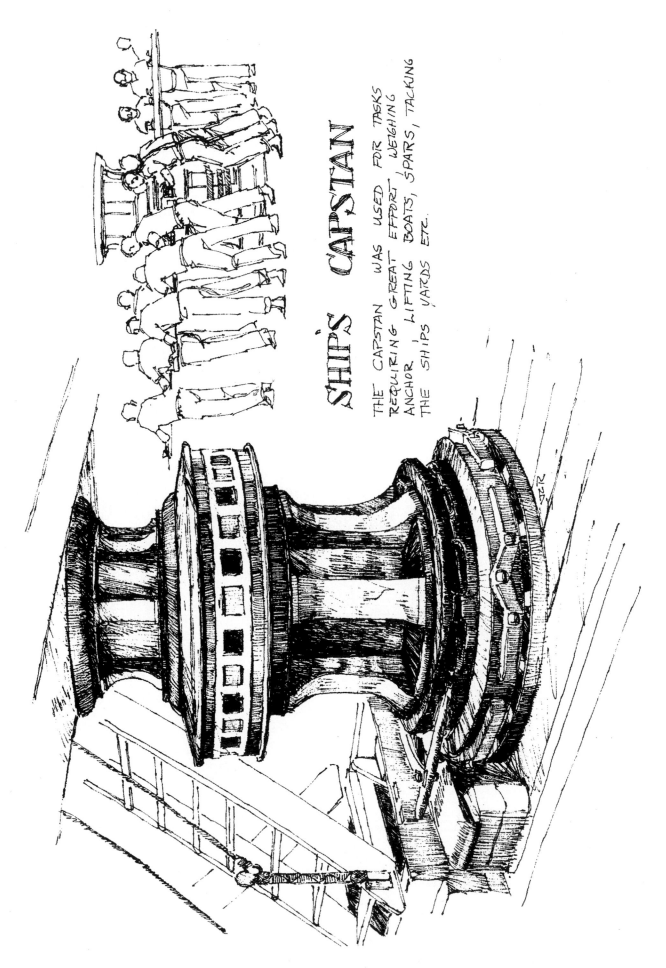

SHIP'S CAPSTAN

THE CAPSTAN WAS USED FOR TASKS REQUIRING GREAT EFFORT. WEIGHING ANCHOR, LIFTING BOATS, SPARS, TACKING THE SHIP'S YARDS ETC.

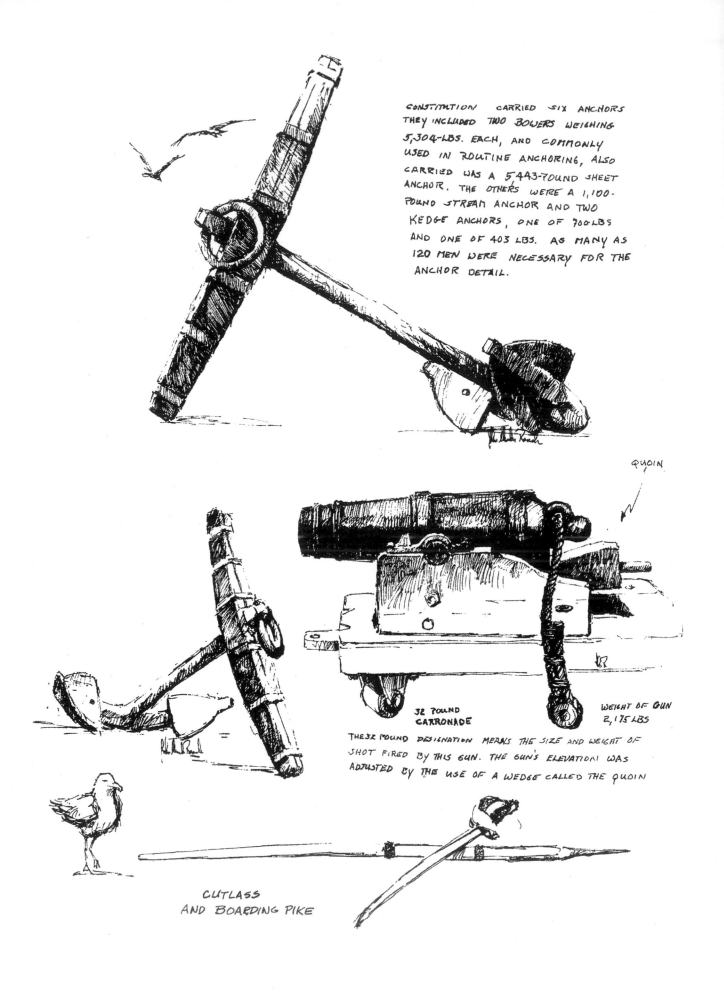

CONSTITUTION CARRIED SIX ANCHORS
THEY INCLUDED TWO BOWERS WEIGHING
5,304-LBS. EACH, AND COMMONLY
USED IN ROUTINE ANCHORING, ALSO
CARRIED WAS A 5,443-POUND SHEET
ANCHOR. THE OTHERS WERE A 1,100-
POUND STREAM ANCHOR AND TWO
KEDGE ANCHORS, ONE OF 700 LBS
AND ONE OF 403 LBS. AS MANY AS
120 MEN WERE NECESSARY FOR THE
ANCHOR DETAIL.

QUOIN

32 POUND
CARRONADE

WEIGHT OF GUN
2,175 LBS

THE 32 POUND DESIGNATION MEANS THE SIZE AND WEIGHT OF
SHOT FIRED BY THIS GUN. THE GUN'S ELEVATION WAS
ADJUSTED BY THE USE OF A WEDGE CALLED THE QUOIN

CUTLASS
AND BOARDING PIKE

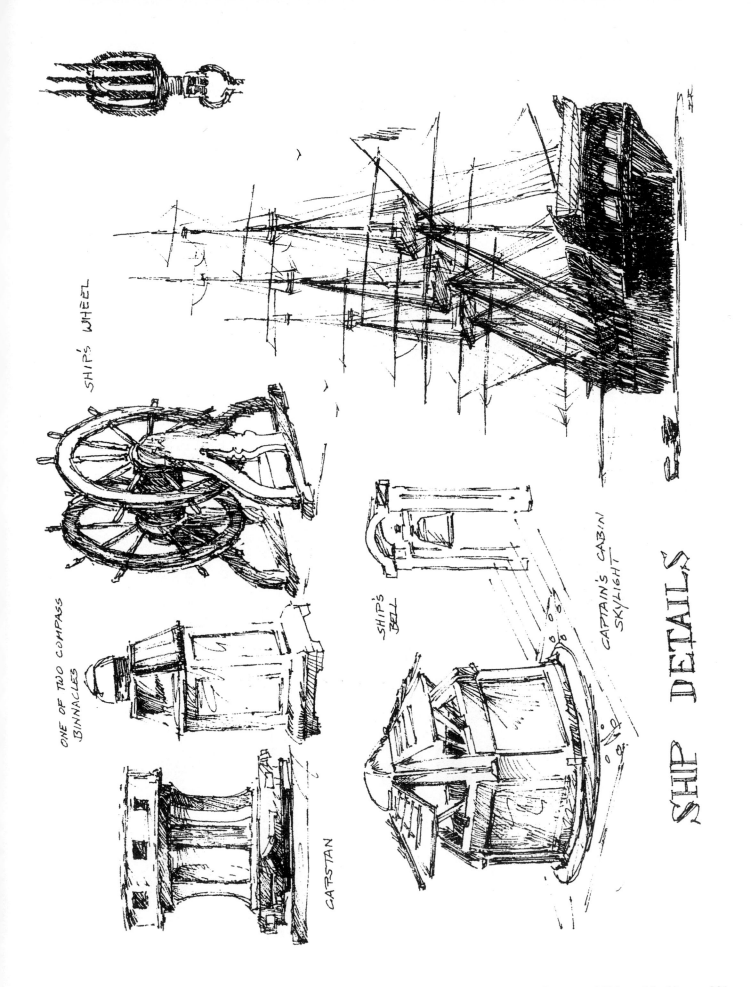

SHIP'S WHEEL

ONE OF TWO COMPASS BINNACLES

CAPSTAN

SHIP'S BELL

CAPTAIN'S CABIN SKYLIGHT

SHIP DETAILS

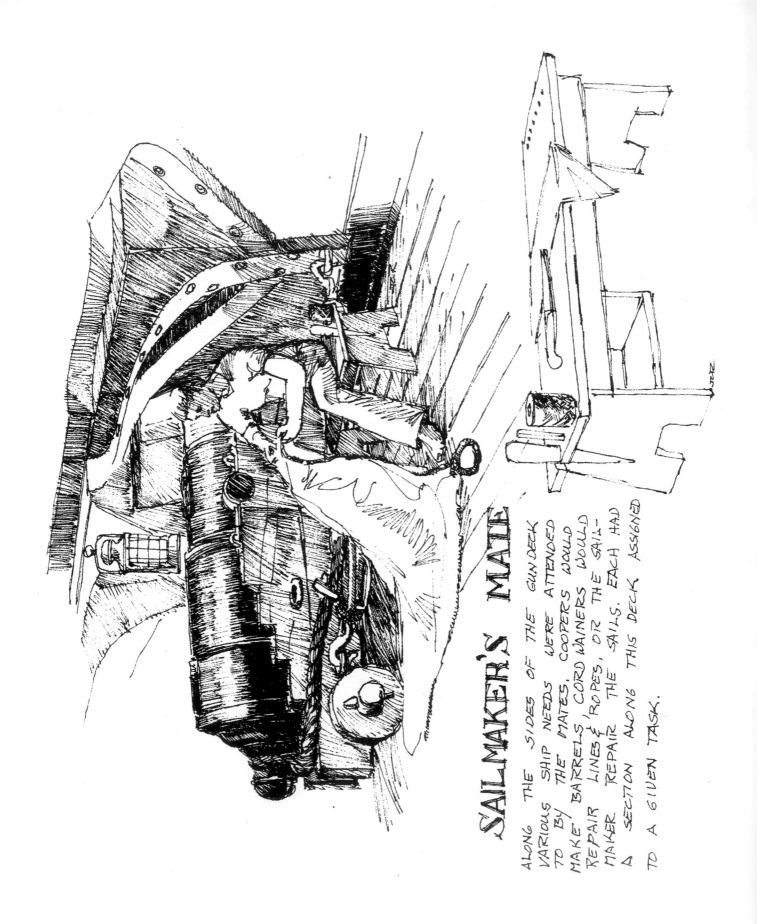

SAILMAKER'S MATE

ALONG THE SIDES OF THE GUN DECK
VARIOUS SHIP NEEDS WERE ATTENDED
TO BY THE MATES. COOPERS WOULD
MAKE BARRELS, CORD WAINERS WOULD
REPAIR LINES & ROPES, OR THE SAIL-
MAKER REPAIR THE SAILS. EACH HAD
A SECTION ALONG THIS DECK ASSIGNED
TO A GIVEN TASK.

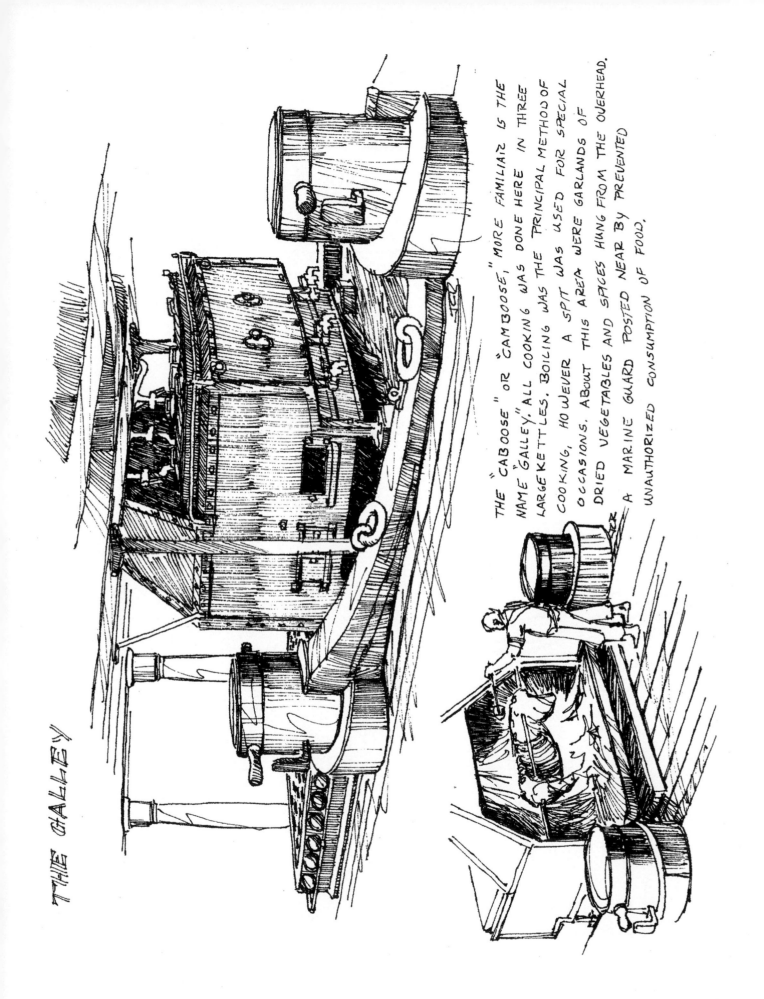

THE GALLEY

THE "CABOOSE" OR "CAMBOOSE," MORE FAMILIAR IS THE NAME "GALLEY." ALL COOKING WAS DONE HERE IN THREE LARGE KETTLES. BOILING WAS THE PRINCIPAL METHOD OF COOKING, HOWEVER A SPIT WAS USED FOR SPECIAL OCCASIONS. ABOUT THIS AREA WERE GARLANDS OF DRIED VEGETABLES AND SPICES HUNG FROM THE OVERHEAD. A MARINE GUARD POSTED NEAR BY PREVENTED UNAUTHORIZED CONSUMPTION OF FOOD.

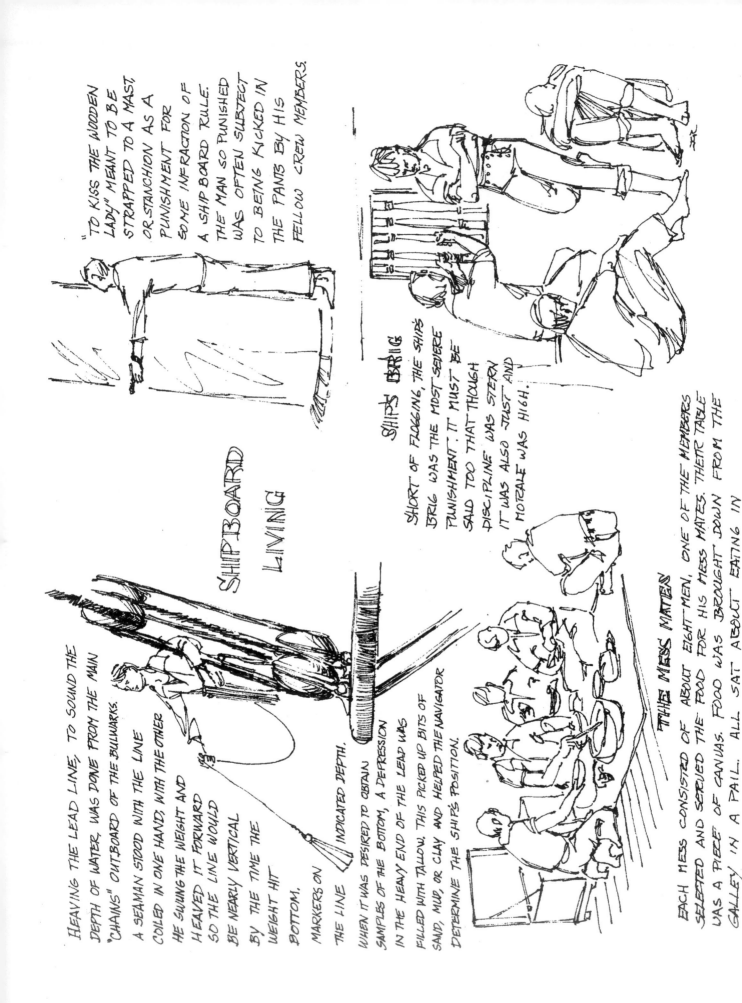

"TO KISS THE WOODEN LADY" MEANT TO BE STRAPPED TO A MAST, OR STANCHION AS A PUNISHMENT FOR SOME INFRACTION OF A SHIP BOARD RULE. THE MAN SO PUNISHED WAS OFTEN SUBJECT TO BEING KICKED IN THE PANTS BY HIS FELLOW CREW MEMBERS.

SHIPS BRIG

SHORT OF FLOGGING, THE SHIPS BRIG WAS THE MOST SEVERE PUNISHMENT. IT MUST BE SAID TOO THAT THOUGH DISCIPLINE WAS STERN IT WAS ALSO JUST AND MORALE WAS HIGH.

SHIPBOARD LIVING

HEAVING THE LEAD LINE, TO SOUND THE DEPTH OF WATER, WAS DONE FROM THE MAIN "CHAINS" OUTBOARD OF THE BULWARKS.

A SEAMAN STOOD WITH THE LINE COILED IN ONE HAND WITH THE OTHER HE SWUNG THE WEIGHT AND HEAVED IT FORWARD SO THE LINE WOULD BE NEARLY VERTICAL BY THE TIME THE WEIGHT HIT BOTTOM.

MARKERS ON THE LINE INDICATED DEPTH.

WHEN IT WAS DESIRED TO OBTAIN SAMPLES OF THE BOTTOM, A DEPRESSION IN THE HEAVY END OF THE LEAD WAS FILLED WITH TALLOW. THIS PICKED UP BITS OF SAND, MUD, OR CLAY AND HELPED THE NAVIGATOR DETERMINE THE SHIP'S POSITION.

THE MESS MATES

EACH MESS CONSISTED OF ABOUT EIGHT MEN, ONE OF THE MEMBERS SELECTED AND SERVED THE FOOD FOR HIS MESS MATES. THEIR TABLE WAS A PIECE OF CANVAS. FOOD WAS BROUGHT DOWN FROM THE GALLEY IN A PAIL. ALL SAT ABOUT EATING IN PICNIC FASHION.

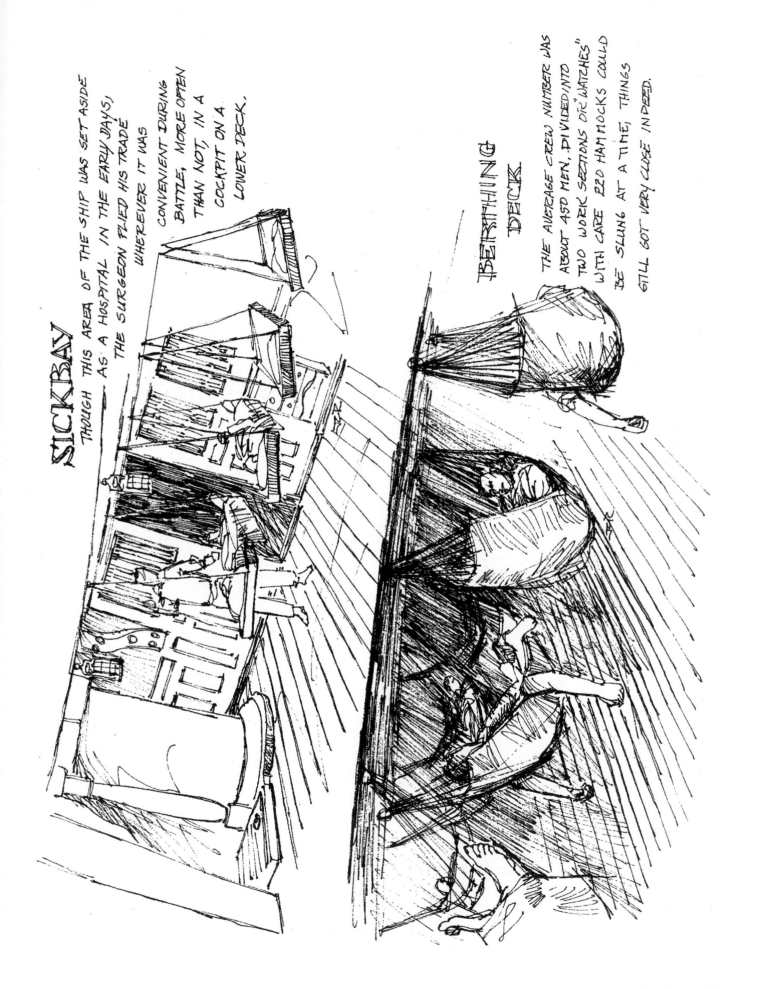

SICKBAY

THOUGH THIS AREA OF THE SHIP WAS SET ASIDE AS A HOSPITAL IN THE EARLY DAYS, THE SURGEON PLIED HIS TRADE WHEREVER IT WAS CONVENIENT. DURING BATTLE, MORE OFTEN THAN NOT, IN A COCKPIT ON A LOWER DECK.

BERTHING DECK

THE AVERAGE CREW NUMBER WAS ABOUT 450 MEN. DIVIDED INTO TWO WORK SECTIONS OR "WATCHES" WITH CARE 220 HAMMOCKS COULD BE SLUNG AT A TIME, THINGS STILL GOT VERY CLOSE INDEED.

THE 8 MAN BILGE PUMP

JUST ABAFT THE MAINMAST THE BILGE PUMP IS PLACED OVER THE DEEPEST POINT OF THE SHIP. WATER WAS PUMPED OUT OF THE BILGES BY MEN WORKING THE PUMP HANDLES. BILGE WATER WAS THEN ALLOWED TO FLOW ACROSS THE DECK AND OUT THE SCUPPERS. IT HELPED KEEP THE DECK MOIST AND PREVENTED THE DECK FROM SPLITTING.

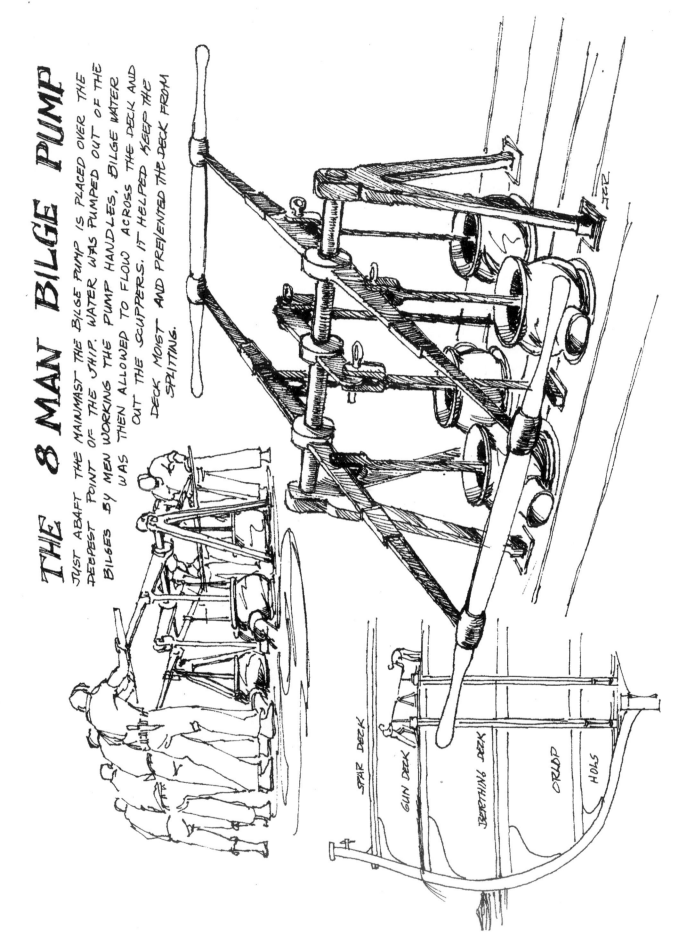

SPAR DECK

GUN DECK

BERTHING DECK

ORLOP

HOLD

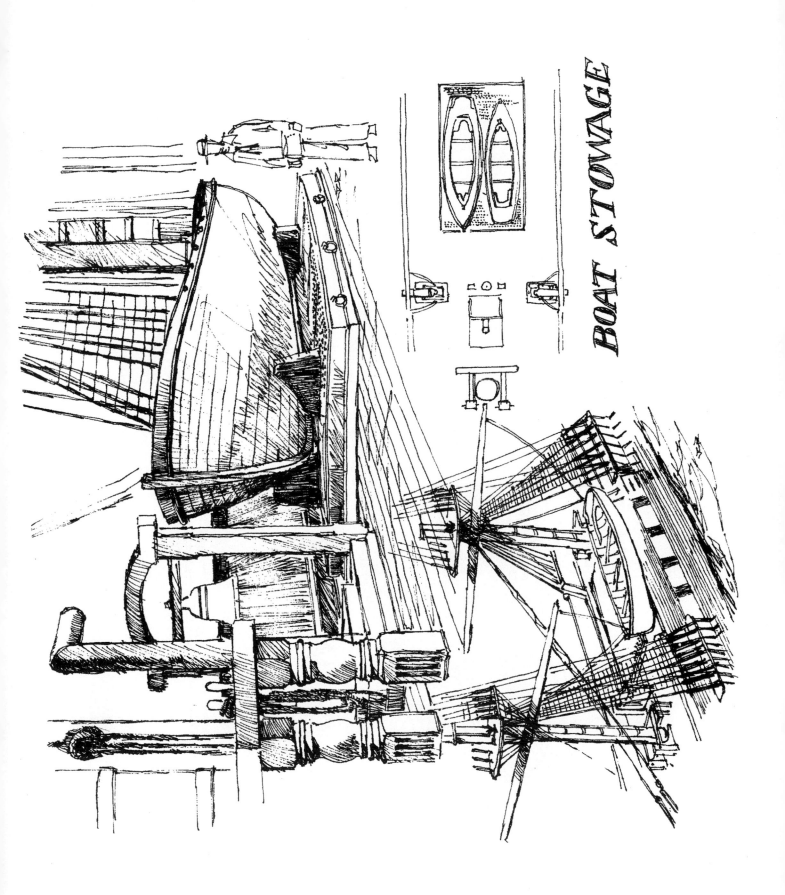

BOAT STOWAGE

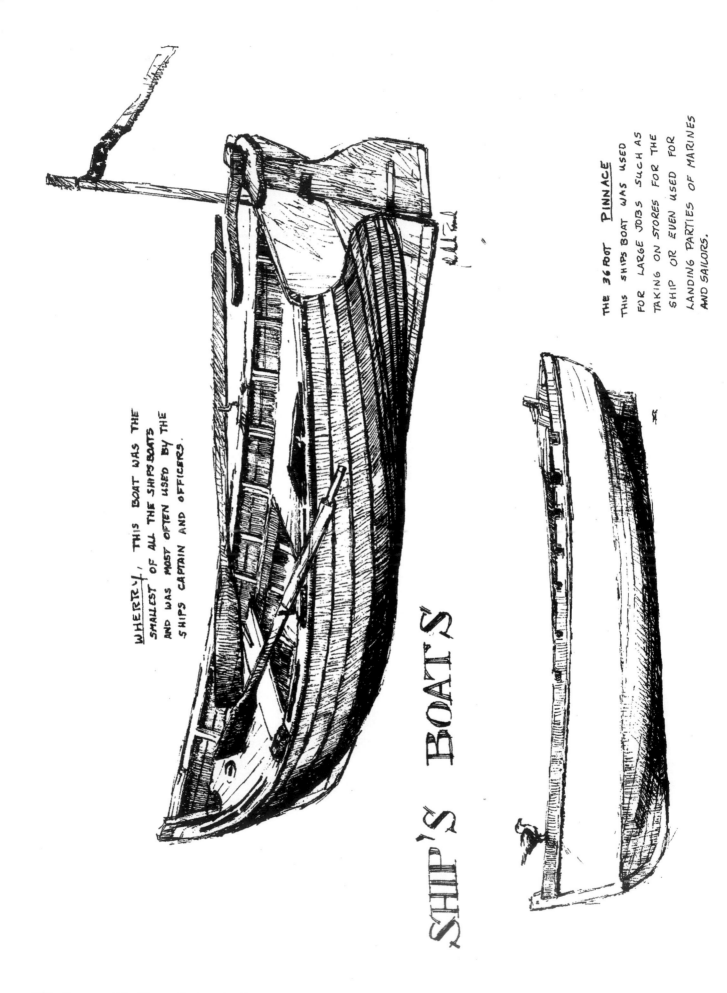

WHERRY, THIS BOAT WAS THE SMALLEST OF ALL THE SHIPS BOATS AND WAS MOST OFTEN USED BY THE SHIPS CAPTAIN AND OFFICERS.

THE 36 FOOT PINNACE
THIS SHIPS BOAT WAS USED FOR LARGE JOBS SUCH AS TAKING ON STORES FOR THE SHIP OR EVEN USED FOR LANDING PARTIES OF MARINES AND SAILORS.

SHIP'S BOATS

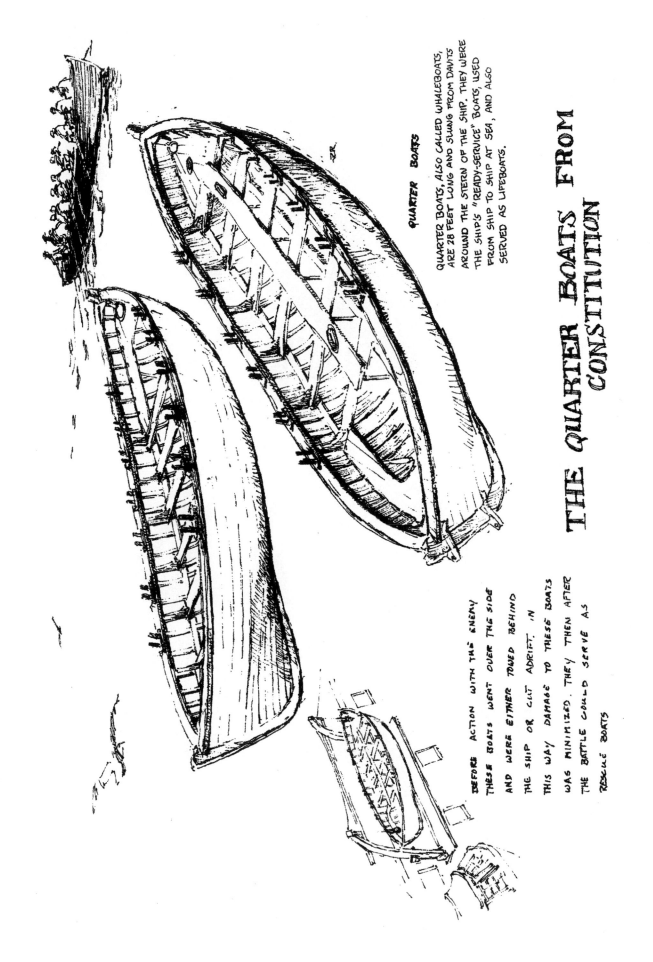

QUARTER BOATS

QUARTER BOATS, ALSO CALLED WHALEBOATS, ARE 28 FEET LONG AND SLUNG FROM DAVITS AROUND THE STERN OF THE SHIP. THEY WERE THE SHIP'S "READY-SERVICE" BOATS, USED FROM SHIP TO SHIP AT SEA, AND ALSO SERVED AS LIFEBOATS.

THE QUARTER BOATS FROM *CONSTITUTION*

BEFORE ACTION WITH THE ENEMY THESE BOATS WENT OVER THE SIDE AND WERE EITHER TOWED BEHIND THE SHIP OR CUT ADRIFT. IN THIS WAY DAMAGE TO THESE BOATS WAS MINIMIZED. THEY THEN AFTER THE BATTLE COULD SERVE AS RESCUE BOATS

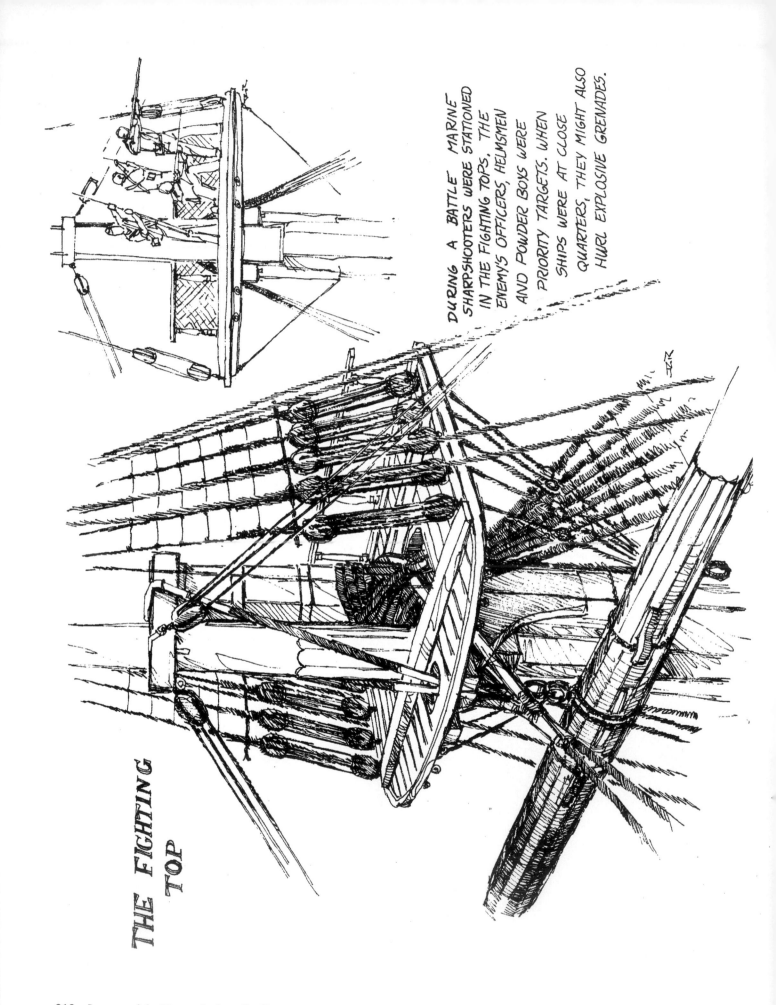

DURING A BATTLE MARINE SHARPSHOOTERS WERE STATIONED IN THE FIGHTING TOPS. THE ENEMY'S OFFICERS, HELMSMEN AND POWDER BOYS WERE PRIORITY TARGETS. WHEN SHIPS WERE AT CLOSE QUARTERS, THEY MIGHT ALSO HURL EXPLOSIVE GRENADES.

THE FIGHTING TOP

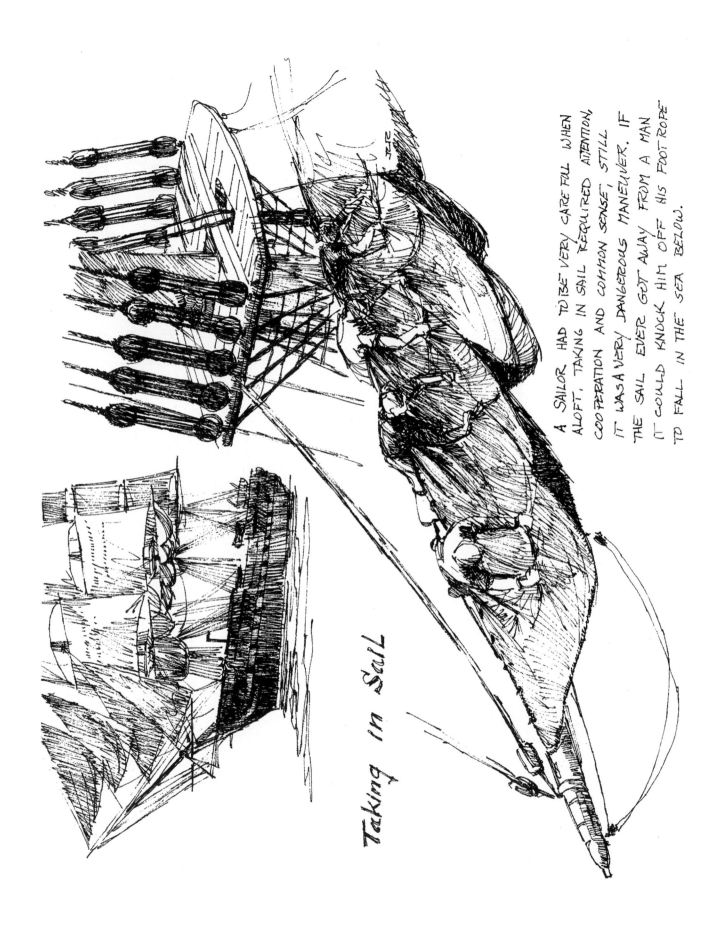

Taking In Sail

A SAILOR HAD TO BE VERY CAREFUL WHEN ALOFT, TAKING IN SAIL REQUIRED ATTENTION, COOPERATION AND COMMON SENSE, STILL IT WAS A VERY DANGEROUS MANEUVER. IF THE SAIL EVER GOT AWAY FROM A MAN IT COULD KNOCK HIM OFF HIS FOOT ROPE TO FALL IN THE SEA BELOW.

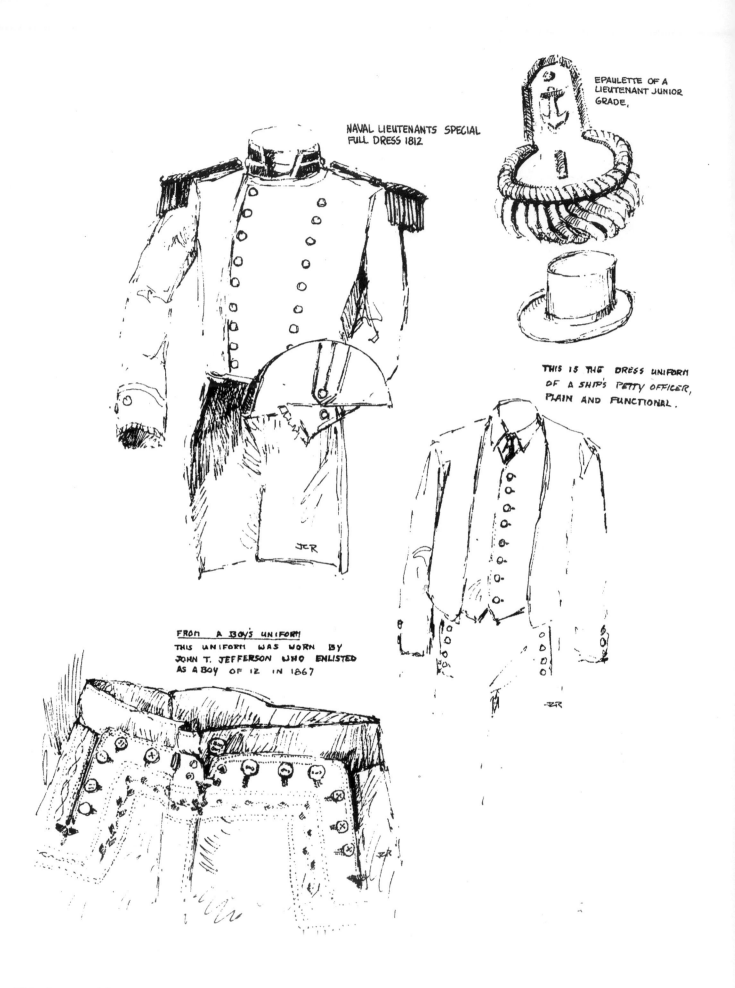

NAVAL LIEUTENANTS SPECIAL
FULL DRESS 1812

EPAULETTE OF A
LIEUTENANT JUNIOR
GRADE.

THIS IS THE DRESS UNIFORM
OF A SHIP'S PETTY OFFICER,
PLAIN AND FUNCTIONAL.

FROM A BOY'S UNIFORM
THIS UNIFORM WAS WORN BY
JOHN T. JEFFERSON WHO ENLISTED
AS A BOY OF 12 IN 1867

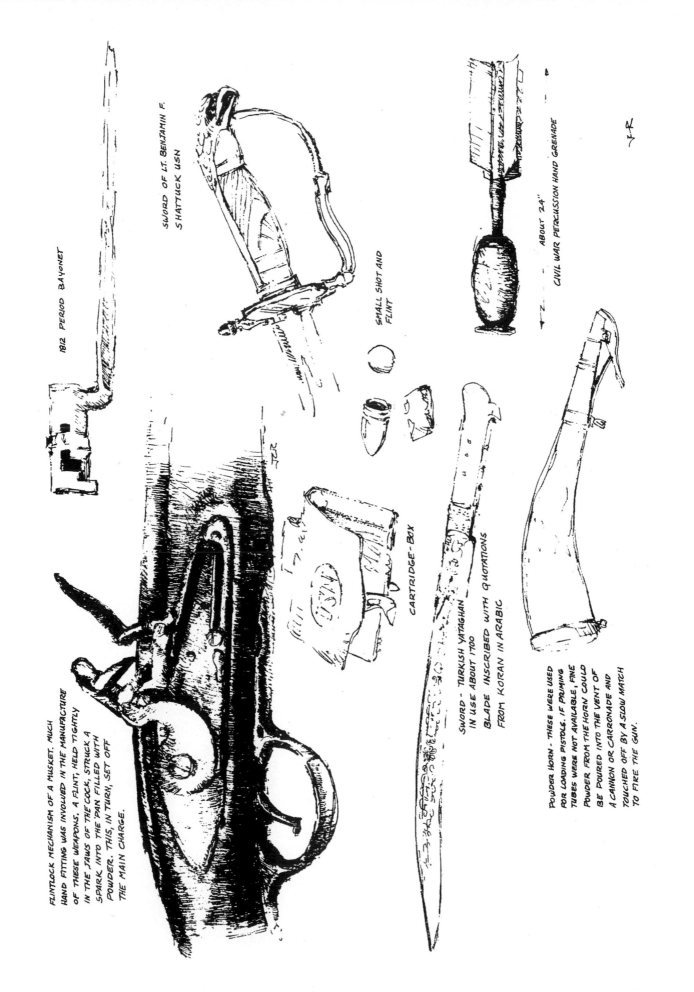

1812 PERIOD BAYONET

SWORD OF LT. BENJAMIN F. SHATTUCK USN

SMALL SHOT AND FLINT

ABOUT 24"

CIVIL WAR PERCUSSION HAND GRENADE

FLINTLOCK MECHANISM OF A MUSKET. MUCH HAND FITTING WAS INVOLVED IN THE MANUFACTURE OF THESE WEAPONS. A FLINT, HELD TIGHTLY IN THE JAWS OF THE COCK, STRUCK A SPARK INTO THE PAN FILLED WITH POWDER. THIS, IN TURN, SET OFF THE MAIN CHARGE.

CARTRIDGE - BOX

SWORD - TURKISH YATAGHAN IN USE ABOUT 1700 BLADE INSCRIBED WITH QUOTATIONS FROM KORAN IN ARABIC

POWDER HORN - THESE WERE USED FOR LOADING PISTOLS. IF PRIMING TUBES WERE NOT AVAILABLE, FINE POWDER FROM THE HORN COULD BE POURED INTO THE VENT OF A CANNON OR CARRONADE AND TOUCHED OFF BY A SLOW MATCH TO FIRE THE GUN.

A Brief History of the English Language
Placing American English in Perspective

As we know, this book deals with the use of nautical words and phrases in our everyday language. However, it is important to place vocabulary growth into perspective by having the answers to questions about our language and its origin. More specifically, how did the English tongue evolve and how does it relate to other languages? In addition, how did it spawn an American English that has created an enormous world of its own?

In order to answer these questions and to fully understand words in English or any language, it is important to know about certain elements of history. According to a number of sources, it is believed that English is a member of the Indo-European family of languages, whose roots sprang about 8,000 years ago in the vicinity of the Black Sea. As a result of geographic dispersion, this mass split into a number of subgroups, which now represent almost all of the languages of Europe and large parts of the Middle East and northern India. Among the subgroups was one that included Slavic (Russian, Polish, Serbo-Croat), Baltic (Latvia and Lithuania) and Celtic (Welsh, Gaelic and Greek) languages.

Two groups were of critical importance to the development of English. The first was the Romance languages that included classical Latin, French, Italian, Spanish and Portuguese and Rumanian. The second of these, the Germanic group, is the one to which English is directly connected. A common Germanic speech community existed about 3000 years ago, and it is believed that its center was on the River Elbe. Three Germanic subgroups evolved from this group and they included: East Germanic (Bulgaria and Crimea); North Germanic (Swedish, Danish, Norwegian and Icelandic); West Germanic (German, Dutch, Flemish, Frisian and English).

The Angles, Saxons and Jutes crossed the Channel into England in the 5th and 6th centuries and these tribes moved into separate parts of England, taking their Germanic-based dialects with them. Individual dialects developed that are described as Old English or Anglo-Saxon.

The Norman invasion of 1066 was the greatest event that ever occurred in the history of the English language. Its crucial element was the introduction of words into the vocabulary by the non-native. The ruling class of England spoke French and there was a major influx of vocabulary from the European continent. Words, phrases, definitions and pronunciations came from different places throughout the world as a result. Importantly, the Norman Conquest represented the start of a gradual transition into the phase that is called Middle English. However, it was the scholarly words of Latin and Greek, which were absorbed during the Renaissance, that had such a major impact.

During the 16th and 17th centuries, the global boundaries of England were greatly expanded because the activities of its merchant fleet. The English sailors brought their speech patterns to foreign ports and continents, and they brought back new and exotic terms that were added to the rapidly growing English language. England formed a powerful navy to defend its merchant vessels and territories. English was the language of its American colonies, and its navy served as the model of structure, terminology and tradition for the newly born Colonial Navy and the future United States Navy.

America did not have an explosion of change as experienced by England in 1066, but it followed the same pattern as its mother country through the influx of seafaring and other terms being brought into the common language. The pattern continues at an increasing pace as the world shrinks through universal television and electronic communication. We are at point in time where there is worldwide participation through Internet, e-mail and many methods of person-to-person communication. And we haven't seen anything yet! The increase in words, vocabulary and international usage are a natural result.

The message is clear! American English is a living, breathing and flexible language that will continue to grow. As with its population, it is a hybrid in which its components have wide and varied origin. The seafaring words and phrases that have entered American language are one of many sources, but they provide a distinct flavor that makes our writing and speech so expressive and unique.

Celebrities in the Naval Services

Millions of Americans served in the naval forces during World War I, World War II, the Korean War, Vietnam, Desert Storm and the years before, between and after those conflicts.

There were a number of persons who were prominent before they entered the naval services, and there were those who became well-known afterwards. Included in this list are the names of recognizable persons who served in the Navy, Coast Guard, Marine Corps and Merchant Marine.

World War II saw the largest number of naval service participants. The June 1945 total of 4,041,598 active duty men and women included 3,380,817 Navy, 474,680 Marine Corps and 186,101 Coast Guard. In describing the time period in which an individual on this list served, World War II is used as a base. Specifically, WWII veterans do not have a war stated after his name. The designations of pre-WWI, WWI, prewar (pre-WWII), postwar (post-WWII), Korea and Vietnam are self-explanatory.

This is much more than a roster of persons who reached a degree of fame before or after their naval experience. Rather, it provides a dramatic view of United States history and the impact of war. It places into perspective how young Americans, as a result of national emergency, ended up in a uniform that they would never have otherwise worn. The well-known persons on this list, as with most veterans, were affected by their service experience. In illustration, World War I sailor Jack Benny got his start as an entertainer by playing his violin before service audiences. World War II sailor Guy Madison embarked upon an acting career when a talent agent spotted the handsome Madison.

The stories of some of the notables are of interest as indicated by some of their experiences. Spencer Tracy and Pat O'Brien were also in the World War I Navy. A number responded to the emergencies in Korea and Vietnam. Others, such as Jack Warden, Ernest Borgnine, George O'Brien, Ed Begley and Jason Robards served in the prewar Depression Navy.

There were genuine heroes among the men on this list. Lt. Eddie Albert was exposed to gunfire when he operated a casualty boat at bloody Tarawa. Wayne Morris flew a F6F-3 Grumman Hellcat and became an ace by downing seven Japanese planes. Lee Marvin received extensive wounds during the invasion of Saipan. Douglas Fairbanks Jr. became a highly decorated naval officer who saw much action in the European and Mediterranean theaters. Sterling Hayden worked with Yugoslav guerillas in OSS commando operations. During the 1944 invasion of southern France, John Howard was awarded the Navy Cross and French Croix de Guerre for his outstanding bravery in the sweeping of mines from the invasion area. Jason Robards survived the attack on Pearl Harbor, earned a commission from the fleet and went on to be awarded the Navy Cross and 13 battle stars. Glenn Ford entered the marines in 1944, became a postwar naval reserve officer afterwards, served in Korea and Vietnam, and retired with the rank of captain. Alex Haley had a different type of distinction: he joined the Coast Guard as a ship's cook in 1939, was appointed that service's first journalist and remained in the Coast Guard for 20 years. (Haley was known as "the cook who writes," and he earned 50 cents for each letter he wrote for a shipmate.) W. Graham Claytor, Commanding Officer of the destroyer escort *USS Doyle* (DE-368) and future Secretary of the Navy, did not wait for orders to turn his ship around and help rescue survivors of *USS Indianapolis* (CA-35) from the shark-filled Pacific Ocean. Further, Captain Claytor took it on his own when he ordered the searchlights be lit in the night sky in order to provide help and morale for the swimming survivors; this was done despite the lurking presence of the Japanese submarine that torpedoed *Indianapolis*.

Based upon the limited information available concerning service records, there is incomplete biographical information for some persons who are listed as serving during a "postwar" period. Therefore, there is no mention of participation during a specific war for those individuals.

United States Navy, Coast Guard and Merchant Marine

George Bush-*USS San Jacinto* (CVL-30)
Jimmy Carter-Submarine Service
Gerald R. Ford -*USS Monterey* (CVL-26)
Lyndon R. Johnson
John F. Kennedy-*PT-109*
Richard M. Nixon-Air Transport Command

Charles Adams-CEO, Raytheon Corp.-CO *USS Steele* (DE-8)
Nick Adams-Actor-USCG
Richard Adler-Composer
Desi Arnaz-Actor
Louis Auchincloss-Author-*LST*
Richard Avedon-Photographer-USMM
Phil Baker-Radio Personality
Russell Baker-Journalist
Wallace Beery-Actor-prewar and WWII
Ed Begley-Actor-*USS Stewart* (DD-224)-prewar
Harry Belafonte-Actor, Vocalist
Jack Benny-Comedian-WWI
Thomas Hart Benton-Author-prewar
Shelley Berman-Comedian
Lawrence "Yogi" Berra-New York Yankees Baseball-*USS Bayfield* (APA-33)
Frank Blair-Broadcast Journalist
Humphrey Bogart-Actor-WWI; *USS Leviathan* (SP-1326); *USS Santa Olivia* (SP-3125)
Richard Boone-Actor-*USS Enterprise* (CV-11); *USS Intrepid* (CV-11); *USS Hancock* (CV-19)
Ernest Borgnine-Actor-*USS Lamberton* (DD-119); *USS Sylph* (PY-12)
Tom Bosley-Actor
Ben Bradlee-Editor, *Washington Post*
Scott Brady-Actor-*USS Norton Sound* (AV-11)
Beau Bridges-Actor-USCG postwar
Albert Broccoli-Actor
Paul Brown-Cleveland Browns Football Coach
Lenny Bruce-Comedian-*USS Brooklyn* (CL-40)
Raymond Burr-Actor
Sid Caesar-Comedian-USCG
Joseph Campanella-Actor
Harry Carey Jr.-Actor
Richard Carlson-Actor
Johnny Carson-TV Personality-

USS Pennsylvania (BB-38)
Gower Champion-Choreographer-USCG
W. Graham Claytor-Secretary of the Navy-*USS Lee Fox* (DE-65) and CO *USS Coyle* (DE-368)
Kevin Conway-Actor
Robin Cook-Author
Jackie Cooper-Actor
Jeff Corey-Actor
Roger Corman-Film Producer
Bill Cosby-Actor-Korea
Frank "Junior" Coughlan-Actor
Tony Curtis-Actor-*USS Proteus* (AS-19)
Glenn Cunningham-Track Star
James Daly-Actor
Dennis Day-Actor, Vocalist
Jack Dempsey-Boxer-*USS Wakefield* (AP-21); *USS Arthur Middleton* (AP-55); USCG
Richard Denning-Actor
Billy de Wolfe-Actor
Howard Dietz-Composer
Paul Dooley-Actor-postwar
Kirk Douglas-Actor-*PC-1139*
Mike Douglas-TV Producer
Eddie Duchin-Bandleader-*USS Bates* (DC-68)
Vernon Duke-Composer-USCG
Buddy Ebsen-Actor-*USS Pocatello* (PF-9)-USCG
Jack Elam-Actor
Dana Elcar-Actor
Ralph Ellison-Novelist-USMM
Leif Erickson-Actor
Chad Everett-Actor-postwar
Tom Ewell-Actor
Douglas Fairbanks Jr.-Actor-*USS Ludlow* (DD-438); *USS Mississippi* (BB-41); *USS Washington* (BB-56)
Clay Felker-Publisher-postwar
Bob Feller-Cleveland Indians Baseball
John F. Floberg-Air Force Secretary-*USS Goss* (DE-444)
Henry Fonda-Actor-*USS Satterlee* (DD-626); *USS Curtiss* (AV-4)

Henry Ford II-Ford Motor CEO
John Ford-Film Director
Bob Fosse-Choreographer
Paul Gallico-Author-WWI
James Garner-Actor-USMM
Dave Garroway-TV Personality-*Minesweeper*
John Gavin-Actor-Korea
Arthur Godfrey-TV Personality-prewar Navy and USCG
Leo Gorcey-Actor *(Dead End Kids)*
Otto Graham-Football Player and Coach-USCG
Farley Granger-Actor
Shecky Greene-Comedian
Fred Gwynne-Actor
Alan Hale Jr.-Actor-USCG
Alex Haley-Author-USCG
Lou Harris-Political Analyst
Mark Hatfield-Oregon Governor
Woody Hayes-Ohio State Football Coach
Don Hewitt-TV Producer
Pat Hingle-Actor-WWII and Korea
Earl Holliman-Actor
Robert Horton-Actor-USCG
John Howard-Actor-*USS YMS-24*
Rock Hudson-Actor
William Bradford Huie-Journalist
Jeffrey Hunter-Actor
Tab Hunter-Actor-USCG
Claude Jarman Jr.-Actor-postwar
Gene Kelly-Actor, Choreographer
Joseph P. Kennedy Jr.-Attorney
Robert E. Kennedy-Attorney General-*USS Joseph P. Kennedy* (DD-850)
Hank Ketcham-Cartoonist
Richard Kiley-Actor
Ralph Kiner-Chicago Cubs Baseball
Harvey Korman-Actor
Otto Kruger-Actor
Julius La Rosa-Vocalist-postwar
Harvey Lembeck-Comedian
Jack Lemmon-Actor-*USS Lake Champlain* (CV-39)
Bill Leonard-TV News Commentator-*DD* and *DE*
Elmore "Dutch" Leonard-Novelist

Russell Long-Louisiana Governor
Jack Lord-Actor
Guy Madison-Actor
Dewey Martin-Actor
Tony Martin-Actor-USCG
Eddie Matthews-Baseball Player-
postwar
Victor Mature-Actor-*USS Storis*
(WMEC-38)-USCG
Bibber McCoy-Wrestler -USCG
Jim McKay-TV Sportscaster-
Minesweeper
Ed McMahon-TV Personality-
WWII and Korea
Robert Meyner-New Jersey
Governor
James Michener-Author
Robert Montgomery-Actor-*PT-107;*
USS Columbia ((CL-56); *USS*
Barton (DD-722)
Robert M. Morgenthau-New York
County District Attorney-
USS Winslow (DD-359); *Harry F.*
Bauer (DM-26); *USS Lansdale*
(DD-486)
Wayne Morris-Actor-Carrier Air
Group 15, *USS Essex* (CV-9)
Robert Morse-Actor-postwar
Stan Musial-St. Louis Cardinals
Baseball
Edmund Muskie-Maine Governor-
(DE) postwar
Edwin Newman-Author, Broad-
caster
Paul Newman-Actor-*USS*
Hollandia (CVE-97)
George O'Brien-WWI and WWII
Pat O'Brien-Actor-WWI
Carroll O'Connor-Actor-USMM
Donald O'Connor-Actor, Dancer
Francis Cardinal O'Connor-VADM,
New York
Joseph Papp-Theatrical Producer-
USS Solomons (CVE-67)
Eddie Peabody-Actor-WWI and
WWII
Sidney Poitier-Actor
Dick Powell-Actor
Richard Quine-Actor-USCG
Logan Ramsey Jr.-Actor-*USS*
Block Island (CVE-106)
Aldo Ray-Actor
Harold "Pewee" Reese-Brooklyn
Dodgers Baseball
Harry Richman-Actor
Don Rickles-Comedian-*USS*
Cyrene (AGP-13)
Phil Rizzuto-New York Yankees

Baseball
Jason Robards-Actor-*USS Hono-*
lulu (CL-48)
Marty Robbins-Vocalist
Cliff Robertson-Actor-
USS Admiral Cole-USMM
Edward G. Robinson-Actor-WWI
Norman Rockwell-Artist-WWI
Wayne Rogers-Actor-postwar
Cesar Romero-Actor-*USS Cavalier*
(APA-37)-USCG
Franklin D. Roosevelt Jr.-Political
Consultant-CO *USS Ulvert M.*
Moore (DE-442)
John A. Roosevelt-Banker-*USS*
Wasp (CV-18)
Carl Rowan-Columnist
Vermont Royster-Publisher, *Wall*
Street Journal- CO *USS Miller*
(DE-410)
Robert Ruark-Novelist
Richard Salant-CBS News Executive
Soupy Sales-Comedian-*USS*
Randall (APA-224)
Pierre Salinger-Journalist-CO *Sub-*
chaser (SC-1368)
Robert Sarnoff-NBC Chief Execu-
tive
Franklin Schaffner-Film Director
Murray Schisgal-Playwright
Budd Schulberg-Author
Willard Scott-TV Personality-
postwar
Artie Shaw-Bandleader-*USS Bates*
(DE-68)
Stirling Silliphant-Movie Producer
Sam Snead-Golf Professional
Benjamin Spock, M.D.-Physician,
Author
Robert Stack-Actor
Harold Stassen-Minnesota Gover-
nor
Edward Steichen-Photographer-
USS Lexington (CV-16)
Rod Steiger-Actor-*USS Taussig*
(DD-746)
Robert Stevens-Actor-USCG
Adlai Stevenson-Illinois Governor-
WWI
McLean Stevenson-TV Personality
Potter Stewart-Supreme Court
Justice
Larry Storch-Comedian
Joe Stydahar-Chicago Bears Foot-
ball Player
Walter Sullivan-Journalist-*USS*
Fletcher (DD-445) and *USS Overton*
(DD-239)

David Susskind-TV Producer-*USS*
Mellette (APA-156)
Jo Swerling Jr.-Movie Producer
Robert Taylor-Actor
Claude Thornhill-Bandleader
Lawrence Tibbett-Opera Singer-
WWI
Spencer Tracy-Actor-WWI
Tom Tryon-Author
Ted Turner-Turner Communica-
tions-postwar USCG
Orrin Tucker-Bandleader
Gene Tunney-Boxer
Rudy Vallee-Bandleader-USCG
Lee Van Cleef-Actor
Mike Wallace-TV Newscaster
Jack Warden-Actor-pre-WWI and
WWII
William Warner-Author
Pat Wayne-Actor-USCG
Fran "Spig" Wead-Author-WWI
Frank Wead-Novelist-WWI
Dennis Weaver-Actor
Sylvester "Pat" Weaver-Media
Executive
Paul Whiteman-Bandleader-WWI
Tom Wicker-Journalist-Korea
Henry Wilcoxon-Actor
Walter Winchell-Columnist-WWI
and WWII
Bob Woodward-Author-postwar
Herman Wouk-Author
Gig Young-Actor-USCG
Tony Zale-Boxer

United States Marine Corps

Sherman Adam-Presidential Aide, New Hampshire Governor
Don Adams-Actor
Burt Bacharach-Columnist
F. Lee Bailey-Attorney-postwar
Dan Bankhead-Brooklyn Dodgers Baseball
Hank Bauer-New York Yankees Baseball
Peter Benchley-Author
Paul Benedict-Actor-postwar
Anthony Drexel Biddle-Consultant-WWI
Larry Blyden-Actor
Joseph Bologna-Actor-postwar
Robert Bork-Jurist
Gregory "Pappy" Boyington-Pilot, Author
James Brady-Columnist
Wilford Brimley-Actor-Korea
Richard Brooks-Film Director
Art Buchwald-Columnist
Dale Bumpers-Arkansas Governor
Bob Burns-Humorist-WWI
Philip Caputo-Journalist-Vietnam
MacDonald Carey-Actor
Philip Carey-Actor
Billy Carter-Presidential Family, Consultant
Hodding Carter-Journalist
John Chafee-Rhode Island Senator -WWI and Korea
Ramsey Clark-US Attorney General
Charles Colson-Nixon Presidential Aide
Bob Crosby-Bandleader
Brian Dennehy-Actor-Vietnam
Brad Dillman-Actor-postwar
Davis Dinkins-New York City Mayor
Paul Douglas-Illinois Senator
David Duncan-Photographer
Dale Dye-Actor-Vietnam
Daniel Ellsworth-Military Analyst-postwar
Leif Erickson-Actor
Don and Phil Everly-Musicians-Vietnam
Jimmy Fidler-Columnist
Joe Foss-Pilot, Governor South Dakota
Glenn Ford-Actor-WWII; Korea; Vietnam
Bill Gallo-Sports Artist
John Glenn-Astronaut, Ohio Senator
James Gregory-Actor

Clu Gullagher-Actor-Korea
Gene Hackman-Actor-postwar
Ernie Harwell-Sportscaster
Sterling Hayden-Actor
Louis Hayward-Actor
Ray Heatherton-TV Personality
Howell Heflin-Alabama Senator
George Ray Hill-Film Director
Thomas Hoving-Museum Director
Don Imus-Radio Personality-postwar
Dick Jurgens-Bandleader
Bob Keeshan-TV Personality-postwar
Harvey Keitel-Actor-postwar
Brian Keith-Actor
Jim Lehrer-Broadcast Journalist-postwar
Robert Ludlum-Author
William Lundigan-Author
Jock Mahoney-Actor
William Manchester-Author
Lee Marvin-Actor
Joseph McCarthy-Wisconsin Senator
Paul N. McClosky Jr.-California Congressman-Korea
Ed McMahon-TV Host-Pilot, *USS Guadalcanal* (CVE-60)
Steve McQueen-Actor-postwar
Guy Molinari-New York congressman-Korea
Clint Murchison-Oil Executive
Michael Murphy-Actor-postwar
Oliver North-Author, Lecturer-Vietnam
Warren Oates-Actor-postwar
Hugh O'Brien-Actor
Lee Harvey Oswald-postwar
Charley Paddock-Olympic Runner
Pat Paulsen-TV Comedian
Sam Peckinpaw-Movie Director
George Peppard-Actor-postwar
Tyrone Power-Actor
Joe Pyne-Radio Personality
Dan Rather-TV Journalist-postwar
Donald T. Regan-US Treasury Secretary
Buddy Rich-Bandleader
Charles Robb-Virginia Governor-postwar
Pat Robertson-Evangelist Leader-Korea
James Roosevelt-Political Consultant
Mark Russell-Political Humorist-postwar

Robert Ryan-Actor
Vincent Sardi-Restauranteur
George Schultz-Secretary of State
George C. Scott-Actor
William Styron-Author
John Charles Thomas-Opera Singer -WWI
Dan Topping-Sports Executive
Merle Travis-Vocalist
Leon Uris-Author
Bill Veeck-Baseball Club Owner
Joseph Wambaugh-Author-postwar
James Webb-Secretary of the Navy-Vietnam
Robert Webber-Actor
James Allen Whitmore-Actor
Ted Williams-Boston Red Sox Baseball-WWII and Korea
Jonathan Winters-Comedian
Ed Wood Jr.-Film Director

IMAGES OF THE NAVY
NOT SO SERIOUS STUFF

Boot Camp Cheerful Service

COMMANDANT

SAMUEL LEVIN

UNITED STATES NAVAL TRAINING CAMP
Gulfport, Mississippi
Boot Camp, 1918
The Gadget Publication

2ND REGIMENT

RIGGING LOFT

W. KUHNE

Commissary Department

ARTHUR W. NUGENT

Reviews

PLUMBING SHOP

ARTHUR W. NUGENT
U.S.N.R.F.

ARTHUR W. NUGENT
U.S.N.R.F.

CAMP DISPENSARIES

"Darn it! Here I am on liberty and I forgot to take my Bluejacket's Manual with me."

NAVAL EXPANSION

"This sure beats milking cows."

"Please remember. Aboard ship you are to refer to me as Admiral, not "Duckie-Wuckie."

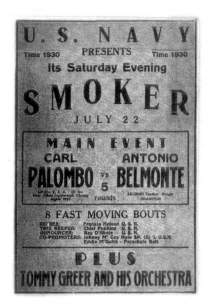

NAVY FABLES
"I know you're sleepy, but gee, all the other fellows get up at reveille."

From your Shipmates on the U.S.S. Minneapolis
Pearl Harbor, Hawaii.

The Sea Gull
(With apologies to Poe)
By J. H. PLANKENHORN

Once upon the rolling briny
Sailed a ship, so bright and shiny
For all hands had finished working,
   Cleaning her from aft to fore.
One tired sailor, rather strapping,
Lay on topside, nearly napping,
Freed of all his body wrapping,
   Just his shorts was all he wore.
He was sunbathing on the deck,
   That was why he only wore
      Just his shorts and nothing more.

Ah, the sun was never ceasing
As it shone upon him, teasing
Forth the tan that's ever pleasing
   Girls a sailor meets ashore.
Lying there so still and dreaming,
Did he know the sun was beaming
On a bird above him gleaming?
   'Twas a sea gull, nothing more.
Worthy of the names the sailors
Use for things that they abhor,
   Names that no one does adore.

Did he know that it was gunning
For a target and some funning,
Just as it had done
   On many, many of its flights before?
Banking, turning, soaring, stunting,
"Target for Tonight" 'twas hunting.
Then it found it in the bunting,
   'Twas the sleeper's shorts, no more.
Striped like the brightest bunting
   Found in any dry goods store.
      Gorgeous shorts and nothing more.

Suddenly the bird was diving;
Closer, closer ever striving
For the point to do the bombing
   Which would add another score.
Then there came a sudden tapping
And it wasn't gently rapping
On his belly; it was slapping,
   Slapping him and he was sore.
He was flustered, lost his course,
   Dropped his load but made no score,
      Just a sea splash, nothing more.

What had hit him? he was sighing;
High and higher he was flying.
Puzzling, thinking as he wondered
   What had spoiled his perfect score.
Then the answer came from under
In a burst of laughing thunder.
For the bird had made a blunder
   Thinking he could make a score
On a sailor, one who did not sleep
   Recalling times before
      When there WAS a perfect score.

That was why he was not sleeping,
But was resting, ever keeping
Watch for birds who go out hunting
   Ways to add another score.
And his means to make them lose it
Was a sling shot armed with babbitt.
Baby, baby, could he use it,
   He, a farmer lad of yore.
That was why the sea gull meant it
   As he fled, still rather sore,
      Shrieking loudly, "Nevermore."

"Can't you forget about your old target practice, even for a few minutes?"

YOU'LL PARDON ME SIR— FOR NOT GETTING UP TO SALUTE

"How do you want them, too large or too small?"

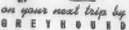

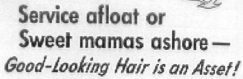

SALTY RHYMES

The Macon

By LESTER J. WILLIAMS, USS *Oklahoma*

She was the Jewel of them all,
This silvery Mistress of the skies;
To every Nation, great and small
She was the spark that electrifies
Their hearts with words of praise su-
    preme,
Her Country's pride, her Country's
    Queen!

To behold her gliding thru the skies,
Her motors tuned to perfect time;
With the sunlight on her silvery sides,
Made her a celestial thing sublime.

Thousands beheld her, thousands hoped
    to see,
This celestial Queen, bold and brave;
Little they knew her destiny
Was to be interred in a watery grave!

Below her, the sea, raging and wild;
Above her, the clouded, ominous sky;
To Nature she was just a wanton child;
To Man, a Queen who could never die!

Brave was her crew of valiant men,
Who guided her on her celestial flights;
Dangers they braved again and again,
As they scouted and observed at dizzy
    heights.

A broken fin, a battered beam,
Crippled this mighty silvery Queen;
Slowly she settled on the greedy foam,
Reluctant to surrender to a Foreign
    Throne!

Greedily she was swallowed by the surg-
    ing sea;
Dying, she surrendered to her fate;
Salute her, to her is the Victory,
She's proved her worth, so why relate?

Her sister suffered a similar fate
Off the stormy Atlantic shore;
Sisters, together they lie in State,
Midst the ferns and flowers of the
    Ocean's Floor.

Others will come to take her place,
But her glory can never be erased;
Their strength will be centered where
    she was weak
And the storms and seas will be ob-
    solete!

They Were Navylets

In a small and furnished flatlet,
With a doglet and a catlet,
    Lived a tarlet and his wifelet
        Who were young and newly wed.
And, considering her agelet
And the smallness of his paylet,
    It was quite a comfy lifelet
        They connubially led.

In their, as you might say, hutlet,
They devoured their daily chowlet,
    And their tealet and their toastlet,
        When their working day was through.

And at times the little flatlet,
With a "welcome" on its matlet,
    Would become the perfect hostlet
        To a partylet or two.

Thus it went until the tarlet
Started working on a planlet
    For a houselet with a yardlet
        And a porchlet and a tree;
Not from any discontentlet
Or the steepness of the rentlet,
    But with wistful, sweet regardlet
        For a little tarlet-to-be.
            —Apologies to "Life."

Success

By LESLIE C. COURTRIGHT, Bug2c, USS
    Altair

I patiently worked in the years gone by
    Tilling the fertile soil,
And often at night my joints would bite
    From the heavy grind and toil.
But now I smile as I see each mile
    That I followed the disc and plow;
And I lazily yawn, those days are gone—
    I'm a bugler in the Navy now!

From fore to aft, I proudly beam
    As thoughts pass in review.
The old cow shed, the mud, the slime,
    The rain, and the wind that blew.
The old cow yard, those days were hard,
    But I'm happy now, instead of blue.
Let memories fade, I've made the grade—
    I'm a bugler in the Navy now!

Rebel's Nook

By A. M. JABLONSKI, USS *Dale*

There's a designated spot
On the good old U. S. Dale
Where all the crew make merry
In the calm, or blowing gale.

It's a very cheerful corner—all hands
From the captain to the cook
Appreciate the value
Of the place called "Rebel's Nook."

Oh! They say we're not so rugged
"You can't take it," they exclaim
But the backbone of the Navy
Is the Rebels just the same.

They ridicule our speech
And rib our education too
But when they get in trouble
Then We Rebels see them through.

So let 'em talk, and let 'em rave
About our "Southern drawl"
The best place on a Navy ship
Is where they say "you all."

Farewell to Arms

By GORDON L. BARNUM, Ex-Navy

My four years have drawn to a close,
    The long "hitch" is over for me;
I'm taking the life on the outside,
    Instead of the wide open sea.

My buddies aboard ship I'm leaving,
    But in memory they'll always remain;
And I can't conceal that I'm lonesome,
    As I take that home-going train.

I'm quitting the life of a rover,
    And the skies of all other climes;
But as I stow my blues in my seabag,
    I dream of those good old times.

The Sailor Returns from a Cruise

In the wake of the ship as she plows
    through the sea
A bright convoy of thoughts keeps me
    gray company....
The warm beauty of jungles asleep in
    the sun,
And the padding of footsteps where wild
    creatures run;
The hoarse call from a tangle of bold
    parakeet,
The mad rythm of "shore-leave" in rol-
    licking feet;
A broad smile from Sabina, a dusky
    brown girl
Who can keep half the sailor boys' heads
    in a whirl!
The deep booming of guns as we pass
    on parade,
And the stillness of death when we go
    on a raid.
O the life of a sailor lacks nothing of
    change
From the workaday world to exotically
    strange . . .
But the pounding of surf turning white-
    and then green
Helps to make me forget other things
    I have seen.

Going South

By W. D. ELEY, F2c, USN, USS *Bass*

Hey! you, bend down on that scrubber;
    Then grab a squilgee, ye blasted lubber;
Scrub the decks, so no spots will show
    For soon to the blistering South we go.

Scrub the decks so they'll beach out white
    Without a spot of dirt in sight.
'Cause on the decks our bunks must go
    To rid ourselves of the heat below.

We're heading South where the sun beats
    down
On arms, 'n Necks, 'n sweating crowns.
And the decks throw off that torrid glare
Like a boiler fireside in the air.

So fix 'em up for the time to leave
    On the blistering trip, through the swel-
        tering seas.
'Cause on the decks our bunks must go
    As it's too damned hot to sleep below.

WELCOME TO BOOT CAMP!

Now Listen Here, Boots! The Navy has its personal language and it is immensely jealous of it. No other service speaks in such a traditional code. It is possible for a civilian to hold a 30-minute conversation with a sailor and not understand one sentence.

A primary rule of the Navy is never to call a ship a "boat." A *boat* is carried on a ship. The universe may measure speed in miles per hour, but the Navy uses *knots*. One *knot* is the speed that it takes for your vessel to travel 2,025 yards in an hour, which is a *nautical mile*, instead of the 1,760 yards recognized by everyone else. The Navy ignores the normal clock and it goes by *bells*---one *bell* every half-hour, cumulatively.

Another code: it's not a rope, it's a *line* and a wall is a *bulkhead*. You walk on a *deck*, not a floor and you clean the deck with a *swab*, not a mop. Above is *overhead*, not the ceiling and you walk down the *passageway*, not the hallway. You open a *hatch* instead of a door. You don't go up the stairs, you climb the *ladder*.

You go to the *head* instead of the bathroom, sailor! You sleep in your *sack* or *bunk* and not in a bed. You eat in the *chow* or *mess hall* where spinach is *seaweed*, ketchup is *red lead* and the other dishes have nicknames that defy publication.

Ahead of you is *forward* and to the rear is *aft*. Right is *starboard* and left is *port*. You don't stop something, you *belay* it. If you want a cigarette, you must wait for the *smoking lamp* to be lit. Candy is *pogey bait* and ice cream is *geedunk*. A sailor does not go on vacation, he goes on *leave*. He keeps his shaving gear in a *ditty bag* and next to his bare skin, he wears *skivvies* instead of underwear.

A ship doesn't get torpedoed, it takes a *fish*. If something needs temporary repair, you *jury-rig* it. If you are ailing you go to *sick bay*. Should your ship sink, you're *in the drink*. If you don't survive, you've *deep-sixed* it.

A battleship is a *wagon* and the commanding officer is *the old man*. A *tin can sailor* serves on a destroyer and a *DE* is a destroyer escort. An *airdale* serves on a *flattop* (aircraft carrier). If he is a member of the flight crew, he is a *hooktail*, and the planes are handled by *deck apes*. Naval aviators are *brown shoes* and seagoing officers are *black shoes*. Navy officers above the rank of full commander are *gold braid*. Soldiers are *dogfaces*, marines are *seagoing bellhops* and Coast Guardsmen belong to the *Hooligan Navy*.

In the 1970s there were attempts to sabotage tradition. Official Navy bulletins directed that the *chow hall* be referred to as *"enlisted dining facility."* The brig was to be called the *"correction facility,"* and the ship would be *"it"* instead of she or her. However, Secretary of the Navy John Lehman, an old Navy hand, came into Office and junked the reform movement.

You'll be sorryeeee!...

Second Injection

"Chow"

"About size 36"

FIRST NIGHT IN HAMMOCKS

"CLEANLINESS IN THE NAVY IS NEXT TO GODLINESS"

HIPP—BY—HIPP....

"ARCHBISHOP'S THRONE"

"OH, YOU EVEN HAVE A LOUNGE CHAIR HERE — HOW COZY!"

SIGNAL BRIDGE
"EXECUTE!"

"AIRCRAFT — PORT BOW!"

"FIRE!"

THE VANITY LINE

ROOM AND BOARD

"ATTENTION!"

LOOKOUT

MONKEY FIST

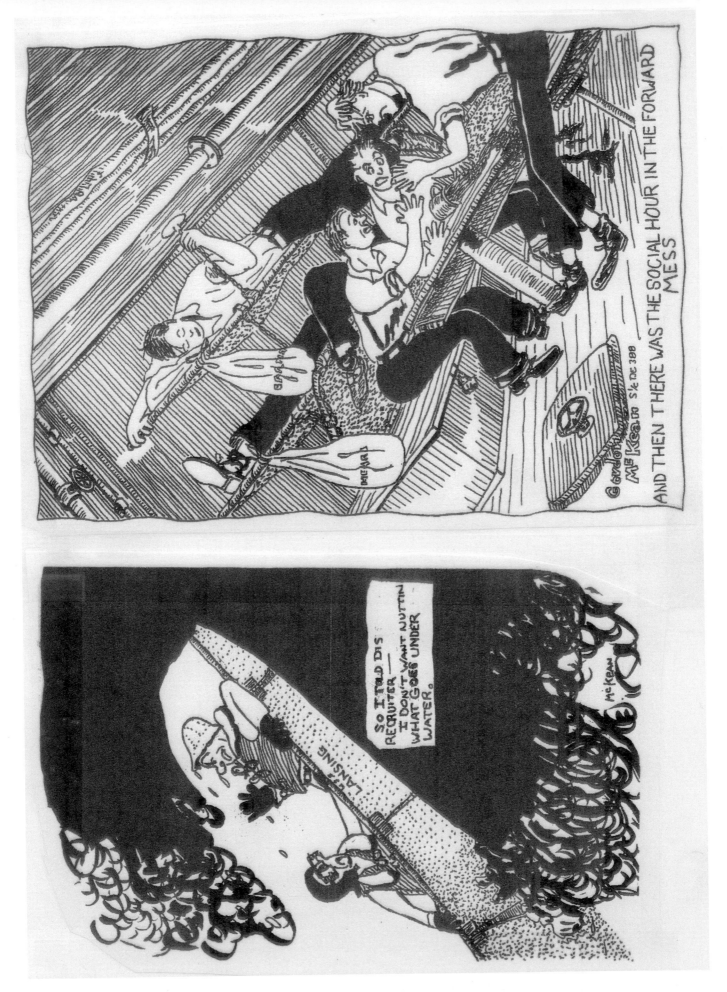

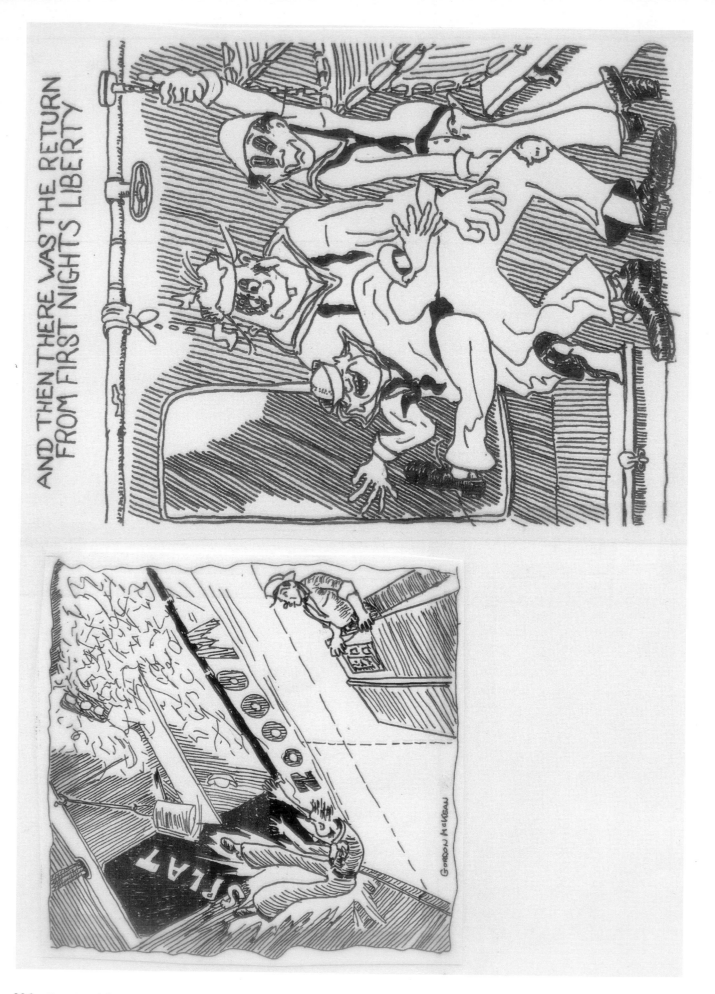

AND THEN THERE WAS THE RETURN FROM FIRST NIGHTS LIBERTY

Traditions and Tales of the Navy - 237 -

"So you used to be on the stage before you enlisted? I've got just the job for you!"

"Now what was the name of that knot?!!!"

"Electrician's mate or no electrician's mate, you leave that light alone."

SALTY RHYMES

John Paul Jones
By EDGAR D. KRAMER

Though I'm berthed here in Snug Harbor,
While I'm sippin' of my grog,
You can verify my statements
By consultin' of the log;
Huh! 'Fore I was old an' crippled,
When youth danced along my bones,
I sailed up an' down the waters
With John Paul Jones.

He was just a runty feller,
Five-feet-seven-inches high,
But he had the Devil duckin'
From the fire in his eye,
An' it's gospel that I'm spillin',
Life was far from jam an' scones,
When we bucked the boundin' billows
With John Paul Jones.

Lord, I'll never be forgettin'
That far misty April day,
When we swooped down on White Haven,
Spiked the guns an' slipped away,
With the shippin' fiercely blazin',
Crimsonin' the fort's gray stones,
As we flung our jeers at England
With John Paul Jones.

As if all that wasn't plenty,
We were nosin' through the swell
In the captured BON HOMME RICHARD,
That was rottener than hell,
When the SERAPIS *came chargin'*
Like a Shylock after loans,
An' we cleared our decks for action
With John Paul Jones.

Well, we took that British frigate
An' just scrambled on our prize,
When the RICHARD *lurched to starboard*
An' went down before our eyes,
While the roarin' of the waters
Swallowed up the yells an' groans;
In them dead days real men went sailin'
With John Paul Jones.

Swab Jockey's Lament
By BORTZ

I've swabbed so many decks,
To make them bright and clean;
I've swabbed a thousand miles of decks,
It's a task that seems so mean.

I often longed to be a Bluejacket,
A real good Navy fighter,
But my only job is swabbing decks
To make the Navy brighter.

My job is bringing back the glow
Of decks, or common flooring;
I'm like an artist at his work,
His masterpiece adoring.

Yes, I've swabbed many a deck,
For sailors' feet to soil;
And no one here to give me praise
In recompense for toil.

Oh, what reward and joy 'twould be
For the Captain's voice, in pity,
To look upon my lovely decks
And say, "How clean and pretty."

Apart
By BONNIE L. STRAYER

We watched the moon rise slowly over-
head,
And wondered at the pang of love we felt.
We watched the stars that shown among
the clouds,
And wondered at our destiny that fate
had dealt.

Silently we watched the dark clouds
gather,
And longed for the comfort of each other's
hand.
Quietly we watched the rain drops start
to fall,
And longed for the power to make us
understand.

Together, yet apart, we watch these
wonders of the sky,
I, from my safety post upon the porch
dream thoughts of you,
While you, on watch in blue, upon your
ship of war,
Are comforted, because you know our
love is true.

Now I'm Wondering!
By CELIA KEEGAN

I just got a letter from someone at sea
And oh, the delight and the joy that it
gave!
For my sailor-beau ended that letter to
me
With: "Oceans of love, and a kiss on each
wave."

But second thoughts wondered: was he
making sport?
My poor head is aching; my jealous
brain whirls.
For sailors, they say, have sweethearts in
each port
And the WAVES *also mean those uni-*
formed girls!

Dan Cupid—Unemployed
By ALOYSIUS COLL

Cupid sat under a yew tree,
Ashiver with sorrow and sob;
Smashing his bow and his arrows,
He muttered: "I've lost my job!

"Jack has gone down in a submarine
To capture a mermaid shy;
John has gone up in a cargo plane
To flirt with an angel on high.

"One chasing a fillet of seaweed,
A jacket of scales and a fin;
The other a harp and a halo—
Oh, where does Dan Cupid come in?"

Deep Gratitude
By LORETTA SAALFIELD

Our thoughts when night begins to fall,
And shadows lengthen over all—
We look back upon that day just past
And mark the good with thoughts that
last.
And so while wars take sons away,
We bow our heads to humbly pray.
We thank Thee, Lord, for those who
stand
Near by our sons, on foreign lands;
Who take our place to lead him right
To show him still, God's right is might.
Near by on every foreign shore
God places chaplains over all.
With courage equal to their task,
Each chaplain stands near God to ask
His ever-present, loving care
For all our sons, found everywhere.

Mothers of Heroes
By VIRGINIA HAGGENJOS BRAGG

We can only remain in the background....
We, once the protecting ones,
Stand fast, full of fear but exultant
At the valor of our sons:
These lads once so awkward and callow,
Have in the short space of a year
Become the invincible heroes,
Deaf to all thought of fear.

One boy once afraid of the darkness
Now flies over tropical sands—
Through starless nights he is winging
With Freedom's bright torch in his hands;
Another has answered the challenge
And is sailing the seven seas. . . .
We wait at home—proud and yet humble
To have mothered such heroes as these.

Cupid on Deck
By ALOYSIUS COLL

I don't believe in Cupid's darts;
I'm mighty much too human
To think that anything so frail
Could subjugate a woman.

More likely 'tis that he bombards
The maid a sailor marries
With something like the eight-inch gun
A battle cruiser carries!

THE SATURDAY EVENING
POST
SEPTEMBER 15, 1945   10¢

Berliners say:
"YOU CAN'T DO THIS TO US"
By ERNEST O. HAUSER

The Christian Science Monitor
By MARQUIS W. CHILDS

Norman
Rockwell

Index 1
Salty Words, Phrases an Sea Stories

Index II
The Drawings of Cedric W. Windas
1936-1942

Index III
Drawings of Cedric Windas
1943-1948

Naval Organizations and Resources

Many hundreds of veteran groups have been formed as a result of the United States' participation in wars and conflicts during the 20th Century. The following list includes some of the more prominent veteran organizations together with historical publications and sources of research or participation..

U. S. NAVY MEMORIAL FOUNDATION
701 Pennsylvania Avenue, Washington, DC 20004-2608
Tel (202) 737-2300   Fax (202) 737-2308
www.lonesailor.org

HISTORIC NAVAL SHIPS ASSOCIATION
C/O US Naval Academy Museum
118 Maryland Avenue, Annapolis, MD 21402-5034
Tel (757) 499-6919   Fax (757) 499-0440
www.maritime.org/hinsa-guide.htm

NAVAL HISTORICAL CENTER
Washington Navy Yard
901 M Street, SE, Washington, DC 20374-5060
www.history.navy.mil

NAVAL HISTORICAL CENTER
Navy Vessel Deck Logs
Textual Reference Branch
8601 Adelphi Road, College Park, MD 20740
(301) 713-7250

US NAVAL INSTITUTE
Naval History Magazine
& Proceedings Magazine
2062 Generals Highway, Annapolis, MD 21401-6780
Tel (410) 268-6110   Fax (410) 224-2406
www.usni.org

Sea Classics Magazine
PO Box 16149, North Hollywood, CA 91615
Tel (818) 700-6282

Sea History Magazine
National Maritime Historical Society
PO Box 68, Peekskill, NY 10566
Tel (914) 737-7878

World WarII Magazine
741 Miller Drive, SE, Leesburg, VA 20175
WorldWarII@thehistorynet.com

NAVY LEAGUE of the UNITED STATES
2300 Wilson Boulevard, Arlington, VA 22201-3308.

USS CONSTITUTION
Charlestown Naval Yard, Boston, MA 02129-1797
Tel (617) 242-5670   Fax (703) 602-4982

DESTROYER ESCORT HISTORICAL FOUNDATION
USS SLATER DE-766
PO Box 1926, Albany, NY 12201-1926
Tel (518) 431-1943   Fax (518) 432-1123
www.ussslater.org

DESTROYER ESCORT SAILORS ASSN.
(DE, DER, DE-APD, FF)
P0 Box 3448, Deland, FL 32721-3448
Tel (904) 738-6900   Fax (904) 738-2299
www.desausa.org

TIN CAN SAILORS
PO Box 100, Somerset, MA 02726
Tel (508) 677-0515   Fax (508) 676-9740

ASIATIC FLEET FOUR-STACK DESTROYERS
1105 Whitehall Drive, Mt. Pleasant, SC 29464
Tel (803) 884-2360

COAST GUARD COMBAT VETERANS
17728 Striley Drive, Ashton, MD 20861-9763
Tel & Fax (301) 570-5664

COAST GUARD SEA VETERANS OF AMERICA
8042 Avery Lane, Sedro-Wooley, WA 08284-9363
(360) 856-2171

PATROL FRIGATE ASSOCIATION
622 Southgate Avenue, Daly City, CA 94015
(650) 756-7931   patrolf@aol.com

LANDING CRAFT SUPPORT (LARGE) ASSN.
PO Box 9087, Waukegan, IL 60079   (847) 623-7450

USS LSM-LSMR ASSN.
(Landing Ship Medium (SM & LSMR)
66 Summer Street, Greenfield, MA 01301
(413) 774-2397

AMPHIBIOUS ATTACK BOATS ASSN.
(LCVP, LCM)
PO Box 3328, Fort Pierce, FL 34948
(561) 468-8875

TORPEDO BOAT VETERANS ASSOCIATION
(PT Boats, Bases & Tenders)
PO Box 38070, Germantown, TN 38183-0070
Tel (901) 755-8440   Fax (901) 751-0522
www.geocities.com/Pentagon/6140/

U.S. NAVY ARMED GUARD WWII VETERANS
115 Wall Creek Drive, Rolesville, NC 27571
(919) 570-0909

U.S. MERCHANT MARINE VETERANS OF WWII
P.O. Box 629, San Pedro, CA 90733
(310) 519-9545

SUBMARINE VETERANS OF WWII
317 North Palm Avenue, Frostproof, FL 33843
(813) 635-2442

LCI NATIONAL ASSN.
(Landing Craft, Infantry LCI)
155 Main Street, Port Monmouth, NJ 07758
(908) 495-0672

ASSOCIATION OF GUNNERS MATES
PO Box 247, Hammond, IN 46325

ESCORT CARRIER SAILORS ASSN.
1100 Holly Lane, Endicott, NY 11760
(607) 748-3284

US SUBMARINE VETERANS
13821 SE Raymond, Portland, OR 97236
(503) 761-3791

NAVY MINE WARFARE ASSN.
(DM, DMS, AMC, YMS, AMS, CM, MSC, ETC.)
224 Angelus Drive, Salinas, CA 909006-3302
(408) 449-5352

USN CRUISER SAILORS ASSN.
55 Donna Terrace, Taunton, MA 02780-2824
(508) 824-0789

NATIONAL ASSN OF FLEET TUG SAILORS
P.O. Box 1507, Sausalito, CA 54965
(415) 331-7757

PATROL CRAFT SAILORS ASSN
4911 S. View Ridge Drive, Green Valley, AZ 85614
(520) 625-1576

U.S. LST ASSOCIATION
P.O. Box 711247, San Diego, CA 92171
(619) 371-6106

SAMPSON WWII NAVY VETERANS
2 Hamlin Drive, Canandaigua, NY 14424
Tel (716) 393-9590   Fax (716) 393-9551

MARINE CORPS HERITAGE FOUNDATION
PO Box 420, Quantico, VA 22134-0420
Tel (703) 640-7961

Bibliography

Alexander, John W., *A Living Tradition*. Washington, DC: U.S. Navy Memorial, 1987.

Ambrose, Stephen E., *Citizen Soldiers*. New York: Simon and Schuster, 1997.

Ayto, John, *Dictionary of Word Origins*. New York: Little, Brown and Company, 1990.

Barrow, Clayton R., Jr., *The Navy Needs You: U.S. Navy Poster Art of the Twentieth Century*. Annapolis: U.S. Naval Institute, 1987.

Baur, Bill and June, eds., *Now Hear This!* Villa Park, IL: NI-DESA, Various Issues, 1989-2000.

Biegel, Harvey M., *The Fleet's In: Hollywood Presents the U.S. Navy in World War II*. Missoula, MT: Pictorial Histories Publishing Company, Inc., 1994.

Beavis, Bill and McLoskey, R.G., *Salty Dog Talk*. London: Adlar Coles Nautical, 1983.

Bloomster, Edgar L., *Sailing and Small Craft Down the Ages*. Annapolis: U.S. Naval Institute, 1940.

Brokaw, Tom, *The Greatest Generation*. New York: Random House, 1998.

Buck, Victor and Davis, Martin, *Trim but Deadly*. Albany, NY: Destroyer Escort Historical Foundation, Various Issues, 1993-2000.

Ciardi, John, *A Second Browser's Dictionary*. New York: Harper and Row, 1983.

Clark, William H., *Ships and Sailors*. Boston: L.C. Page & Co., 1938.

Carpenter, Joseph and Dorinson, Joseph, *Anyone Here a Sailor?* Great Neck, NY: Brightlights Publications, 1993.

_____ , *Anyone Here a Marine?* Vol. 1 and 2. Great Neck, NY: Brightlights Publications, 1995.

Cosgrove, John P., *DESA NEWS*. Washington, DC, VA: Destroyer Escort Sailors Assn., Various Issues, 1977-2000.

Cutler, Carl S., *Greyhounds of the Sea*. Annapolis: U.S. Naval Institute, 1967.

Davis Martin and Saylor, Samuel, *We Brought USS Slater Home: Trim But Deadly*. Albany, NY: Destroyer Escort Historical Foundation, 1994.

Engle, Eloise and Lott, Arnold S., *America's Maritime Heritage*. Annapolis: U.S. Naval Institute Press, 1975.

Evans, Ivor H., *Brewer's Dictionary of Phrases and Fable, rev*. New York: Harper and Row, 1970.

Funk, Charles E. and Charles E., Jr., *Horsefeathers*. New York: Harper & Row, 1958.

Funk, Wilfred, *Word Origins*. Avenel, NJ: Random House, 1950.

Gard, Alex, *Getting Salty*. Washington, DC: U.S. Navy, 1943.

_____ , *Sailors in Boots*. Washington, DC: U.S. Navy, 1943.

Greenbie, Sydney and Marjorie, *Gold of Ophir*. Garden City: Doubleday, Page and Company, 1925.

Heinl, Robert Debs, *Dictionary of Military and Naval Quotations*. Annapolis: U.S. Naval Institute, 1966.

Hendrickson, Robert, *Salty Words*. New York: Hearst Marine Books, 1984.

Horgan, Thomas F., *Old Ironsides*. Camden, ME: Yankee Publishing Company, 1963.

Jeans, Peter D., *An Ocean of Words*. Secaucus, NJ: Carol Publishing Group, 1998.

Langer, William L., *An Encyclopedia of World History*. Boston: Houghton Mifflin Company, 1960.

Lott, Arnold S., ed., *Almanac of Naval Facts*. Annapolis: U.S. Naval Institute Press, 1964.

_____ , ed., *Bluejackets' Manual*. Annapolis: U.S. Naval Institute Press, 1973.

_____ , *Traditions of the Navy*. Annapolis: Leeward Publications, 1978.

Maltin, Leonard, *Leonard Maltin's Movie Encyclopedia*. New York: Penguin Books, 1998.

Martin, Tyrone, "Salty Talk," *Naval History*. Annapolis: U.S. Naval Institute, Various Issues, 1994-1999.

May, W.E., *History of Marine Navigation*. New York: W.W. Norton & Co., Inc., 1973.

McCloud, A.S., *The Spirit of Hawaii*. New York: Harper and Brothers, 1946.

McCombs, Don and Worth, Fred L., *4,139 Strange and Fascinating Facts of World War Two*. New York: Random House, 1983.

McKean, Gordon and Parker, Charles A., eds., *Life on USS Lansing DE-338 Sketches*. Raleigh, NC: *USS Lansing* Association, 1993.

McReady, Lauren S., *The Men and the Ships of the War Years 1942-1945*. Kings Point, NY: U.S. Merchant Marine Academy Alumni Association, 1993.

Morris, William and Mary, *Morris Dictionary of Word and Phrase Origins*. New York: Harper & Row Publishers.

Mostrert, Noel, *Supership*. New York: Alfred A. Knopf & Co., 1974.

Neaman, Judith S. and Silver, Carole G., *Kind Words*. New York: Facts on File, 1983.

Paullin, C.O., *American Voyages to the Orient*. Annapolis: U.S. Naval Institute, 1971.

Peltin, Thomas, *Tin Can Sailor*. Somerset, MA: Various Issues, 1986-1999.

Pohjanpalo, Jorma, *Sea and Man*. New York: Stein & Day, 1970.

Rankin, Robert H., *Uniform of the Sea Services*. Annapolis: U.S. Naval Institute, 1971.

Ritter, Theodore J. and Gadbois, John, *Bet Your Boots*. Great Lakes, IL: U.S. Naval Training Station, 1943.

Roach, John Charles, *Old Ironsides: An Essay in Sketches*. Washington, DC: Department of the Navy.

Silverstone, Paul H., *U.S. Warships of World War 2*. London: Ian Allen, Ltd., 1982.

Smith, Gernie. *Joy of Trivia*. Chatsworth, CA: Brook House Publishers, 1976.

Soule, Charles C., *Naval Terms and Definitions*. New York: Van Nostrand Co., 1926.

Van Osdol, William R., *Famous Americans in World War II*. St. Paul, MN: Phalanx Publishing Co., 1994.

Whall, W.B., *Romance of Navigation*. New York: Robert M. McBride & Co., 1926.

Wiener, J.L. and Brandow, E.C., *The Gadget*. Albany, NY: 1919.

Windas, Cedric W., *Traditions of the Navy*. New York: Our Navy, 1942.

Wise, James E. and Rehill, Anne C., *Stars in Blue*. Annapolis: Naval Institute Press, 1997.

Worcester, C.R.G., *Junks and Sampans of the Yangtse River*. Annapolis: U.S. Naval Institute, 1971.

Zucker, Channing and McCarthy, Anne, *Anchor Watch*. Annapolis: Historic Naval Ships Assoc., Various Issues, 1924-2000.

_____, *All Hands*. Washington, D.C.: U.S. Navy Bureau of Naval Personnel, Various Issues 1941-1946.

_____, *California Gold Rush*. New York: American Heritage Publishing Company, 1961.

_____, *Commandant'a Bulletin*. Washington, DC: U.S. Coast Guard, Various Issues, 1984-1991.

_____, *Dictionary of Modern English Usage*. London: Oxford University Press, 1965.

_____, *Naval Orientation*. Washington, DC: Bureau of Naval Personnel, June 1945.

_____, *Our Navy Magazine*. New York: Various Issues, 1935-1948.

_____, *Quarterdeck Log*. Westfield Center, OH: Coast Guard Combat Veterans Association, Various Issues, 1991-2000.

_____, *Skylab, Our First Space Station*. NASA SP38. Washington, DC: GPO, 1977.

_____, *War Years Derry 1939-1945*. Derry, North Ireland: Guildhall Press, 1992.

_____, *What's In a Word?* Nashville, TN: Abington Press, 1954.

_____, *Why Do We Say It?* Secaucus, NJ: Castle Book Sales, 1985.

USS Slater DE-766

We Brought Her Home!

Defying all odds, the members of the Destroyer Escort Sailors Association (DESA) raised $286,000 to save the World War II destroyer escort *USS Slater DE-766* from the scrap heap and bring her back to the United States. Commissioned in April 1944, *Slater* participated in both the Battle of the Atlantic and the Pacific War. Donated to Greece under the Mutual Defense Assistance Program in 1951, she sailed as the Hellenic Navy *Aetos* until she was decommissioned in 1991. After temporarily berthing at the Intrepid Sea-Air-Space Museum in New York City, the ship is now at her permanent home on the Hudson River in Albany, New York.

Today, the ship is in a magnificent state of restoration. This is the result of the efforts of historic ship restorer Tim Rizzuto and more than 100 volunteers. Every part of the vessel has been brought back to its 1945 appearance and the ship looks as if it can go to sea and battle with U-boats and fight off Kamikaze attacks. *Slater* serves as an historic, educational and patriotic resource, and is a keystone in the City of Albany's waterfront improvement and economic development program. In 1999 and 2000, 81 destroyer escort reunion groups visited the vessel.

Only a few of the 565 Navy and Coast Guard DE's are in existence and *Slater* is the only one afloat in North America. A major honor has been bestowed upon the ship through its selection to the National Register of Historic Places. Plans are to activate the propulsion system and to make this destroyer the only American World War II warship in sailing operation.

You are invited to become a member of the non-profit Destroyer Escort Historical Foundation and to join us in this great adventure.

Destroyer Escort Historical Foundation
PO Box 1926, Albany, NY 12201-1926
Tel (518) 431-1943   Fax (518) 432-1123
Website – www.ussslater.org

About the Author

The author, Dr. Martin Davis is Director of the Destroyer Escort Sailors Association and Executive Director of Destroyer Escort Historical Foundation. He produced the documentaries, "Fighting Destroyer Escorts of World War II" and "Proudly We Serve: Men of the *USS Mason* (DE-529). Dr. Davis earned his doctorate degree at Columbia University and he writes and lectures on World War II naval affairs. He served aboard the *USS Pettit* (DE-253) in both the Atlantic and Pacific theaters. His videos and books are available through Pictorial Histories. Dr. Davis, who lives in Huntington, New York, is the retired Superintendent of Schools at Cold Spring Harbor, New York, and is a former professor at Hofstra University.